Essays in Honor of Edmond Malinvaud

volume 3: Empirical Economics

Essays in Honor of Edmond Malinvaud

volume 1: Microeconomics (with introduction by J.-C. Milleron)

volume 2: Macroeconomics

volume 3: Empirical Economics (with bibliography)

Essays in Honor of Edmond Malinvaud

volume 3: Empirical Economics

edited by
Paul Champsaur
Michel Deleau
Jean-Michel Grandmont
Roger Guesnerie
Claude Henry
Jean-Jacques Laffont
Guy Laroque
Jacques Mairesse
Alain Monfort
Yves Younès

The MIT Press
Cambridge, Massachusetts
London, England

Published in French as part of a single volume entitled *Mélanges économiques: Essais en l'honneur de Edmond Malinvaud* (Paris: Economica, 1988). Translations provided by the authors.

Set in Palatino by Asco Trade Typesetting Ltd. in Hong Kong. Printed and bound in the United States of America.

Library of Congress Cataloging-in-Publication Data
(Revised for vol. 3)

Essays in honor of Edmond Malinvaud.

Includes bibliographical references.
Contents: v. 1. Microeconomics—v. 2. Macroeconomics—v. 3. Empirical economics.
1. Economics. 2. Malinvaud. Edmond. I. Malinvaud, Edmond. II. Champsaur, Paul.
HB173.M4213 1990 330 89-48826
ISBN 0-262-03158-2 (v. 1)

volume 1
ISBN 0-262-03158-2

volume 2
ISBN 0-262-03159-0

volume 3
ISBN 0-262-03160-4

3-volume set
ISBN 0-262-03174-4

Contents

I Empirical Studies

25 Having Confidence in the Future and a Successful Life

Christian Baudelot

At the end of *French Growth* (Carre et al. 1972), there is a three-page questionnaire which the authors address to their sociologist colleagues. Economic analysis has identified the main factors in growth, measured the explanatory power of each one, and shown the existence of a considerable residual which resists any explanation in terms of the accumulation of productive work or of labor activity. The improvement in the labor training schemes, the professional migrations, and the modernization of equipment acount for only half of this residual.

Questions from the Economist to the Sociologist

It is on the basis of this assessment that the appeal to the sociologists comes in. They were asked two things: to reflect on the unexplained residual and to try, for five identified factors, to discover the roles played in the way they are used by the different sociological factors of which one thinks.

The task which has been passed on to the sociologists by the economist consists in providing for the progress in production, which he has himself established and measured, explanations based on an analytic description of the *behavior* of the main economic agents having contributed to this growth: firm managers, executives, workers, women, and so on.

More accurately still, the economist expects the sociologist to distinguish among these different types of behavior, between those suggested to or even imposed on individuals by development or economic necessity and those which appeal rather to will, to aspirations, or to conscious acceptances of the agents only concerning one's free will. The search for a division between what one is subjected to and what is deliberate, the conscious and the subconscious, can be found all through the questionnaire. Therefore:

> Was the maintaining at a high level of the weekly working hours desired by the workers? If yes, can this be explained by the general longing for bourgeois consumer habits . . . or by the high birth rate and the expenses that a bigger family involves? Do the maintaining of the length of work time and the birth rate both result from *a more confident attitude towards the future* [our italics]?
>
> Is the increase in feminine activity purely due to the existence of wider employment possibilities or must one attribute them to a modification of people's behavior? Is this possible modification a result of the alteration of the role which the predominant ethic gives women in society, or has it been made possible by the development of household equipment or certain community services (e.g., child care).
>
> Can one conclude that there has been an intensification in the labor produced from 1950 up to the present day? If this is the case, is it due to a stricter supervision of workers or to the spontaneous acceptation of more sustained effort? Is it exact that the consciousness of the needs of expansion and that of the French technology being so behind was particularly acute at the end of the last war? Could it then be that the desire for achievement had become stronger? Can one establish the existence of a revival of the spirit of enterprise in France between 1955 and 1960? Could this be linked to an *increased confidence in the future* [our italics] or to a modification of the predominant ethic in favor of taking risks and to the detriment of security?

For once the sociologist is at a loss to answer a questionnaire. It is not that the economist, through his questions, places the sociologist on foreign ground: spirit of enterprise, predominant ethic, modification of consumer habits, length of work time, birth rates, female activity, intensification of work, distinctions between executives and heads of firms and workers—these are all factors, all aspects of the economic and social life which he is used to taking into consideration and to working into a pattern. The general meaning of the questions is also familiar to him. It is part of the mainstream of the great sociological tradition, started by Max Weber, that tries to understand and sort out the relationship between ethics, economy, society, and religion. The difficulty is elsewhere. It is with regard to the nature of the demand, which asks an explanation of the sociologist while at the same time providing a general explanatory outline. The identified and measured economic facts (labor activity, accumulation of capital, and remaining factors) are nothing but the effects of causes which must be found by the sociologists in the agents' behavior, the agents being either complete masters of their acts (will, consciousness, confidence in the future) or motivated by ethnic values which go over their heads but to which they adhere.

Or take for example *increased confidence in the future,* which is mentioned twice in the questionnaire. The economist wonders whether one cannot here look for one of the causes of the maintenance of a high level of length of working time and the birth rate as a revival of the spirit of enterprise in France between 1955 and 1960. How can the sociologist decide? He must, before anything else, explain these three points:

1. Can he impute to this confidence in the future such a causal sociological function as the economist's questions lead us to suppose?
2. Can one isolate and give a clear empirical status to the notion of "confidence in the future"? What are, in fact, the status and the degree of reality of the existence of this notion? Is it a feeling, a belief, a quantity of knowledge, a faith, or a more complex behavioral system? Is confidence in the future a single phenomenon, or does one observe different forms?
3. What empirical indications does the sociologist dispose of to identify, grasp, and strictly measure it to be able to transform it into one or many variables and therefore be able to evaluate the specific incidence which it brings to bear, among other factors, on different behavior? Is it possible to measure the variations of its intensity in the course of time or within the same period for different social groups? How?

Three interrogations but only two questions: the two last points are linked. They are concerned with problems of measuring, that is to say with the difficulties for the sociologist that are posed by the empirical grasping of behavior that one considers for sure as pertinent to having confidence in the future. As regards the first one, it is very close to the position that can be reserved for this notion in an explanatory system.

There is an exemplary sociological answer to these two questions. Alain Darbel and Pierre Bourdieu (1966) formulate it in a chapter of *The Sharing of Benefits* which is entitled "The End of a Malthusianism." The answer even anticipates the question, because the text dates from 1966. Reflecting on the progression of fertility recorded in France during the postwar period of growth, they observe first that the classification of socio-professional categories according to their fertility level has stayed the same, the number of children decreasing as one goes up the social scale from the middle-class categories to the upper categories. They then notice that, starting from an identical level of fertility before the war, the increase in the average number of children is more marked for salaried workers, and that the relative growth is all the more pronounced in that the average number of children was low before the war. Then they construct, to illustrate this demographically established fact, a certain number of hypotheses, which they formalize into a pattern. It is supposed that the expected child is earmarked with a certain cost, which depends on the attitudes as regards the future; it is very low in the working classes, and this relative cost goes up considerably when one goes toward very upwardly mobile families, who are, for this reason, inclined to invest in education ("the supreme instrument of social ascension"). Low among the small incomes, as it is among the very high, the incremental cost of the child then reaches a maximum in homes which are in the middle of the salary scale: the average executive at the time. This explains the U curve.

The model constructed is similar to that used by economists (there is at the end the incremental cost of the child), but the attitudes and types of behavior which are listed as being factors susceptible to vary this cost have no direct relation to the area of the quantities usually manipulated by the economists. The pattern is coherent; one can even believe that there was a predictive value, because it suggested as early as 1966 the fragile character of the resumption of fertility. The pattern adopts the hypothesis formulated by the economist when he confirms that the attitude and the confidence as regards the future, like the increasing feeling of security, can be considered as the "predominant factor in the increased fertility."

The economist marks the difference, however, when he shows that, far from being *straightaway* given as a perceptible and univocal fact, this relationship with the future is itself the complex and socially conditioned product of a whole set of objective conditions which define an individual's or a household's situation at any given moment: income, job, educational level, living conditions, sort of accommodation, etc. The attitude as regards the future, itself strongly linked to the aptitude for mastering the future through calculation and rational predictions, depends greatly therefore on the present situation and on the objective future which is inscribed. The individual determines his relationship with the future through referring to the future inscribed in the present. The objective future is therefore potentially inscribed in the present as if the positive or negative chances of being, having, or doing something predisposed, by predestinating, toward acting so that these chances can be realized. This is what Pierre Bourdieu (1974) was later to call "the causality of the probable."

It follows from this analysis that the forms and the degrees of confidence in the future vary a great deal from one social group to another, and that these variations, for which there is no question of denying the real effects that they can exercise on different types of behavior, can be explained only by taking into account objective conditions, past and present, which define the situation of a group of individuals.

This sociological analysis enables one to answer the economist's first question in the following way: Yes, the relationship with the future is a determining factor in social behavior; however, its causal status is not simple, because this confidence is both a cause and an effect. In particular, it varies a good deal in its forms and intensity according to the different social groups.

To the second question, that which concerns the empirical grasping of concrete indicators, the sociologist's answer is less clear. Although the pattern is very convincing in its desire to sociologically explain the U-shaped curve, it suggests more than it proves or measures. The sociographical work, which consists in measuring or identifying separately the variables which are supposed to grasp in their diversity and complexity the different forms of this confidence, has yet to be done: we still do not know the aptitude for rational calculation or the confidence in the future of the parents concerned. There is an excellent reason for that! One only need have a try at it to become conscious of the enormous amount of work involved in going from such a concept, which is both specific and general, to concrete indicators susceptible of being able to identify the forms and measure their intensity. One single example taken from literature will be enough to give an idea: Fabrice del Dongo and Eugène de Rastignac can both be said to have a high degree of confidence in the future. But it is obvious that one cannot compare the two: while the former confidence comes from a naive adherence to the presence of the youth and history, the latter is heavily steeped in roots and is laid out like a path by a mind educated about the cogs governing the workings of the "chimes of social order," and is shown as a well-thought-out genealogical shift. One group can believe in the future in the perspective of an eternal recurrence and another in the hope of original solutions to be invented. How can one measure these fundamental differences which are far from being only those of Stendhal's and Balzac's heroes?

Two solutions are possible: resorting to indirect indicators and resorting to direct indicators of social agents. Fertility, schooling for children, debts, and savings are generally considered good indirect indicators of confidence in the future. But two difficulties immediately appear. First, the causality induced by this form of validation of the hypothesis has a circular character: fertility being recognized as a pertinent indicator of confidence in the future, one deduces that this confidence is quite simply what the fertility rate measures. Second, the ambiguity of the indicator is not always easy to remove: regularly putting money aside in a savings bank account can be interpreted either as a sign of confidence or as a sign of mistrust in the future. Is it simple foresight (postponing one's consumption to protect oneself against the risks and hazards of an uncertain future), or is it rational budgeting (saving for future expenses by taking into account the comparison between the interest rate and the rate of inflation)?

Direct interrogation of the agents involved falls far short of filling the gaps opened by resorting to indirect indicators. What can one find out about the relationship people have with their future by questioning them about it? The experience accumulated by sociologists in this field makes one very prudent. For example, Vaquin (1982) has shown through interviewing mothers of a very young child on the reasons why they hope (or hope not) to have other children that it is very difficult to give an univocal content to the notion of confidence in the future. Effectively everything depends on the dimensions that the woman being interviewed implicitly takes into account when she answers the question: whether the mother places herself from the angle of humanity and the paper, whether she consults immediate property facts or considers herself as a future school-parent or a potential grandmother, one will have, for the same woman, three types of answers engaging different forms and degrees of confidence in the future and especially a different relationship between this confidence and the plans to procreate again. The same thing happens when one tries through interviews to grasp the aptitude for rational calculation and its transposition to contraceptive practices.

Answer from a Sociologist

Very difficult to grasp and to measure empirically, confidence in the future cannot be reduced to a simple causal factor. Diverse and variable according to the different social groups, it is itself the effect of the objective taking into account of their situation by the actors, and of the probable future which is inscribed. These differences and effects can be felt right down to microsocial levels. This is what we want to bring to the fore, but using completely different data from that which served as the empirical basis of Bourdieu and Darbel's reasoning. It is not a question of fertility but of the symbols that certain youngsters have of a successful life. These symbols are not national but regional and even local; they concern a population of 594 pupils going to an LEP (a secondary school giving professional training and diplomas comparable to those given by the RSA or the guild in Britain) in the town of Nantes. They are situated in an economic and social climate which is the complete reverse of the previous one: in 1986 there is neither growth nor a demographic boom but rather an economic slump and a decrease in the birth rate.

"To you what does the expression 'a successful life' (to succeed in one's life) mean?" This is the wording of one of the open questions asked in the questionnaire. Not bearing directly on the confidence that the youngsters interviewed might individually have in the future they hoped for, this question theoretically opened up a large range of possibilities for the answers. The purposely general and impersonal terms of the question did not condemn the response to realism or to individual projections; on the contrary, they left the imagination completely free to express itself. In fact, the immense majority of the answers, refusing dream or utopia, seem to express the wishes and hopes that the youngsters questioned came out with themselves about their future. One can appreciate this from the following extracts, the object of which is to familiarize the reader with the answers collected. They have been pulled out at the rate of one in ten at random.

Have a family and a job.

Find a well-paid job, have children.

Have a trade, money, a wife, and children.

Have a position, a family, and a trade.

Have a family home.

Have a trade, a house, a car, a good wage, win the lotto.

Have a job, a family home, good friends.

Be in a place where this gives me pleasure.

Have a professional activity which one has chosen, be a happy couple.

Work, earn money, doing a job one likes, travel, find happiness, and then die.

A trade one likes, warm love, enough money to live and be able to do what one likes when one likes.

Have a good position, no money worries nor family problems.

Have a good trade which one likes, have a family, be happy, at peace with oneself.

Have a family, a job, a house, be at peace with oneself.

Have a good salary, a profession one likes, a family life, and do what one wants.

Have a good social rank, like one's job, be in good health, and have a girlfriend one gets on well with.

Have a good position, be satisfied with one's job, a good salary, a family.

Obtain what one wants.

Have a job which one likes, a decent salary, and some fun.

Succeed in everything one attempts to do.

Be happy living a family life.

Have a trade, a child, someone to love, a lot of money.

Have an interesting trade, a family, be loved, and love one's own.

Have a family, a good position, and have friends.

Have a good position at work, take the time to make the most of life.

Find a good job which interests me, live with a girl I like in my own flat.

Be able to succeed in the three things that give man the incentive to live: sentimental and family life, professional life, power; the climax: live luxuriously without working.

Be happy and have all your ambitions come true.

Be known, have money, love and be loved.

Have a stable position, have friends.

Have a good well-paid trade and live happily as a couple.

Have a good trade, a pleasant life, and be at peace with oneself.

I would be very happy to succeed in my own life and in others.

Have a good trade, a happy life, a good salary.

Have a trade and earn a good living.

Have a trade and be happy.

Be at peace with oneself, have the trade one wants, a job, and a good salary.

Have a professional qualification to be able to bring up one's children, food, clothing, a good education, teach them a trade.

Have a good position, accommodation, a family.

Have a job, a wife, children, and car.

Have a steady job with a good salary in order to be able to manage alone.

Have a recognized trade, have a family and a house.

Have a good position.

Have a good job.

Earn a lot of money, have a beautiful wife and children.

Work, eat, drink, sing, earn money, sleep with a woman I fancy.

Earn money, have a steady job and a family.

Have a job.

Have a position you like, be at peace with yourself.

First of all, have work, be at peace with oneself, and no longer have the present problems between countries.

First have a decent profession and have a happy married life and give oneself certain pleasures.

Be at peace with oneself, in one's interesting and instructive job, have a woman.

What can the material we have collected contribute to our subject? The data is fragile because it is only words and sentences expressing opinions and interpretations of youngsters who are still at school, and this in a survey which was imposed on them. Very variable from one individual to another, the degree of commitment of the person in his answer is not verifiable. The remarks collected do not lend themselves to any confrontation with observable or measurable practices.

It is, however, not impossible to consider these remarks as many interpretations which the pupils at the age we are referring to (16–18), and on the day we questioned them, make of the future they desire for themselves. Because they are not unrelated to a hoped for or idealized future, they contain, in the wording of those wishes and desires, a relationship with the future, and can in this way clarify the idea of confidence.

A supplementary element that prompts us to take this set of sentences seriously is the high rate of answers obtained. The answers were both numerous and abundant, a sign that the question asked meant something to the population concerned: only 79 failed to respond, that is to say a reply rate of 87%. We should point out as a comparison that a closed question about one's dream job (that which one would love to have if there was nothing against it) came up against a great number of refusals to answer (17%) and that all the questions about marriage, living together, life as a couple, and friends with whom one goes out had refusal rates ranging between 15% and 33%. In these conditions, getting only a 13% refusal rate for an open question with young pupils who are not enthusiastic about written composition and of whom 20% do not answer when asked their father's age can be considered a good result. This high rate must be connected with the high proportion of answers obtained for all the questions linked to guidance in courses to be followed at school and to the professional future.

Diverse characteristics of a successful life come to the fore right from the first reading of the above sample. A successful life is exclusively associated with the individual and domestic dimensions of existence: work, happiness, family, wife, children, car, money. The collective and political dimensions are conspicuously absent: no sign of revolt, no reference to struggles or to adventure, no plans for changing life or the world: neither Marx nor Rimbaud. The absence of collective references is coupled with great caution as regards the level of ambitions: in a period of unemployment and economic crisis, the future holders of a CAP or a BEP fix the target they want ideally to reach during their life at the level of security which a steady and interesting job, a family life (or being in a couple), and reasonable accommodations will give them. Individualism prevails; at least this is what comes out of the first reading. On this point the results of our survey match the results of several surveys carried out on young people in recent years. One can say that the (apparent) degree of confidence in the future is very low because minimum security, far from being taken for granted, is here given as an aim in life and as something that is difficult, even impossible, to reach.

It is clear that even if it gives a general idea this first commentary remains insufficient. A certain number of themes come to the fore as being constructive elements of a successful life (work, security, family happiness, money), but each of these items can in turn be broken up into component parts: "have work," "have a trade/profession," "have an interesting job," "have a trade or profession that one likes." All these comments show that work is a key element for succeeding in life, but they also show the number of aspects and assessments of the entity of work that have to be taken into account. It is the same for all the other themes mentioned: "have a house, a wife, and children" is an answer which puts "family happiness" right on the front line, but in a completely different way from those who say "have a close family" or "being happy with the person one loves" or "be loved and make those around one happy." One can even wonder if the category "family happiness" is really meaningful. Going through the answers given, one can only be struck by the opposition which goes right through the questionnarie between those who answer the question with the verb *to have* (have work, have a wife, have a house, have children, have money, have a motor-bike, have leisure activities), even if they qualify more subtly the object of their success (have a trade/profession one likes, have a wife who loves you) and those who answer with the verb *to be* (be happy with oneself, be loved, be happy, be well paid, be married, be rich, not be unemployed). The choice of the auxiliary is not socially neutral: there are two distinctly different philosophies about the future and success which do not necessarily stem from the same populations. The CAP and the boys are on the *to have* side of success while the girls and the BEP find themselves on the *to be* side.

On this point the intuitive analysis of the material is complicated by the fact that certain themes which are abstractly isolatable find themselves very closely tied up in certain answers where we notice an odd mixture of the themes of work, security, family happiness, money, and even *to be* and *to have* in specific combinations which cannot (as in other situations) be reduced to a simple addition of the different parts.

In order to be objective, we have resorted to a way of analyzing the contents which is based on statistical word-counting tools and factor analysis applied to the numerical variables of the survey (the answers to closed questions: sex, age, speciality, careers, parents' social category) and to the texts collected on the open question. The programs used (SPAD) were devised by Ludovic Lebart and his CREDOC team (Lebart 1982; Lebart et al. 1984, 1985, 1987).

The analysis principle is simple: it consists of constructing a table where the complete answers to the questions are shown on lines and the different graphic forms present in these answers are shown in columns. At the intersection of these lines and columns one can calculate the number of times that the graphic form Y is used in the answer X. So that we do not clutter up the analysis with too great a number of tool words (*to, of, and, the*) and rare words, it has been decided to keep in the analysis only the words that appear more than five times in the corpus as a whole. The 594 answers (including the blanks) contain a total of 4266 graphic forms (of which there are 567 distinct graphic forms), but only 102 distinct graphic forms of more than two letters appear more than five times. The chart of occurrences to be analyzed therefore has 594 lines and 102 columns. The lines of the table can easily be related to the numerical variables of the survey: sex, age, parents' jobs, etc. It is therefore possible to project into the same factor-space the social, educational, and cultural characteristics of the pupils and the qualitative answers which they made to this open question.

The sociological advantages of this style of analysis are clear: over and above the meanings intended by the actors, one can grasp the objective indicators of their attitudes and opinions in the shape of words and the combinations of words they use. Whether verbs, adjectives, nouns, or conjunctions, the words which are meaningful to them are significant on two levels: the meaning that those who pronounce the words give them and that which the position they have in the space drawn by the other words used by the other pupils gives them. The actor thinks "object" or "predicate" (*wife, car, happy*); the sociologist records these objects but also takes into account the verbs and the tool words by which the actors are doubtless unaware of differentiating themselves from others. However, these words, the way they are used, and the words with which they are associated succeed, unknown to those who pronounce them, in marking differences or similitudes, in drawing profiles, and in sketching representative systems. This is why it is essential to start the analysis by breaking the collected material down into as many lexical forms as it makes up: the unity here is *the word* (or more accurately the graphic form), which is compared to other words, independent of the specific context in which they have been spoken.

The Count: *To Be* and *To Have*

The first operation is simple: we give the computer the task of counting the lexical forms and classifying them according to their frequency. The quantitative variable being integrated into the plan of action, these word counts can be exploited according to sex, age, and section as well as the other forms of variables that the previous analyses have enabled us to isolate as being significant.

In the first hundred words, one distinguishes itself very clearly: the infinitive of the verb *to have* appears 451 times, outstripping by over three times the second and third nouns encountered, *being* and *work* (respectively used 151 and 149 times). The articles *one* (275) and *some* (106)—doubtless like "a," which was eliminated because it has (in French) only two letters—are automatically produced by the transitive construction of the auxiliary *have*, which needs a direct object preceded by an article.

For the youngsters we are studying, doing their second consecutive year in an LEP in Nantes, succeeding in life is therefore first and above all *to have*. This word comes first for all the categories considered: boys and girls, BEP and CAP, plasterers, tradespeople, caterers, and electricians. It remains true that the frequency varies clearly according to the subgroups considered: the CAPs of industrial drawing, carpentry, roofing, and general mechanics are singled out by a much-higher-than-average use of this verb (over two and a half points higher), whereas with the BEP sales, technical

Table 1.
The 102 Most-Used Words (Graphic Forms)

N	%	Lexical form	*N*	%	Lexical form	*N*	%	Lexical form
451	13	have	25	0.8	much	9	0.3	especially
275	7.9	one	24	0.7	job	8	0.2	all
151	4.3	be	21	0.6	for	8	0.2	is
149	4.3	work	21	0.6	(to) love	8	0.2	health
106	3	some	21	0.6	us	8	0.2	set
106	3	trade	20	0.6	not	8	0.2	enjoy
102	2.9	life	19	0.5	love	7	0.2	fix
101	2.9	money	19	0.5	on	7	0.2	want
82	2.3	family (famille)	19	0.5	(to) work	7	0.2	fact
80	2.3	good (bonne)	18	0.5	skin	7	0.2	by
80	2.3	happy (heureux)	18	0.5	home	7	0.2	loved
74	2.1	who	17	0.5	car	7	0.2	problems
73	2.1	which	17	0.5	all	7	0.2	cash
69	2	earn	15	0.4	wants (il veut)	7	0.2	miss
67	1.9	position	13	0.4	pals	7	0.2	go out
66	1.9	well	13	0.4	flat	7	0.2	nothing
65	1.9	good (bon)	12	0.3	family (familial)	7	0.2	maximum
59	1.7	in	12	0.3	professional	7	0.2	(to) desire
57	1.6	do	12	0.3	paid	7	0.2	must
54	1.5	children	12	0.3	(to) start	7	0.2	you
47	1.3	wife	11	0.3	happy (heureuse)	6	0.2	(to) benefit
46	1.3	with	11	0.3	more	6	0.2	world
45	1.3	please	10	0.3	wage	6	0.2	accommodation
45	1.3	live	10	0.3	others	6	0.2	problem
40	1.1	friends	10	0.3	(to) marry	6	0.2	diplomas
37	1.1	salary	10	0.3	oneself	6	0.2	(to) feed
33	1	be able to	10	0.3	grind	6	0.2	happiness
32	0.9	succeed	10	0.3	(to) travel	6	0.2	(to) give
32	0.9	find	9	0.3	studies	6	0.2	profession
31	0.9	his/hers (ses)	9	0.3	beautiful	6	0.2	quiet
31	0.9	the	9	0.3	enough	6	0.2	trade
30	0.9	his/hers (son)	9	0.3	without	6	0.2	get on
29	0.9	house	9	0.3	good (bons)	6	0.2	married
28	0.8	steady	9	0.3	leisure	6	0.2	someone

and car servicing, quantity surveying, refrigeration, and climatization subgroups and the CAP wallpapering subgroup its relative infrequency is noticed (between three and five points under average). Variations in the same direction but not so extreme can be observed between the boys (+) and the girls (—), between the pupils who chose neither their LEP nor their section (+) and those who affirm that they did choose them, and between the pupils who repeated one or several classes in primary school (+) and those who did not repeat a year (two and half points under average). A common point within this population, the identification of a successful life with *to have* seems to be found most among those who have the least (table 1).

Sociology being a comparative discipline, it will be particularly interesting to give the same questions to other populations who would accept the same treatment but who belong to groups having different economic, educational, and social capital. This is the only way to relativize the weight of *to have*.

The counts also enable us to take other measurements. Let us take, for example, the two following lists, and compare the five nouns encountered more than a hundred times both among the girls and among the boys. The list starts with the most used word (table 2).

Have is first on both lists, but *money* appears in the top five only in the boys' list and *life* only in the girls'. *Work* and *trade* appear also in the top five in the girls' list, but they prefer, contrary to the boys, the verb *be*.

In the same way it is instructive to make lists of the above-average use of words by both the boys and girls. Here are, starting from the most frequently used, the top 25 words (table 3).

Have is masculine and *be* feminine. *Work, trade,* and *professional* appear on the girls' list, and in association with words about happiness, pleasure, friendship and love. Money, family, earn/win, position, children, wife, salary, house, job, and car are elements that make for a successful life according to

Table 2.

Boys	Girls
Have	Have
Work	Be
Be	Work
Money	Trade
Trade	Life

Table 3.

Boys	Girls
Have	Be
One	Work
Some	Trade
Money	Life
Family	Happy
Good	Who
Win/earn	What
Position	In
Well	Do
Good	With
Children	Please
Wife	Friends
Live	Succeed
Salary	His/hers
Power/be able to	The
Find	For
His/hers	Us/we
House	Love
Steady	Sure
Job	Skin
Love	Home
Not	Flat
Work	Professional
Car	Create
Want	Happy

the men. Line 19 gives us precious information. Two different adjectives conjure up security: *steady* (*stable*) for the men and *sure* (*sûr*) for the women. The words deceive us while at the same time expressing our feelings; the simple fact of counting, classifying, and exploiting the words used in an answer enables one to bring together and trace coherent and clear descriptions of the future and of success. In the masculine model organized around acquiring material goods (house, money, car), economic wealth (positions, job) and family ties (wife, children, family), contrasts with a feminine model where the work and one's trade take an important place next to friends, being well-balanced oneself, pleasure, and happiness.

The Correspondence Analysis: The Triangle of Success

In the places where the count insisted on frequencies, ranging from generalities to specific cases, from the most common to the exceptional, the factor analysis will, by measuring the divergencies from the average profile, bring to light the system of differences by which such or such a subgroup of pupils diverge or come close to one or several other groups.

It is neither *having* nor *being* nor their opposition that "makes" the first axis, but a trio, placed toward the negative pole of this axis and made up of the words *that/what*, *do*, and *want*. The word *that/what* is endowed with the highest contribution. Those of the two verbs are also very high. At the other end of the first axis we find *one* with a high contribution, then *having* (used with certain direct objects: house, wife, position) with a lesser one.

The second axis is also pulled down by the same trio which made up the first one: *that*, *do*, *want*. Four words which distinguish themselves very clearly from the others—*lack*, *nothing*, *in*, and *be* (these words are given in decreasing order)—make up the opposite pole of this second axis. Figure 1 enables us to picture the shape of this construction: *do what one wants* is a sufficiently clearing choice to be opposed both to answers which identify a successful life with *have* and to all these direct objects like *to be* with all its predicative phrases but also *to lack nothing*.

There are therefore not two models of a successful life but three: *do*, *have*, and *be*. *Be* and all its predicative phrases are the essential part of a vast model defined by *not lacking anything*. Although it uses negative expressions to explain what others express with positive ones (having something), this expression does not have any less meaning. *Not lacking anything* is doubtless one of the necessary conditions for being, whereas *having* places itself at an even earlier stage in the accumulation: there is a very real fear of having nothing. These three points clearly define a triangle in which

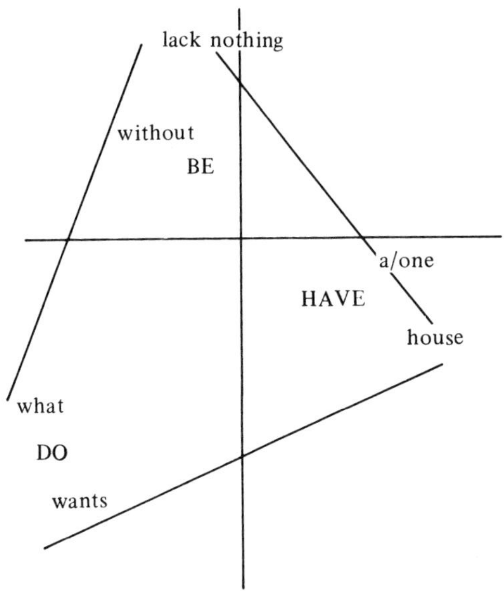

Figure 1.

are placed each of the words used in the answers. The populations associated with these three peaks do not resemble each other.

One is not surprised to find on the *have* side those who have the least: pupils preparing CAPs (sheet metal, plastering, metal work, painting), having repeated years more than others at primary school, finding themselves in a school and a particular field which they did not want, wanting to get into the labor market as early as possible and get out of the school as quickly as possible. This group is essentially made up of boys coming from the second form, but also from SES and CPPN (specialized sections for children in difficulty). Their parents are workers on employees with no qualifications; asked to indicate the job they would like to have if given complete freedom, they quote trades which by field and social level are very close to those which they learn in the LEP (mason, for example).

In contrast, the pole *lack nothing* and *being* attracts the girls and the BEP service industries (sales, commerical services). They have seldom repeated primary-school years, and have gone to school until the end of the fourth form; they are satisfied with the teaching at the LEP, a school in which one has chosen one's field; their favorite subjects are French and the workshops; they have rarely chosen to do the same job as their father; in fact they feel that the latter is not satisfied with his job or his life. Unemployed more frequently than elsewhere but also skilled workers, the fathers of these pupils do not distinguish themselves from others by any particular trades or social positions; all the trades are represented. As regards the dream job, it is to be found as an extension of the learned skill, but at a much higher level than that of the probable job at the end of the studies. The possibility of having free time, the atmosphere, and the interest value of the work are always considered more important than the salary.

The third peak (*do what one wants*) gathers around it both boys and girls preparing for a CAP in wallpapering, the boys preparing for industrial BEPs, the girls getting BEPs in perishable products, and to a lesser extent the BEPs in sanitary and thermic fitting; there again there is very little repeating of primary school years, a secondary education followed until the fourth form; the children are from big families, often those of average executives, and their relationship with the LEP and the school is positive: satisfied with the training they receive, they envisage repeating a year in the event of failing their exams. They hope, if they obtain the BEP, to continue their studies in a grammar school. Far from being dead ends, these industrial specialities have selective recruitment and pride themselves on regrouping the best elements. The lesson these students like best in the LEP is the workshop.

Another complementary and perhaps more accurate way of studying the relationship between the school and social characteristics of the youngsters studied and the image they have of a successful life consists in analyzing in a way which is both symmetrical and the reverse of the one on which we have just commented. Instead of using lexical forms as active variables and specialities as supplementary variables, the contrary is done.

The space thus constructed is that of the specialities. On one side here (on the right) are the CAPs, particularly those in building; on the other are the BEPs, which divide themselves into two: at the top left the service industries and training attracting girls, and at the bottom the industrial and masculine BEP. The triangle *do-be-have* is to be found where we expected it: *have* on the side of the CAPs and building, *be* for the girls, and *do* in the southwest associated with the industrial BEPs.

Reading the factor analysis presented above is instructive both in the confirmations it shows and in the new facts it enables us to notice.

What is new here is the dispersion in space of synonymous terms, insofar as they exist in French. Some examples:

relationships: *pals* used by the CAP, *friends* used by the girls in the service industries

incomes: *cash, salary, wage* used by the CAP, *money* halfway between them all and no substitution word used by the girls activity: *job, trade, grind, work* used by the CAP, *position* used by the BEP, *profession* between both, nothing used by the girls

security: *permanent, steady, sure*; three words, three particular positions, three different conceptions.

Confirmations:

1. The openly "materialistic" character of the image of success that the building and the CAP students have; image controlled by *having* and its "direct objects": very materialistic in the bottom quadrant (plastering): salary, wage, cash, accommodation, car, trade, job, eating; more symbolic in the top one (carpentry, roofing, metalworking, painting): qualifications, studies, pals, home, wife.

2. The association of success and freedom for the industrial BEPs (do what one likes, what one wants to do, what one desires, what pleases one, without problems, leisure).

3. More of a question of relationship and affectivity with the girls in the commercial and service industries of the northwest quadrant (friends, others, harmony, loved, happy, happiness, travel).

The results are clear: one could have supposed a high level of homogeneity among the student population going to an LEP in Nantes in a given year, and a low level of variation in the picture one another could have of the future. The previous analysis brings very clearly to light two facts: the existence of important factors of differentiation of status, school situations, and the behavior within that population (boys and girls, CAP and BEP, professional specializations, building, industry, services) on the one side and on the other a correspondence between the main factors of differentiation and the nature of the relationship that these youngsters have with the future and success (or at least what the question asked enables us to grasp from this idea).

This is how the model "do what one wants, what gives pleasure . . ." can be assimilated to a maximum degree of confidence in the future and the mastering of same, which is shown in the population studied. However, far from being uniformally shared in the population, it belongs to pupils who, owing to the fact they had a good school record, could be accepted in renowned and selective departments and have a right to hope (based on passing the BEP) that they can integrate "A" level classes and prepare the "baccalaureate" (G.C.E. "A" level). The hopes they place in the school are directly related to the hopes that the school places in them. Of all the pupils who were interviewed, it was these who actually had the most chance of "doing what they wanted," thanks to an increase on their school investment. Realistic in spite of an apparently hedonistic formula concerning their wishes (do what pleases me), these pupils have objective reasons for being able to think that they have in their hands enough school and social assets to control, as far as possible, part of their fucture; their relative confidence comes from this.

It is not the same for the pupils who find themselves preparing for a CAP in building after repeated school failures and forced and negative advising on courses to be followed. If *do* is a verb of action implying the notions of realization and of project and therefore a projection into the future, *have*, only referring to the idea of possessions, excludes this controlling of the future. Money, grind, salary, car, house, wife, etc., the "objects" one hopes to possess, represent both the strict minimum necessity and the maximum that the pupils who have constantly been failures at school can perhaps objectively aspire to in a period of unemployment, hitting in particular the youth and the least qualified. Here again there is a relative adjustment of the level of aspiration as regards the future one will probably have by taking into account, rationally or in a diffuse way, the objective chances which are given them by a future that their past has already blocked. This is confirmation, should it be necessary, of the very solid nature of the connections which associate the attitude as regards the future to the aptitude to control it by calculation and rational prediction.

As for those, both boys and girls, who associate a successful life with being (being at ease with oneself, happy, happy in one's work life) as long as they lack nothing (no problems), the girls preparing the BEP service industries want to create a balance between the professional necessities of these jobs demanding a great deal of social contact with others (commerce, community employees) and their affective, relational, and family life (love others, make happy, with, be loved, harmony). The wish that is expressed here anticipates a future in which women have to reconcile their traditional female functions with the status of a worker who has not given up the idea of succeeding.

This is confirmed by the edition of the modal answers given by the girls, that is to say the answers which use the largest number of words characteristic of their group. Whether they are selected by the average row (which favors short answers) or by the χ^2 distance (which favors the longer answers), the results are very close: the two dimensions, family and professional, are clearly linked. The importance given to work and professional life is in keeping with the increasingly important role that women play in the working population.

A steady job, being happy.

Be satisfied with the way we are spending our lives (in a way corresponding to what we wished for).

Make the most of everything, that is to say traveling and being happy for as long as possible.

Succeed in one's professional life and second on the labor market.

Succeed in overcoming one's shortcomings, one's fears, be happy with oneself, succeed in one's professional and private life.

Be happy within oneself, succeed in one's professional life and make the most of life.

Reach the target one has fixed oneself in life.

Work, love, by happy.

Do a job which pleases one, be happy within oneself.

Do what pleases me, be free, have a trade which interests me.

Let us now come back to the original question the economist asked the sociologist, in which was implied the hypothesis of rational behavior—a permanent bone of contention between these two disciplines. The answer could be the following. It is clear that the relationship with or the confidence in the future constitutes a decisive dimension in different social behaviors. One can even attribute to it a causal status insofar as it succeeds, associated with other factors, in explaining behaviors (fertility, savings, schooling, choice of a job). One must, however, understand it as a complex product of a whole set of social determinations in which are brought into play, without necessarily being clearly and rationally conscious, consideration of the present situation, past experience, and the objective future engraved in this present. Individual in its process, this taking into account refers to collective experiences. This is where the "causality of probability" (Bourdieu 1974) is sociologically resorted to. From this, too, comes the diversity of relationships with the future which can be observed in apparently homogeneous populations. In particular, this confidence in the future puts up, for those who try to give it a strict empirical status, a fierce resistance: going from the imaginative sociology of models (imagination that must be encouraged!) to the realistic sociography of indicators, which may or may not enable us to decide on the validity of the models, implies mobilizing an immense arsenal of theoretical reflections capable of giving suitable relevance to the observation and the display of the treasures of experimental imagination. There is no question, in what is said here, of refusing to contribute to the modelizing imagination and to its necessary simplifications, but merely of measuring the distance which separates an elegant and fertile theoretical paradigm from a slight observation that tallies well and is susceptible to validation.

References

P. Bourdieu, "Avenir de classe et causalité du probable," *Revue française de sociologie* 15, no. 1, 1974.

P. Bourdieu and A. Darbel, "La fin d'un malthusianisme," in *Le Partage des bénéfices* (Minuit, 1966).

J. J. Carre, P. Dubois, and E. Malinvaud, *La Croissance française, un essai d'analyse économique causale de l'après-guerre* (Seuil, 1972), Annexe 8, pp. 667–670.

L. Lebart, "L'analyse statistique des réponses libres dans les enquêtes socio-économiques," *Consommation*, no. 1, 1982.

L. Lebart, A. Morineau, T. Aluja, E. Brian, E. Ganon, H. Joannes, A. Laporte, T. Lambert, P. Pleuvret, L. Pradel, P. Richardot, and H. de Roquefeuil, *SPAD, système portable pour l'analyse des données*, volumes 1, 2, 3 (Cesia, 1984, 1985, 1987).

V. Vaquin, Fécondité et scolarité, l'importance de l'école dans la stratégie de fécondité, Mémoire de maîtrise de sociologie soutenu à l'Université de Provence, 1982.

26

Executives' Promotion in an Internal Labor Market: An Econometric Analysis

François Bourguignon and
Pierre-André Chiappori

I. Introduction

In recent years, a number of articles have been devoted to internal labor markets. According to Malcomson (1984), the latter are characterized by three main features:

• The hierarchical structure of the organization, in which internal promotion, rather than external hiring, plays a key role. Moreover, turnover rates are low, most agents spending their whole career within the organization (Doeringer and Piore 1971).

• Wages are related to job, rather than to workers; also, wage increases usually result from collective bargaining (Williamson, Wachter, and Harris, 1975).

• The average wage increases with seniority faster than productivity does (Medoff and Abraham 1980); in addition, the variance of earnings also increases with seniority.

The analysis of internal labor markets is important for several reasons. First, a large number of workers are employed in this kind of organization (government offices, state-owned and large private firms, etc.). Second, from a theoretical viewpoint, internal markets provide examples of contractual relationships between a principal and an agent, outside the scope of (traditional) competitive market models. Lastly, the conclusions of such an analysis will clearly improve our understanding of labor market phenomena, hence of their relevant representation in macroeconomic modeling. This point, is stressed by Malinvaud (1985), who claims that the multiplicity of (internal and external) rules and mechanisms on the labor market is likely to be a major cause of disequilibria. He insists, in particular, upon the need to analyze precisely the nature and the role of long-term contractual relationships.

A number of theoretical models have been developed, in order to explain the main features of internal labor markets; they will be discussed briefly below. However, econometric studies are far less numerous, at least at the micro level. This is for two reasons. First, data are quite difficult to gather, since one should ideally use panel data covering a "sufficient" number of individuals and for a "sufficient" length of time. Second, such studies require highly specific tools. In particular, it is clear that a "career," within this context, consists in a discrete sequence of promotions, rather than in a continuous wage path. A consequence is that such models will require a nonlinear approach applied to panel data.

In this paper, we develop and estimate an econometric model of internal labor market, based upon an analysis of hierarchical promotions. Our approach is essentially *positive*. Our aim is *not* to explain the internal market structure, by deriving its main features as optimal answers to a well-chosen optimization problem. Rather, we shall take the structure as given, and try to estimate its main characteristics, as well as its consequences upon agents' behavior.

The theoretical model is set forth in section II. Section III presents the method we use for estimations; results are given in section IV.

II. The Model

1. Information Asymmetries and Internal Markets

Traditional explanations of internal market phenomena rely upon the concept of *specific human capital*. If we assume that the agent's productivity depends on the mastery of a given stock of knowledge, *specific to the organization*, we can easily explain a very low turnover rate. On the one hand, the firm will promote its employees, rather than hire new entrants, since the former have already acquired (part of) the necessary know-how. On the other hand, the agent cannot leave the firm without losing part of his stock of human capital; hence, he will generally stay within the firm for his whole career. So, the environment of the firm can be neglected.

This kind of explanation, however, is far from satisfactory. It suggests that the internal labor market should concern only those firms in which the level of *specific* human capital is high—a fact which is not confirmed by empirical observation. Also, this argument explains the low turnover rate, but it fails to justify other features of internal labor markets sketched above—job-related wages increasing with seniority, careers as sequences of promotions.

In contrast, recent approaches emphasize the role of information asymmetries between the employer and the employees. Two types of arguments are generally considered. First, when hiring a worker, the firm may be unable to fully observe his "ability" (adverse selection). The agent's performances, during the first years with the firm, will provide information about his characteristics. This explains why the firm will rather promote "old" workers than hire new entrants. Moreover, since the differences in ability between workers are progressively revealed, the variance of wages will increase throughout time.

On the other hand, the firm may, at any moment, fail to fully monitor the agent's behavior (moral hazard). Specifically, the firm cannot precisely observe the "actions"—e.g., "effort," "investment"—chosen by the agents; it only observes a "performance," which depends on both the agent's action and some random shock. This results in a conflict between risk sharing, on the one hand, and incentives, on the other hand: the contract cannot fully ensure the agents against the risk conveyed by the random part of his performance, since, in that case—i.e., a fixed wage—the agent would be incited to choose a "low" level of effort. Several consequences follow. First, wages should increase with seniority (apart from any productivity effect), since this will discourage cheating behavior by the agents. Second, it may be efficient to incite the agents through a promotion scheme based upon "tournaments" (Lazear 1981; Green and Stockey 1983).

In addition, Malcomson (1984) notes that the observation of performances may itself be asymmetric; specifically, the records made by the firm will not, in general, be *verifiable* by the agent. A consequence is that a contract that would directly link wages to observed performances is simply not feasible in this context, since the firm would have a strong incentive to underreport performances. However, *tournament* schemes are still available, because the firm may commit to the number of agents it will promote and the corresponding increase in wages, both being fully verifiable. Once committed, the firm cannot reduce its costs by underreporting performances. This argument explains both the hierarchical structure and the job-related wage structure; typically, it suggests, that a "career" should indeed consist in a discrete sequence of promotions.

2. A Dynamical Model

The ideas briefly presented above can be formalized in the following way. We consider an agent i, spending T periods within an organization with K

hierarchical levels. In what follows, $K_t^i \in \{1, \ldots, K\}$ is the level reached by agent i at period t. Let e_t^i denote the agent's effort and x_t^i his performance; then

$$x_t^i = f_i(e_t^i, \varepsilon_t^i),$$

where ε_t^i is some random shock.

Promotions are based upon observed performances. Specifically, promotion at date t depends upon the sequence $x_1^i, \ldots, x_t^i$ of present and past performances. We can, thus, define *direct promotion probabilities*, which to any effort sequence $(e_1^i, \ldots, e_t^i)$ associate the probability (over $\varepsilon_1^i, \ldots, \varepsilon_t^i$) of being promoted from level k to level $k+1$:

$$P_k(e_1^i, \ldots, e_t^i) = \mathbb{P}[K_{t+1}^i = k + 1/K_t^i = k, e_1^i, \ldots, e_t^i].$$

Here, P_k depends on the promotion scheme; moreover, for any given scheme, it depends on the probability distribution of $(\varepsilon_1^i, \ldots, \varepsilon_t^i)$, the latter being assumed independent of i.[1]

Lastly, the agent's utility depends (negatively) on "effort" and (positively) on the hierarchical level. In addition, we assume intertemporal separability of preferences:

$$U = \sum_{t=0}^{T} \rho_i^t U^i(K_t^i, e_t^i).$$

Hence, the agent's program, at date θ, writes down

$$(P) \quad \begin{cases} \displaystyle\max_{e_\theta^i, \ldots, e_T^i} E\left[\sum_{t=\theta}^{T} \rho_i^t U^i(K_t^i, e_t^i)\right] \\ P(K_t^i = k + 1/K_t^i = k) = P_k(e_1^i, \ldots, e_t^i), \quad \begin{cases} t = \theta, \ldots, T \\ k = 1, \ldots, K-1. \end{cases} \end{cases}$$

Let us briefly comment on this program. At date θ, efforts $e_1^i, \ldots, e_{\theta-1}^i$ are bygones; the agent's decisions only concern present and future efforts. The agent's *commands*, hence, are $e_\theta^i, \ldots e_T^i$. Moreover, the hierarchical level K_t^i can be considered as a *state variable* of the system. Relation (P) only describes the (stochastic) evolution of this state variable (which, incidentally, also depends on past values $e_1^i, \ldots e_{\theta-1}^i$).

The optimal decision e_θ^{*i} at date θ—assumed to be unique—depends on all exogenous variables at that date, including θ itself, the past career $(K_1^i, \ldots, K_\theta^i)$, and the vector of past actions $(e_1^i, \ldots, e_{\theta-1}^i)$:

$$e_\theta^{*i} = \tilde{e}_\theta^i(\theta, K_1^i, \ldots, K_\theta^i, e_1^i, \ldots, e_{\theta-1}^i).$$

In particular, e_1^{*i} can be expressed as a function of K_1^i alone. Replacing e_1^i by $\tilde{e}_1^i\ (K_1^i)$ in $\tilde{e}_2^i$, we see that e_2^{*i} can be expressed as a function of K_1^i and K_2^i alone. By forward induction, hence, e_θ^{*i} can be written as a function of $(K_1^i, \ldots, K_\theta^i)$, which, for simplicity, is denoted $e_\theta^{*i}(K_1^i, \ldots, K_\theta^i)$. The complete resolution of the program up to θ will lead to some optimal path:

$$e_{\mapsto\theta}^{*i} = (e_1^{*i}(K_1^i), \ldots, e_\theta^{*i}(K_1^i, \ldots, K_\theta^i)).$$

Lastly, if we assume that the agent effectively follows his optimal strategy, then the promotion probability at date θ can itself be written as a function of his past career:

$$\Pi_\theta^i(K_1^i, \ldots, K_\theta^i) \stackrel{\text{def}}{\equiv} P_{K_\theta^i}[e_1^{*i}(K_1^i), \ldots, e_\theta^{*i}(K_1^i, \ldots, K_\theta^i)].$$

Here, Π_θ^i can be interpreted as *the indirect promotion probability* of agent i at period θ. Note that, while the P_k did not depend on i, the Π_θ do, because the optimal effort path depends on preferences.

From an econometric viewpoint, this presentation is of interest, because indirect probabilities only depend on *observable* variables (i.e., past career); on the contrary, direct probabilities would depend on effort (or performances), which are unknown, at least to the economist analyzing those indirect probabilities.

3. Information Asymmetry and Promotions

It remains to see which properties the theoretical framework mentioned above implies for indirect probabilities. The basic idea is the following. In the general model there is no restriction on the *memory* of the promotion process; each of the (direct) promotion probabilities depends on the *whole* history of past efforts (or performances). However, in many cases, promotion depends only on "recent" performances; we shall show that, in such a case, we can derive *testable* restrictions upon indirect probabilities.

Let us first briefly remember some results of the repeated principal-agent literature. A first case is that where information is incomplete and symmetrical, i.e., neither the principal nor the agent knows some relevant parameter (say, the agent's ability). Both of them gradually discover its true value by observing performances. In that case, it can be shown (Harris and Holmström 1982) that the optimal contract will take into account *all* past performances. On the contrary, consider the pure adverse selection model, in which the agent perfectly knows his own characteristics whereas the principal does not. If the principal is able to *commit* on the long run, then the optimal contract is memoryless; in fact, the best strategy, for the principal, is to commit not to use the information revealed by the agent at each period, and to simply repeat the optimal one-period contract (Holmström 1979; Freixas, Guesnerie, and Tirole, 1985).

Lastly, even when the optimal contract is with memory, only part of the available past information may be relevant. Assume, for instance, that each hierarchical level requires specific abilities, which are not revealed by performances at inferior levels. In that case, *direct* promotion probabilities will only depend on performances (hence efforts) obtained at the present level:

$$\forall \tau \leqslant t, \quad K_\tau < k \Rightarrow \frac{\partial P_k}{\partial e_\tau}(e_1, \ldots, e_t) = 0. \tag{1}$$

We now come to the second polar case, namely moral hazard. The main features of (finitely) repeated moral hazard problem are by now well known (see Chiappori, Macho, Rey, and Salanié 1988 for a general survey). First, the structure of the optimal contract heavily depends on the one hand on whether the principal and the agent are able to commit on the long run, and, on the other hand, on whether the agent has (free) access to a (perfect) financial market. Second, the optimal long-term contract entails memory in general. However, there are at least two situations in which this is not the case. The first one is where the agent's utility is exponential and the cost of effort is purely monetary (Holmström and Milgrom 1987; Fudenberg, Holmström, and Milgrom 1987); the second one is where the agent cannot commit, has no access to financial markets, and his productivity increases "fast enough" with time—so that his reservation utility at any period is "much higher" than before (Chiappori and Macho, forthcoming).

Whenever the optimal contract is memoryless, direct promotion probability depends only on the most recent performance:

$$\forall \tau < t, \quad \frac{\partial P_k}{\partial e_\tau}(e_1, \ldots, e_t) = 0. \tag{2}$$

We now show that properties (1) and (2) can be translated in terms of *indirect* probabilities in a straightforward way.

Proposition. If (1) is satisfied, then Π_t^i depends only on the present hierarchical level, K_t^i, and the agent's seniority *at this level*:

$$\Pi_t^i(K_1^i, \ldots, K_t^i) = \Pi_t^i(K_t^i, t - t'),$$

where $t' = \inf\{\tau \text{ s.t. } K_\tau^i = K_t^i\}$.

If (2) is satisfied, Π_t^i depends only on K_t^i:

$$\Pi_t^i(K_1^i, \ldots, K_t^i) = \tilde{\Pi}_t^i(K_t^i).$$

Proof.[2] Assume that (1) is satisfied, let $t' \leqslant t$ be the data of entrance at level K_t^i. For any $\theta \in [t', t]$, the agent's program at date θ writes

$$\left| \begin{array}{l} \operatorname{Max} E \left\{ \sum_{\tau=0}^{T} \rho^{\tau} U(K_\tau^i, e_\tau^i) \right\} \\ P[K_{\tau+1}^i = k + 1 / K_\tau^i = k] = P_k(e_{t'}^i, \ldots, e_\theta^i, e_\tau^i). \end{array} \right.$$

In particular, the optimal effort at date θ, e_θ^{*i}, depends only on K_θ^i and $e_{t'}^i, \ldots, e_{\theta-1}^i$; by backward induction, it depends only on K_θ^i and on $t - t'$. Hence the conclusion. The proof of the second part of the proposition is exactly similar.

III. Data and Econometric Specification

In the rest of this paper, we seek to test some of the previous hypotheses about the role of time memory in individual careers, on the basis of panel data coming from a large French government-owned company. More precisely, we estimate an econometric model where the dependent variable is the promotion of an executive in a company from a ladder—i.e., "level"—in the earnings hierarchy to the next, and independent variables are the past career of executives in the company—i.e., the memory of his/her promotion process. As all personal characteristics are not observed and since the test of the proposed hypotheses requires those characteristics to be fixed, we also include a personal fixed effect, which is estimated thanks to the panel nature of the data.

As the past career of an executive in the company essentially is, at each point of time, a multidimensioned variable—hierarchy levels at each point of the past—which is somewhat uneasy to comprehensively account for, we use only two variables to summarize it. In accordance with the preceding theoretical arguments they are the number of years with the company (company seniority) and the number of years at the current job level (level seniority). We also use age as a personal characteristic, but because of the obvious redundancy with company seniority, only the age at which the individual joined the company is relevant.

This general specification is used to test the following hypotheses presented in the previous section:

1. No memory in the promotion process: pure adverse selection or special case of moral hazard;

2. Promotion depending on level seniority: symmetric incomplete information and assimilated cases—with level-specific abilities;

3. Promotion depending on level and company seniority: all other cases.

Note moreover that, depending on the hypothesis, the coefficients of level seniority and company seniority must have definite signs. For instance, under symmetric incomplete information as well as moral hazard, company seniority must have a positive effect upon promotion at given level in the hierarchy, level seniority and age. Indeed, in such a case, company seniority is smaller for those individuals who have been promoted sooner at the level of the hierarchy that is considered, which is synonymous with superior performances. Likewise, in the same situation, company seniority must have a negative effect upon promotion at given age, level, and level seniority, since it took more time for the individual to get to the job level he is observed to hold, revealing poor past performances. In the case of level-specific characteristics, on the other hand, company seniority should have no effect on promotion—all other variables being fixed. Finally, in the other cases, the optimal effort depends on the whole past career and the total effect of level seniority and company seniority is ambiguous.

1. Data and Variables Definition

The sample consists of 732 executives of a large French government-owned company, all of them were recruited before 1970 and were still with the company in 1982. For each individual in the sample, we observe:

- Personal characteristics: sex, diploma, year of birth, marital status as of January 1, 1984, number of children at the same date and their dates of birth.
- Career characteristics: year of recruitment in the company, job level at recruitment, dates of promotion at the next level, dates of job changes (at the same level), or changes across branches or production units of the company, number and dates of special retraining sessions within the company.

The career of the oldest individuals in the sample is known since 1960, the time at which the job-level classification used until 1982 has been set to work.

The dependent variable in the analysis is a dummy variable, A_{it}, which takes the value 1 or 0 according to whether individual i was promoted at a higher job level in year t or not. As mentioned before, our representation of the past career of an individual is not based upon the whole sequence of $A_{i\tau}$, $\tau < t$, but on three summary variables:

• The job level attained at time t, that is a set of dummy variables K_{it}^k, $k = 1, 2, \ldots, N$, where N is the total number of job levels ($N = 7$).

• Company seniority, C_{it}, controlled by the job level at time t, that is $C_{it}K_{it}^k$, $k = 1, 2, \ldots, N$.

• Level seniority S_{it}, controlled by the job level attained at time t, that is $S_{it}K_{it}^k$, $k = 1, 2, \ldots, N$[3].

Other explanatory variables include the following:

• age, N_{it}, also controlled by the job level, K_{it}^k, in order to account for expected utility before retirement

• number of children (E_{it}), which is the only time-dependent personal characteristic.

In order to test for the various types of human capital investments, we also include variables that describe the mobility of the individual within the company: CBR is the number of division changes, CUN the number of changes of production units, CEP the number of changes in job types and NFP the number of retraining sessions. However, the status of these variables is not clear. They may reflect either the voluntary choice of an individual pursuing its optimal strategy within the company, in which case they are fully endogenous, or exogenous involuntary shocks like the restructuring of a division or a production unit.

Fixed individual characteristics are accounted for in the following alternative way:

• a dummy variable for each individual i (D_i) whose coefficient summarizes the effect of *all* observed (e.g. diploma) and unobserved (e.g. social background, special abilities) personal characteristics

• observed personal characteristics (which is essentially the nature of the diploma, sex, and marital status as of 1984).

2. Econometric Specification

For the sake of convenience, we use a Logit specification. The probability of promotion at time t, P_{it}, is based upon the latent variable y_{it} according to

$$P_{it} = P_r\{A_{it} = 1\} = P_r\{y_{it} > 0\}. \tag{3}$$

The latent variable y_{it} is given, with the previous notations, by

$$y_{it} = \sum_k (a_k + b_k C_{it} + c_k S_{it} + d_k N_{it}) K_{it}^k + eE_{it} + \sum_i \delta_i D_i + u_{it}. \tag{4}$$

This corresponds to the general case where all individual characteristics are summarized by the dummy variable D_i. The coefficients to be estimated are a_k, b_k, d_k, e, and δ_i. To avoid colinearity, the sum of the δ_i must be constrained or a job level k must be taken as a reference. We opted for the latter solution. Concerning the disturbance term, u_{it}, finally, we assume that it is logistic i.i.d. across individuals and years. Note that, in effect, this is equivalent to assuming that our representation of the influence of the past career upon current promotion is correctly summarized by the three variables K_{it}^k, C_{it}, and S_{it}. Otherwise the u_{it} could be expected to be autocorrelated through time. We do not test for that possibility here.

Deriving the sample likelihood associated with model (4) is easy. However, maximizing it is a little more difficult than in the standard logit case because of the prohibitively large number of explanatory variables due to the inclusion of fixed effects. The sample of 732 individuals leads to more than 13,000 observations—i.e., a little less than 20 observations per average individual. The total number of explanatory variables is approximately 800, because of the personal dummy variables D_i, which precluded using a standard logit package. An original maximization algorithm was designed, the detail of which is given in the Appendix to this paper.

The above specification is a straight generalization of the well-known "variance component" model often applied to the analysis of personal earnings dynamics.[4] In the present case, the variance decomposition is applied to a discrete rather than a continuous variable. The problems associated with this type of estimation are similar, however. We emphasize here the most relevant ones for the interpretation of the results that follow.

The variance component model in the continuous case is

$$y_{it} = X_{it}\beta + v_{it}, \quad v_{it} = \delta_{it} + u_{it}, \tag{5}$$

where β is the vector of coefficients to be estimated and X_{it} the set of explanatory variables. The problem is to estimate β with the following stochastic specifications:

$$\underset{i}{E}(\delta_i) = \underset{t}{E}(u_{it}) = 0, \quad E(\delta_i u_{it}) = 0,$$

$$\underset{t}{V}(u_{it}) = \sigma^2 I_{T_i}, \qquad \underset{i}{V}(\delta_i) = s^2 I_n,$$

where T_i is the number of observations for individual i, n is the number of individuals in the sample, and I_j the identity matrix of dimension j. Since the random term $\delta_i + u_{it}$ is correlated across all observations of a given individual, the model is estimated by generalized least squares (GLS). It may be shown that this method is asymptotically equivalent—i.e., when $T_i \to \infty$ for all i—to ordinary least squares with individual dummy variables (OLSID)[5]:

$$y_{it} = X_{it}\beta + \sum_i \delta_i D_i + u_{it}. \tag{6}$$

It is that estimation technique that we generalize to the case of a latent variable which defines a discrete process. Using directly the specification (5) would in fact be difficult since it would require integrating the density of the vector of nonindependent random variables $(v_{i1}, v_{i2}, \ldots, v_{iT_i})$ over a linear subspace of $\mathbb{R}^{T_i}$.

In the discrete as in the continuous case, introducing fixed instead of random individual effects leads to consistent estimations only if the number of individual observations T_i is sufficiently large. For instance, Andersen (1973) has shown that, in the Logit model, where

$$y_{it} = \begin{cases} 0 \\ 1 \end{cases} \text{if } X_{it}\beta + \sum_i \delta_i D_i + u_{it} \begin{matrix} \leqslant \\ > \end{matrix} 0 \qquad \begin{matrix} t = 1, 2, \ldots, T_i \\ i = 1, 2, \ldots, n \end{matrix} \tag{7}$$

with $T_i = 2$, the maximum-likelihood estimator $\hat{\beta}$ tends toward 2β when n becomes infinite.

An alternative solution to get consistent estimators for the preceding model with small T_i is "conditional likelihood" maximization (see Chamberlain 1984). The idea is to eliminate the δ_i by considering the probability that y_{it} be 0 or 1 *conditional* on the total number of occurrences $y_{it} = 1$ over the observation period T_i of each individual. Instead of maximizing the Logit likelihood,

$$\log V(\beta, \delta) = \sum_{i=1}^{n} \sum_{t=1}^{T_i} y_{it} \operatorname{Log} \frac{1}{1 + e^{-x_{it}\beta - \delta_i}} + (1 - y_{it}) \operatorname{Log} \frac{e^{-x_{it}\beta - \delta_i}}{1 + e^{x_{it}\beta - \delta_i}},$$

this transformation leads to maximizing the multinomial Logit likelihood:

$$\log V(\beta) = \sum_{i=1}^{n} \operatorname{Log}\left[\exp\left(\beta \sum_{t=1}^{T_i} x_{it} y_{it}\right) \Big/ \sum_{d \in B_i} \exp\left(\beta \sum_{t=1}^{T_i} x_{it} d_t\right)\right]$$

or

$$B_i\left\{d \in R^{T_i}/d_t = 0 \text{ or } 1, \sum_{t=1}^{T_i} d_t = \sum_{t=1}^{T_i} y_{it} = D_i\right\},$$

D_i being now the total number of occurrences of the event $y_{it} = 1$ for individual i.

Of course, if T_i is large, the preceding technique becomes much too heavy to implement. In the present case, with T_i being 20 on average and the mean number of promotions D_i being 3, the total number of alternatives to be considered in B_i would be C_{20}^3—that is, 1140! We thus preferred to stick to the simple Logit model with fixed effects, assuming that 20 observations for each individual on average was sufficient to ensure that maximum-likelihood estimation were consistent. Rigorously this should be tested with some Monte Carlo experiments.

Another important problem in variance component models is that of the estimation of the coefficients of those individual variables, X_{it}, that stay constant over time. Assume that the vector of explanatory variables may be decomposed into

$$X_{it} = (X_{it}^1, X_i^2);$$

that is, time-dependent personal characteristics (X_{it}^1) and fixed personal characteristics (X_i^2) like sex or diploma. The continuous model with fixed effects (4) now writes

$$y_{it} = X_{it}^1\beta^1 + X_i^2\beta^2 + \delta_i + u_{it}.$$

It is well known that in this case OLS (or GLS) yields consistent estimates of β^1 but inconsistent estimates of β^2, because of the likely correlation between δ and X^2. Hausman and Taylor (1981) have shown that this bias could be corrected by using those variables in X_t^1 and X^2 uncorrelated with δ as instruments.

Such a procedure cannot be used in the discrete case. Besides, when fixed effects are postulated there is an obvious identification problem. The model then writes

$$y_{it} = X_{it}^1\beta^1 + X_i^2\beta^2 + \sum_i \delta_i D_i + u_{it}. \tag{8}$$

Clearly, the variables X_i^2 and D_i play the same role. In terms of explanatory power this model is not different from the model in which β^2 is zero. The fixed individual effect upon y_{it} results from the observed fixed characteristics X_i^2 and from the unobserved fixed characteristics implicit in D_i. Setting β^2 to zero, the estimate of the δ_i's corresponds to the sum of all these effects. With fixed effects—i.e., model (8)—including the variables X^2 thus is redundant if the objective is to estimate only the coefficients β^1 and the distribution of fixed effects δ_i. This is the choice made in what follows. However, we shall give some indications about the effect of the observables X^2.

Taking the opposite view, it might be thought that the inclusion of the fixed characteristics X^2 makes the fixed effects δ_i redundant, in which case OLS—or a simple Logit model in the discrete case—could be used (setting $\delta_i = 0$). This is true, however, only if the X^2 variables are assumed to describe *completely* the effect of fixed personal characteristics. If this is not the case—and, in particular, if the time-dependent variables X_{it}^1 are correlated with these fixed characteristics (as is obviously the case in our model with the job level attained by an individual at time t)—then the random term u_{it} in (6) is necessarily correlated with the X_{it}^1 and the estimates of β^1 are biased. As it is certainly not the case that all the fixed characteristics that determine the career of an individual may be observed, estimating the fixed effects δ_i cannot be avoided. For the sake of completeness, we nevertheless report in the next section the results obtained when applying a simple Logit model over the sole variables X_{it}^1 and X_i^2.

IV. Estimation Results

The estimates obtained from the methods which have just been described are reported in tables 1 and 2. The first table corresponds to the model without individual fixed effect but including the observed fixed personal characteristics—sex and diploma. Table 2 includes individual fixed effects without distinction between observed and unobserved characteristics. It also shows the likelihood obtained at the first iteration of the maximization algorithm, where fixed effects are set to zero.

Comparing this last figure to the likelihood reported in table 1 shows that the observed fixed personal characteristics have a significant effect upon individual careers, most noticeably the nature of the diploma and the marital status. The model reported in table 1 appears of limited interest, however, when comparing its likelihood with that of the fixed effect model in table 2. The log-likelihood ratio is above 1,000, an extremely significant figure, even when accounting for the fact that the fixed effect model has approximately 700 more degrees of freedom than the model reported in table 1.[6] Clearly, then, sex, marital status, and education represent only a small proportion of all fixed characteristics that may determine the career of an individual. In accordance with the argument in the preceding section,

Table 1.
Career Model without Fixed Effects.

Past career

Job level	Constant	Age	Company seniority	Level seniority
0	a	−0.01	0.69	b
		(−2.3)	(18.0)	
1	−0.81*	0.04*	−0.07	0.36
	(−1.2)	(1.6)	(−2.3)	(8.5)
2	2.08	−0.07	−0.08	0.37
	(2.8)	(−2.8)	(−2.9)	(11.6)
3	4.77	−0.2	0.09	0.34
	(4.3)	(−5.5)	(2.7)	(9.1)
4	5.00	−0.16	−0.00*	0.28
	(2.4)	(−2.8)	(−0.0)	(4.0)
5	2.26*	−0.19*	0.34	0.24*
	(0.4)	(−1.3)	(2.4)	(1.5)
6	2.53*	−0.08*	−0.08*	0.40
	(0.8)	(−1.0)	(−1.4)	(2.4)

Other variables

Time-dependent characteristics		*Fixed characteristics*	
Retraining:	−0.03*	School 1:	0.23
	(−0.7)		(2.0)
Change of division:	−0.24	School 2:	−0.22
	(−4.0)		(−3.1)
Change of job:	0.09	School 3:	−0.19
	(3.4)		(−2.4)
Change of unit:	−0.05*	Additional degrees 1:	−0.07*
	(−1.7)		(−0.6)
Number of children:	0.09	Additional degrees 2:	−0.06*
	(3.3)		(−1.4)
Division 1:	−0.40	Widower or single	−0.47
	(−6.2)		(−3.3)
Division 2:	0.14*	Divorced:	−0.44
	(1.96)		(−2.5)
		Married with working spouse:	0.02*
			(0.4)
		Sex (male):	−1.47
			(−8.8)

Log-likelihood: −5191.5.

[a] Reference level.
[b] This variable is colinear with the previous one.
* Nonsignificant coefficient at 95% confidence (standard errors in parentheses).

Table 2.
Model with Fixed Effects.

Career variables

Job level	Constant	Age	Company seniority	Level seniority
0	*a*	*b*	2.05	*c*
			(28.7)	
1	−0.08*	−0.09	1.19	0.09*
	(−0.1)	(−2.1)	(16.9)	(1.3)
2	4.41	−0.31	0.98	−0.20
	(3.4)	(−6.6)	(16.5)	(−4.0)
3	12.63	−0.61	0.88	0.10
	(7.8)	(−10.6)	(13.4)	(2.0)
4	15.58	−0.52	0.31	0.51
	(5.6)	(−6.2)	(4.0)	(4.9)
5	15.00	−0.70	0.91	0.26*
	(2.3)	(−3.4)	(5.0)	(1.4)
6	12.89	−0.35	−0.03*	0.75
	(2.9)	(−3.0)	(−0.3)	(3.3)

Other variables

Number of children	0.00*	Changes of division	−0.20
	(0.0)		(−2.4)
Retraining	−0.15	Changes of job	0.15
	(−2.9)		(3.2)
Division 1	0.10*	Changes of unit	−0.14
	(0.6)		(−2.7)
Division 2	−0.9		
	(−6.6)		

Log-likelihood without fixed effects: −5443.7

Log-likelihood: −4147.4

[a] Reference level.
[b] Excluded to avoid colinearity problems.
[c] This variable is colinear with the previous one at that job level.
* Nonsignificant coefficient at 95% (standard errors in parentheses).

this also implies that the estimates of the coefficients of the variables which describe the past career of an employee in the model without fixed effect are biased. In effect, important differences in these estimates are readily apparent when comparing both tables.

Now that we have put into evidence the prominent role played by fixed individual characteristics in shaping the career of agents, we turn to the influence of their past career on their prospects for promotion. Before coming back to the hypotheses set forth in the theoretical section above, it is worth mentioning how to interpret the coefficients of the corresponding variables K_{it}^{t}, C_{it}, S_{it}, and N_{it} in the tables. It must be kept in mind that the model is multiplicative with respect to the dummy job-level variables K_{t}^{k}, so that the effect of being at a given job level upon the probability of being promoted is not to be read under the heading "constant" but must be calculated using the age, level seniority, and company seniority of the agent. Note also that all coefficients corresponding to a given job level must be understood "other things being equal." In table 2, for instance, for given level seniorities and company seniorities, the probability of promotion decreases with age whereas, on the whole, it increases with time—i.e., the sum of the coefficients of C_{it}, S_{it}, and n_{it} is positive.

With these precautions in mind, we now turn to the test of our theoretical hypothesis about the determinants of agents' careers. Promotion probabilities clearly depend very significantly upon age, level seniority, and company seniority of employees, these three variables being considered separately. We may thus reject the "no memory promotion process" that rules out any influence of the past over the future career. In other words, promotion is not a "pure" incentive device as under the hypothesis of a pure adverse selection, or moral hazard with monetary effort cost and constant risk aversion. Likewise, we may reject the hypothesis of symmetric imperfect information with level-specific abilities. Indeed, that hypothesis is consistent with a significant influence of level seniority but not of company seniority upon promotion. We are thus led to accept the hypothesis of a more general model of promotion.

The stability of past-career effects upon promotion across job levels is also to be stressed. The effect of age is, other things being equal, always negative, and that of seniority, at a job level or within the company, is always positive, but for one exception. The total effect of an additional year at any job level is always positive or zero, and significantly different form zero at lower levels. Note at this respect the importance of the correction brought about by the inclusion of personal fixed effects. The estimated coefficients for company seniority are always smaller in table 1 and sometimes significantly negative. This reflects the fact that, in the corresponding model, past career achievements partly reflect the innate abilities of an individual. For instance, a brilliant person, who may thus expect a faster than average career in the future, will in general have attained a given job level sooner than most other employees, and will thus have less company seniority than other individuals currently observed at that job level. This example puts into light the way in which not accounting for personal fixed effect may severely bias the estimates; in this case the seniority variables summarize at the same time the true effect of seniority and the indirect effect of ability differences among employees.

Concerning now the variables describing the mobility of executives within the company, the results shown in table 2 also are of interest even though we have seen that their exogeneity status was unclear. Moving around within the company appears to be a disadvantage for future promotion, a result which is consistent with the hypothesis that such moves are involuntary accidents in the career of an individual or that the "information" capital of an employee decreases when he switches from a division or

Table 3.
Mean Characteristics of the Sample.

Job level	Age	Company seniority	Level seniority	Percentage of individuals who went through that level	Number of observations[a]
0	26.9	1.5	1.5	94.6	2475
	(21–44)	(0–11)	(0–11)		
1	31.0	5.4	1.9	96.1[b]	2784
	(24–46)	(0–21)	(0–17)		
2	35.9	10.1	2.8	96.3[b]	3957
	(27–54)	(0–21)	(0–15)		
3	39.8	13.7	2.7	74.3	2691
	(30–57)	(0–22)	(0–17)		
4	42.2	15.6	2.0	30.3	815
	(32–52)	(0–22)	(0–14)		
5	42.2	14.3	2.5	4.2	108
	(35–50)	(0–22)	(0–13)		
6	43.9	15.3	1.8	7.6	172
	(35–53)	(0–22)	(0–8)		

[a] Observations correspond to a given year and a given individual.
[b] Increase due to direct entry at that level.

a productive unit to another. On the contrary, a change in the nature of the job, when it does not imply changing department or division, has a positive influence on promotion. Finally, retraining sessions appear to slow down an individual's career. A possible explanation for this paradoxical result is that such retraining programs may rather be a consequence than a cause of promotion. People are not promoted thanks to retraining; on the contrary, retraining becomes necessary after being promoted to a new job.

To get some feeling about the role of individual characteristics, we now examine what differences in estimated fixed effects between individuals may imply for their career. Consider, for instance, two persons who joined the company at the same age and have attained job level 4, without having changed division or type of job. Table 4 shows the promotion probabilities of these two employees to job level 5 under the assumptions that the first one stands at the first quartile of the ability distribution within the sample, ability being measured by the estimated fixed effect, whereas the second one stands at the third quartile. These probabilities are shown as functions of level seniority at job level 4 and company seniority at the time job level 4 was reached. They are defined "at the margin"; in other words, figures reported in table 4 correspond to the probabilities of being promoted to job level 5 precisely at time *t*—time coinciding here with

Table 4.
Promotion Probability according to Level Seniority and Company Seniority, and Individual Fixed Effect.

(Job level 4) Level seniority	0	1	2	3	5	10
Company seniority when entering job level						
0	1.7	2.6	4.1	6.3	14.4	62.7
	0.2	0.4	0.6	0.9	2.2	18.5
1	2.7	4.2	6.5	10.0	21.7	73.5
	0.4	0.6	0.9	1.5	3.6	27.3
2	4.4	6.8	10.3	15.4	31.4	82.1
	0.6	1.0	1.5	2.4	5.8	38.2
5	17.1	24.6	34.1	45.0	84.8	95.3
	2.7	4.2	6.5	10.0	21.7	73.5
10	71.5	79.9	86.3	90.9	96.2	99.6
	25.3	35.0	46.0	57.4	77.2	97.1

The upper figure corresponds to an individual with fixed effect equal to first quartile (from top), the lower figure to the third quartile. Both individuals are supposed to have joined the company at age 25.

level seniority—and not at some time before t—note that such cumulative probabilities may also be computed. Results conform what could be expected. The probability of promotion increases both with level seniority and company seniority, promotion being most unlikely for individuals who would have reached job level 4 only after 3 or 4 years with the company. The differences between the individual with high and with low innate ability—i.e., estimated fixed effects—is more interesting. Indeed differences in abilities are shown to produce important disparities between individuals careers; the probability of being promoted to job level 5 after one year at level 4 is 5 times larger for the most able individual when both individuals have reached level 4 after 5 years with the company.

This simple-minded example shows the usefulness of the model developed in this paper. For lack of space, we do not exhibit here other applications that can be made with the estimates that come out of the model: determination of the probability of a given career, of having reached some job level at a given time, etc., as functions of the estimated personal fixed effects, or on a given sample of individuals. The possibility of using the model "backward" must also be mentioned. In effect, our estimates also permit estimation of the probability distribution of the fixed effect of a given individual from his/her past career and to infer from it the probability distribution of his/her future career. All these instruments may prove useful in personal management and will be investigated more carefully in subsequent work.

As a conclusion to this paper, it seemed interesting to relate the estimated fixed effects with the observed fixed characteristics of the individuals in the sample. From the simple regression reported in table 5 it appears that:

- The tiny fraction of individuals who joined the company at a job level greater than or equal to 2 have an advantage over other employees; however, for those joining the company at job levels 0 and 1, age has a favorable influence upon the future career.
- Two types of diploma are much different from the others, but additional degrees do not significantly improve career prospects.
- Marital status—as of 1984—has no significant effect.
- Being a male has a strong positive effect—comparable to that of the best diploma.
- There is only one significant cohort effect: people who joined the company before 1965 fared better than those who came later.

Table 5.
Simple Regression of Fixed Effects on Observed Individual Characteristics.

Entry job level	Constant	Age at entry
0	−9.40	0.28
	(−4.3)	(6.6)
1	−15.88	0.58
	(−2.2)	(2.4)
3	−14.51*	−0.19*
	(−1.06)	(1.2)
4	−2.20	0.08*
	(−0.182)	(0.3)

School 1:	0.79	Single or widower:	−0.34*
	(2.2)		(−0.9)
School 2:	−0.82	Divorced:	−0.53*
	(−4.0)		(−1.0)
School 3:	−0.14*	Married with active spouse:	−0.07*
	(−0.6)		(−0.4)
Additional degree 1:	−0.36*	Sex (male):	2.03
	(−1.1)		(2.3)
Additional degree 2:	0.02*		
	(0.2)		

Year of entry

Before 1963	1963	1964	1965	1966	1967	1968	1969
0.41*	0.59*	0.58*	0.80	−0.28*	0.15*	0.33*	−0.02*
(1.4)	(1.7)	(1.6)	(2.3)	(−0.7)	(0.4)	(0.9)	(−0.1)

Constant: −4.35
(−2.0)

$R^2 = 0.25$ $F = 7.23$

*Statistically nonsignificant at 95% confidence (t statistics in parentheses).

Finally, it must be stressed that all these variables explain only a quarter of the variance of the fixed effects, which fully justifies inclusion of these effects in the estimation procedure.

Several improvements could be made to reinforce the conclusions obtained in this paper and the tests that can be made of the specificity of the "internal labor market." In addition to several points already mentioned, including the demand side of the market—that is the expansion of the company—into the analysis must be considered at a later stage of this work.

Appendix Maximum-Likelihood of the Logit Model with Fixed Effects: The Resolution Algorithm

The model writes

$$\Pr\{A_{it} = 1\} = \Pr\{y_{it} = X_{it}\beta + \delta_i + u_{it} > 0\}$$

$$= \frac{1}{1 + \exp(-X_{it}\beta - \delta_i)}.$$

The log likelihood of the sample thus is

$$\log L = \sum_i \sum_t A_{it} \log\left\{\frac{1}{1 + \exp(-X_{it}\beta - \delta_i)}\right\}$$

$$+ (1 - A_{it}) \log\left\{1 - \frac{1}{1 + \exp(-X_{it}\beta - \delta_i)}\right\},$$

which also writes

$$\log L = -\sum_i \sum_t \{(1 - A_{it})(X_{it}\beta + \delta_i) + \log[1 + \exp(-X_{it}\beta - \delta_i)]\}.$$

The maximum-likelihood estimators, $\hat{\beta}$ and $\hat{\delta}$, are obtained by equalizing the derivatives to zero. This yields the following two sets of equations:

$$\frac{\partial \log L}{\partial \hat{\beta}_k} = -\sum_i \sum_t X_{it}^k\{(1 - A_{it}) - [1 + \exp(X_{it}\hat{\beta} + \hat{\delta})]^{-1}\} = 0,$$

$k = 1, 2, \ldots, K$

$$\frac{\partial \log L}{\partial \hat{\delta}_i} = -\sum_t \{(1 - A_{it}) - [1 + \exp(X_{it}\hat{\beta} + \hat{\delta})]^{-1}\} = 0,$$

$i = 1, 2, \ldots, N$

where K is the number of explanatory variables and N is the number of individuals.

The preceding system is solved by iterations. Let $\hat{\delta}_i^n$ be the estimates obtained for the fixed effects at iteration n. The estimates of β at iteration $n + 1$, $\hat{\beta}^{n+1}$, are given by the resolution of

$$-\sum_i \sum_t X_{it}^k \{(1 - A_{it}) - [1 + \exp(X_{it}\hat{\beta}^{n+1} + \hat{\delta}_i^n)]\} = 0.$$

Given $\hat{\beta}^{n+1}$, we then solve

$$\sum_t (1 - A_{it}) - [1 + \exp(X_{it}\hat{\beta}^{n+1} + \hat{\delta}_i^{n+1})]^{-1} = 0$$

for each individual i. The first resolution is a slight modification—because of the $\hat{\delta}_i^n$—of the standard resolution of the Logit model. The second resolution conerns only one parameter for each individual. We use a Newton algorithm which requires 3 to 4 iterations on average.

The whole algorithm is necessarily convergent since the likelihood increases at each iteration. Even though it is relatively slow, it is a convenient alternative to the resolution of a standard Logit with more than 700 variables.

Asymptotically, the covariance matrix of the estimations $(\hat{\beta}, \hat{\delta})$ is given by the inverse of the second derivative matrix, I. The iterative procedure described above avoids the computation of that matrix. After convergence, an additional operation is necessary. It is relatively simple. The matrix I may be decomposed into

$$I = \begin{bmatrix} \dfrac{\partial^2 \log L}{\partial \beta^2} & \dfrac{\partial^2 \log L}{\partial \beta \partial \delta} \\ \dfrac{\partial^2 \log L}{\partial \delta \partial \beta} & \dfrac{\partial^2 \log L}{\partial \delta^2} \end{bmatrix} = \begin{bmatrix} B & C \\ C' & D \end{bmatrix}.$$

We must evaluate the covariance matrix V_β of the $\hat{\beta}$ estimators, which is the upper left block of I^{-1}. Indeed the covariance matrix of the fixed effects, $\hat{\delta}_i$, has no particular interest. Only the global significance of these coefficients matter, which may be tested with a conventional likelihood ratio test. We thus want to compute

$$V_\beta = [B - CD^{-1}C']^{-1}.$$

But D is a diagonal matrix:

$$D_{ii} = \frac{\partial^2 \log L}{\partial \delta_i^2} = -\sum_t F_{it}(1 - F_{it}),$$

with $F_{it} = [1 + \exp(-X_{it}\hat{\beta} - \hat{\delta}_i)]^{-1}$.

On the other hand, it is easily determined that

$$C_{ki} = \frac{\partial^2 \log L}{\partial \hat{\beta}_k \partial \delta_i} = -\sum_t X_{it}^k F_{it}(1 - F_{it}).$$

Hence,

$$(CD^{-1}C')_{kl} = -\sum_i \left[\frac{\sum_t X_{it}^k F_{it}(1 - F_{it}) \sum_t X_{it}^l F_{it}(1 - F_{it})}{\sum_t F_{it}(1 - F_{it})}\right]$$

for $k = 1, \ldots, K$ and $l = 1, \ldots, K$.

The matrix $(CD^{-1}C')$ may thus be computed easily individual by individual, whereas B in the above expression of V_β is evaluated at each step of the likelihood-maximization procedure.

Acknowledgments

This paper has been presented in various seminars. We thank the participants to those seminars for useful comments, and, in particular, A. Monfort, A. Trognon, and P. Sevestre. We also thank the company that made its staff files available to us, and B. Sabatier-Labeyrie for computational assistance. We remain fully responsible for possible errors.

Notes

1. We neglect the strategic aspects linked to the fact that *i*'s promotion probability also depends on other agents' strategies. This assumption, frequently made in the literature, can be accepted when the number of agents is great enough. The case of a small number of agents—which requires strategical aspects to be explicitly considered—will be the topic of further research.

2. Of course, the proposition applies for a *given* individual characteristics, including the agent's *age* at date *t*. In particular, promotion probabilities always vary with *t*, since age does.

3. A referee suggested that seniority variables might be partly endogenous, since only the agents with "high" promotion probabilities will remain within the firm. This selectivity bias, however, can probably be neglected here because of the very low turnover rate.

4. See Atkinson, Bourguignon, and Morrisson 1988 for a short survey.

5. See Maddala 1977, pp. 327–328.

6. For a χ^2 distribution with 700 degrees of freedom, the 99% threshold is 576, while λ is over 2000.

References

Andersen, E. B. *Conditional Inference and Models for Measuring*. Copenhagen: Mentalhygiejnisk Forlag, 1973.

Atkinson, A. B., F. Bourguignon, and C. Morrisson, "Earnings Mobility." *European Economic Review*, March 1988, pp. 619–631.

Chamberlain, G. "Panel Data." In *Handbook of Econometrics*, ed. Z. Griliches and M. Intriligator (North-Holland, 1984).

Chiappori, P. A., and I. Macho. Contrats de travail répétés: le rôle de la mémoire. *Annales d'Economie et de Statistiques*, forthcoming.

Chiappori, P. A., I. Macho, P. Rey, and B. Salanié. Repeated Moral Hazard: The Role of Memory, Commitment, and the Access to Credit Markets. Mimeo, Paris, 1988.

Doeringer, P. B., and M. J. Piore. *Internal Labor Markets and Manpower Analysis*. Lexington Books, 1971.

Freixas, X., R. Guesnerie, and J. Tirole. "Planning under Incomplete Information and the Ratchet Effect." *Review of Economic Studies* 52, 1985, pp. 173–191.

Fudenberg, D., B. Holmström, and P. Milgrom. Short Term Contracts and Long-Term Agency Relationships. Mimeo, 1987.

Green, J., and N. Stockey. "A Comparison of Tournaments and Contracts." *Journal of Political Economy* 91, no. 3, 1983, pp. 349–364.

Harris, M., and B. Holmström. "A Theory of Wage Dynamics." *Review of Economic Studies* no. 6, 1982, pp. 315–333.

Hausman, J. A., and W. E. Taylor. "Panel Data and Unobservable Individual Effects." *Econometrica* 49, 1981, pp. 1377–1398.

Lazear, E. P. "Agency, Earnings Profiles, Productivity, and Hours Restrictions." *American Economic Review* 71, no. 4, 1981, pp. 606–620.

Lazear, E. P., and S. Rosen. "Rank-Order Tournaments as Optimum Labor Constract." *Journal of Political Economy* 89, no. 5, 1981, pp. 842–864.

Maddala, G. *Econometrics*. McGraw-Hill, 1977.

Malcomson, J. M. "Work Incentives, Hierarchy and Internal Labor Markets." *Journal of Political Economics* 92, 1984, pp. 486–607.

Malcomson, J., and F. Spinnewyn. The Multiperiod Principal-Agent Problem. D. P. 8511, Southampton, 1987.

Mincer, J. A. *Schooling, Experience and Earnings.* Columbia University Press, 1974.

Malinvaud, E. "Le marché du travail en déséquilibre." In *Keynes aujourd'hui: théories et politiques* (Economica, 1985).

Medoff, J., and K. Abraham. "Experience, Performance and Earnings." *Quarterly Journal of Economics* 95, 1980, pp. 703–736.

Rey, P., and B. Salanié. Long Term, Short Term and Renegotiations. To appear in *Econometrica.*

Williamson, O., M. L. Wachter, and J. E. Harris. "Understanding the Employment Relation: The Analysis of Idiosyncratic Exchange." *Bell Journal of Economics* 6, 1975, pp. 250–278.

27

Disequilibrium on the Labor Market: An Estimation Relying on Survey Data

Frédéric Gagey,
Jean-Paul Lambert, and
Benoît Ottenwaelter

I. Introduction

Spurred by the early theoretical works of Barro and Grossman (1971), Benassy (1975), and Malinvaud (1977), the development of macroeconometric rationing models improved our understanding of a number of economic issues. Thanks to the parallel development of "disequilibrium econometrics" (Fair and Jaffee 1972; Maddala and Nelson 1974), empirical applications of such models could be performed, mostly on European data: France (Artus, Laroque, and Michel (1984), the Netherlands (Kooiman and Kloek 1985), or Belgium (Sneessens 1983).

Since disequilibrium models incorporate Keynesian and classical elements in a natural way, deeper insights could be gained in the analysis of the labor market.

In these models, total unemployment is traditionally identified as the sum of three components:

- frictional unemployment, which accounts for the difference between the registered labor force and effective labor supply,
- Keynesian unemployment, which represents the share of unemployment attributable to deficient demand for goods, and
- classical unemployment, the balance, i.e., what remains after deduction of the frictional and Keynesian components of unemployment.

Such a decomposition is not without conceptual problems. Classical unemployment, for instance, defined as a residual, is somewhat peculiar: since its link with rationing appears as only indirect, specific policy measures aimed at alleviating it are more difficult to identify.

Moreover, the estimation of frictional unemployment meets with technical difficulties. Indeed, only the episodes characterized by tensions on the labor market, i.e., by some rationing of the demand for labor, are likely to be informative about the labor supply. In most European countries, however, such tensions have been infrequent in recent years. Hence, the usual adoption of a very rudimentary specification for labor supply, the estimation of which remaining nevertheless rather flimsy. (See Laroque 1986.)

In the present paper, we aim to refine the analysis of the labor market, through the estimation of a disequilibrium model characterized by the systematic use of "tension indicators" yielded by business surveys.

The use of business survey data enables us to enrich the specification of labor supply and to get hopefully more robust estimates of frictional unemployment. Classical unemployment also is much more precisely identified with lack of productive capacity.

Our model, while clearly inspired by the one proposed in Sneessens and Dreze (1986), presents however a number of distinctive features, due as much to the systematic use of survey data as to the emphasis placed on the labor market.

The model presents a block recursive structure. The first block describes the production structure. Available capacity margins are explicitly taken into account. The adopted procedure yields estimates of short-run technical coefficients (indeed, the substitution possibilities are assumed to be large in the long run but very limited if not nonexistent in the short run).

The second block, which contains the consumption, export, and import equations, yields an estimate of the extent of demand rationing and spillover effects, due to the tensions on production capacities and/or available labor. The results of this block may be used to estimate the notional demand addressed to the domestic sector.

The last block of the model, which relies on the results obtained in the preceding blocks, handles the determination of employment as a function of demand and supply in a rationing context. It consists of three jointly estimated equations, which yield a slightly different decomposition of unemployment as the one summarized above.

II. The Model

II.1. The Production Structure

Let us assume a representative firm that produces a unique good, used as well for consumption, exports etc. The firm uses two inputs, capital K and labor L. While fairly large substitution possibilities between factors are assumed in the longer run, technology is in the short run completely described by rigid technical coefficients:

$$A = \frac{\bar{Q}}{LP}$$

and

$$B = \frac{\bar{Q}}{K},$$

where K is the stock of capital, $\bar{Q}$ the production capacity, and LP the level of potential employment (i.e., the amount of labor necessary for the firm to produce up to full capacity, given the technology prevailing in the short run). Since investment behavior is not examined here, production capacity is thus treated as exogenous.

The choice—in a longer run perspective—of the prevailing technology is analyzed as follows. The substitution possibilities between factors in the longer run are assumed to be adequately described by a CES production function with constant returns to scale:

$$Q = [a(Le^{\gamma t})^{-p} + b(Ke^{\gamma' t})^{-p}]^{-1/p}. \tag{1}$$

At each date, production technology is chosen in order to maximize profit:

$$\Pi = pQ - \omega L - qK, \tag{2}$$

where ω = hourly wage, q = usage cost of capital, p = output price, and L = labor measured in number of hours.

The solution of the firm's program yields the equations

$$\log\left(\frac{\bar{Q}}{LP}\right)^* = (1 - \sigma)\gamma t + \sigma \log(\omega/p) - \sigma \log a \tag{3}$$

and

$$\log\left(\frac{\bar{Q}}{K}\right)^* = (1 - \sigma)\gamma' t + \sigma \log(q/p) - \sigma \log b \tag{4}$$

with $\sigma = 1/1 + \rho$, which define the optimal technical coefficients:

$$A^* = \left(\frac{\bar{Q}}{LP}\right)^* \tag{5}$$

$$B^* = \left(\frac{\bar{Q}}{K}\right)^* \tag{6}$$

and hence determine the production possibilities available in the short run:

$$Q = \mathrm{Min}[A^*L, B^*K]. \tag{7}$$

Due mainly to labor hoarding and the absence of direct information on the share of effectively used equipment, the observed ratios Q/L and Q/K may not be considered as suitable proxies of the optimal values 5 and 6.

Hence, observed productivities of capital and labor have to be "corrected," before estimation, by incorporating outside information about the degree of capacity utilization. Such an information is provided by regular business surveys conducted by INSEE (refer to the appendix for the precise definition and proposed interpretation of available indicators).

Let us denote by MACSE the "capacity margin without additional hiring," i.e., the supplementary output (expressed as a percentage of current output) which could be produced with the presently occupied labor force (in absence of any labor hoarding). The availability of such a statistic allows us to determine the "optimal" value of labor productivity as

$$A^* = \frac{Q}{L}(1 + \mathrm{MACSE}). \tag{8}$$

Denoting similarly by MACAE the "capacity margin with additional hiring," i.e., the supplementary output (expressed as a percentage of current output) which could be produced by recruiting all the additional labor needed, we may determine the optimal value of capital productivity as

$$B^* = \frac{Q}{K}(1 + \mathrm{MACAE}). \tag{9}$$

Since it may be possible that some firms report on all their physically installed capacities instead of only the economically profitable ones and since the available surveys cover only the manufacturing sector (while we are concerned here with the whole private sector), we will assume the "true" value of the margins to be a simple nonlinear function of the reported margins:

$$1 + \text{"true margins"} = f(1 + \text{reported margins})^c.$$

Combining (3) and (9) leads to the following specifications for the observed technical coefficients:

$$\log\left(\frac{Q}{L}\right) = -c_s \log(1 + \mathrm{MACSE}) + \rho\sigma\gamma t + \sigma \log\left(\frac{\omega}{p}\right) + a' \tag{10}$$

with $a' = -\sigma \log a - \log f_s$

$$\log\left(\frac{Q}{K}\right) = -c_a \log(1 + \text{MACAE}) + \rho\sigma\gamma' t + \sigma \log\left(\frac{q}{p}\right) + b' \qquad (11)$$

with $b' = -\sigma \log b - \log f_a$.

If the survey answers about MACSE and MACAE had to be interpreted as reflecting the "true" values of the margins, then c_a, c_s, f_a and f_s would be equal to 1.

Estimation of (10) and (11) allows to obtain estimates of the parameters c_a and c_s and to test this hypothesis. The parameters f_a and f_s are, however, not identified at this stage.

The production model, as it has been exposed above, is purely static. Dynamic specifications are however needed to analyze real data in order to account for the existence of adjustment costs and the formation of expectations on the basis of all available (present and past) information. Assuming that the adjustment of technical coefficients toward their optimal long run targets (defined by equations 3 and 4) follows an error-correction mechanism, we write

$$\begin{aligned}
&\log\left(\frac{Q_t}{L_t}(1 + \text{MACSE}_t)^{c_s}\right) \\
&\quad = \log\left(\frac{Q_{t-4}}{L_{t-4}}(1 + \text{MACSE}_{t-4})^{c_s}\right) \\
&\qquad + d_0(\log A_t^* - \log A_{t-4}^*) \\
&\qquad + (1 - d_3)\left(\log A_{t-4}^* - \log\left(\frac{Q_{t-4}}{L_{t-4}} f_s (1 + \text{MACSE}_{t-4})^{c_s}\right)\right)
\end{aligned}$$

and

$$\begin{aligned}
&\log\left(\frac{Q_t}{K_t}(1 + \text{MACAE}_t)^{c_a}\right) \\
&\quad = \log\left(\frac{Q_{t-4}}{K_{t-4}}(1 + \text{MACAE}_{t-4})^{c_a}\right) \\
&\qquad + d_0(\log B_t^* - \log B_{t-4}^*) \\
&\qquad + (1 - d_3)\left(\log B_{t-4}^* - \log\left(\frac{Q_{t-4}}{K_{t-4}} f_a (1 + \text{MACAE}_{t-4})^{c_a}\right)\right),
\end{aligned}$$

where four periods lags are taken since we work on quarterly data.

These two equations are jointly estimated on quarterly national accounts data covering the period 1964.1 to 1986.2 (with dummy variables for the quarters 68.2, 69.2, and 74.3). Relying on results obtained in previous work, the usage cost of capital has here been specified as being simply proportional to the price of investment goods.

Estimation results suggest a few comments.

All the coefficients are statistically significant with the expected sign, except the capital improving technical progress which appears to the negative: this might be partly attributable to possible modifications of the capital depreciation rate since the mid-1970s, which are not adequately taken into account in the data used.[1] The estimates of the dynamic coefficients reject the simple partial adjustment model in favor of more general error correction mechanism (d_0 being indeed statistically different from $1 - d_3$).

Estimates of the Production Block

c_s	0.46	(5.4)	
c_a	0.56	(7.9)	
d_0	0.51	(4.3)	$DW_1 = 1.9$
d_3	0.69	(15)	$DW_2 = 1.9$
γ	0.007	(6.1)	$RMSE_1 = 0.014$
γ'	-0.006	(-3.8)	$RMSE_2 = 0.015$
σ	0.48	(4.1)	

The estimates of c_s and c_a differ significantly from 0 but also from 1, which might be attributable to the two reasons mentioned above (inadequate reporting by the firms and insufficient sectoral coverage of the survey data). Finally, the estimate of the elasticity of substitution (0.48) conforms to the findings of other authors (Artus and Bismut 1980).

II.2. The Notional Demand for Goods

Estimating demand equations is necessary for the further estimation of what is called "Keynesian employment," i.e., the level of employment that would be needed to satisfy the whole demand for goods addressed to the domestic production sector.

To assess the level of this "notional" demand, we need in particular to get estimates of the importance of the spillover effects arising from insufficient production capacities in some domestic firms. We will assume here that, in the case of excess demand for goods, demand for investment and public consumption are never rationed, while private consumption and export might be rationed. Also excess demand might spill over into increased imports.

Estimation of possible demand rationing and spillover effects is performed through the estimation of the following demand block, composed of three equations and an accounting identity:

$$C_t = C_t^* - \gamma_c(Y_t^* - Y_t), \tag{12}$$

$$X_t = X_t^* - \gamma_x(Y_t^* - Y_t), \tag{13}$$

$$M_t = M_t^* + \gamma_m(Y_t^* - Y_t), \tag{14}$$

$$Y_t = C_t + X_t - M_t + EXO_t + CI_t, \tag{15}$$

$$Y_t^* \underset{\text{def}}{=} C_t^* + X_t^* - M_t^* + EXO_t + CI_t^*, \tag{16}$$

where C_t, X_t, M_t, Y_t, CI_t, and EXO_t are the observed values of private consumption, exports, imports, production, intermediary inputs, and exogenous demand components (investment, public consumption, and changes of stocks) and where an asterisk designates the "notional" (ex ante) value of the considered variable.[2]

The parameters γ_c, γ_x, and γ_m are expected to be positive. If the ratio of intermediary consumption to output is assumed to be constant and equal to π, the relations imply the following constraint:

$$\gamma_c + \gamma_x + \gamma_m = 1 - \pi. \tag{17}$$

Some business survey data may be informative about the discrepancy between the "notional" demand Y^* and the output level Y. Relying on a result obtained by "smoothing by aggregating" over micromarkets in diverse disequilibrium situations (see Lambert 1984), one writes

$$\frac{Y^*}{Y} = (1 - P_G)^{-1/\rho_0}, \tag{18}$$

where P_G is the proportion of firms which, according to the business surveys, are in excess demand (see appendix) and ρ_0 is a parameter measuring the degree of mismatch between demands and supplies of goods at the micro level.

The specifications adopted for "notional" import, export, and private consumption demand and rather conventional.

The "notional" export equation writes

$$\log X^* = (x_0 + x_1 t) \log \mathrm{DM} + x_2 \log\left(\frac{\mathrm{PE}}{\mathrm{PX}}\right), \tag{19}$$

where DM represents world demand and PE/PX is a distributed lag of foreign competitors' prices relative to French export prices (the dynamic structure for these relative prices has been imposed on the basis of extensive work on this subject conducted at INSEE). The elasticity of exports with respect to world demand has been allowed to vary with time, in order to capture the steady decrease of French products in world market shares.

The "notional" import equation also exhibits a quite conventional specification:

$$\log M^* = m_0 + m_1 t + m_2 \log(\text{EXO} + C^* + CI^*) + m_3 \log\left(\frac{\text{PE}}{\text{PP}}\right). \tag{20}$$

The trend term is intended to capture the progressive international integration of the French economy; here also the term PE/PP stands for a distributed lag of foreign suppliers' prices relative to French production prices. One verifies that the level of "notional" imports M^* depends on the level of "notional" consumption demand C^*.

The long-run specification of "notional" consumption demand is

$$\log(\text{CONSO}) = \log(R) + c_1 \dot{p} + c_3,$$

where R is the households' disposable income and $\dot{p}$ the annual inflation rate. The specification proposed for estimation exhibits a dynamic error-correction mechanism structure:

$$\log(C^*) = \log C_{-1} + c_0\left(\log\frac{R}{R_{-1}} + c_1(\dot{p} - \dot{p}_{-1})\right) + c_2(\log C_{-1} - \log R_{-1} - c_1 \dot{p}_{-1}) + c_3. \tag{21}$$

The three equations (12), (13), (14) are estimated simultaneously under the following approximate form[3] (where the notation $(y)_{tl}$ stands for the linear trend of the variable y).

Estimates of the Demand Block

x_0	1.33	(31)	
x_1	−0.0010	(−7.5)	$\text{DW}_x = 1.6$
x_2	0.74	(4.5)	$\text{RMSE}_x = 0.027$
$\dfrac{\gamma_x}{\rho_0}$	0.14	(2.6)	
m_0	−11.4	(−30)	$\text{DW}_m = 1.0$
m_1	0.006	(17)	$\text{RMSE}_m = 0.018$
m_2	1.70	(55)	

m_3	-0.56	(-5.3)	
$\frac{\gamma_m}{\rho_0}$	0.08	(2.9)	
c_0	0.30	(2.4)	$DW_c = 2.5$
c_1	-0.70	(-1.9)	$RMSE_c = 0.007$
c_2	-0.06	(-2.6)	
c_3	0.13	(21)	
$\frac{\gamma_c}{\rho_0}$	0		

$$\log C_t = \log C_t^* + \frac{\gamma_c}{\rho_0}\left(\frac{Y}{C}\right)_{tl} \log(1 - P_G), \tag{22}$$

$$\log X_t = \log X_t^* + \frac{\gamma_x}{\rho_0}\left(\frac{Y}{X}\right)_{tl} \log(1 - P_G), \tag{23}$$

$$\log M_t = \log M_t^* - \frac{\gamma_m}{\rho_0}\left(\frac{Y}{M}\right)_{tl} \log(1 - P_G). \tag{24}$$

The "conventional" parameters are statistically significant and conform to previous knowledge. The Durbin-Watson statistics of the foreign trade equations suggest, however, that the dynamics of these equations should be improved.

The spillover parameters, which are of direct interest to us here, call for a few remarks. First, the parameter intended to capture a possible rationing of consumption demand showed up as insignificant and was thus set equal to zero. This absence of rationing of private consumption conforms to previous findings by other authors (see, for example, Artus, Laroque, and Michel 1984).

The spillover parameters of the export and import equations are significant and exhibit the expected sign, suggesting a stabilizing role of export contractions and import increases in the case of tensions on the goods market.

The estimation results allow us to compute the excess demand as the difference between the observed output level Y and the level of notional demand Y^*.

Excess demand appears as a permanent feature, being particularly important in periods of boom (amounting to 2.4% of actual production in 69.3, 2.0% in 74.2, 1.3% in 80.1) and very minor in periods of slack (0.7% in 68.1, 0.5% in 75.2 and in 81.2). Fluctuations of the ratios M^*/M and X^*/X are of course more pronounced: in 74.2 for example, according to our results,

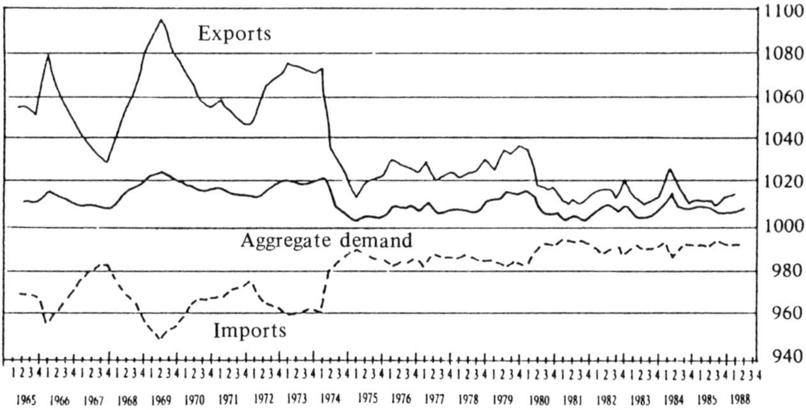

Figure 1.
Ratios of notional to observed values (%).

additional imports amounted to 4% and export reductions to 7% (see figure 1).

II.3. The Labor Market

Some results of the first two blocks will now play a crucial role, namely the estimate of the notional demand Y^* addressed to the production sector and the estimates of the technical coefficients (A^*, B^*) (remember, however, that these coefficients are only estimated up to an unknown constant factor, since the parameters f_a and f_s were not identified).

On the basis of $\hat{A}^*$ (labor productivity) and Y^*, one may thus define, up to a multiplicative constant, the level of employment LD which would be strictly needed, taking into account the prevailing technology, to satisfy the "notional" demand addressed to the firms:

$$\widehat{\mathrm{LD}} = \frac{\hat{Y}^*}{\hat{A}^*}. \tag{25}$$

Combining $\hat{A}^*$, $\hat{B}^*$ (capital productivity), and the installed stock of capital allows us to compute potential employment LP, i.e., the level of employment that would result from the full utilization of production capacities:

$$\widehat{\mathrm{LP}} = \frac{K\hat{B}^*}{\hat{A}^*}. \tag{26}$$

The core of the third block will consist of the confrontation of LP, LD, and a labor-supply function.

At the micro level, one may define a firm's labor demands l^a as the minimum of its potential employment level l^p and the level of employment needed to satisfy demand:

$$l^a = \min(l^p, l^d). \tag{27}$$

The actual employment level of the firm will be equal to the minimum of this labor demand and the labor supply available to the firm:

$$l = \min(l^s, \min(l^p, l^d)). \tag{28}$$

By aggregating over micromarkets one obtains, under suitable distribution hypotheses (see Lambert 1984), simple relationships between aggregate labor supply LS, aggregate potential employment LP, "Keynesian" labor demand LD, effective labor demand LA, and aggregate employment L:

$$\mathrm{LA} = [\mathrm{LD}^{-\rho_1} + \mathrm{LP}^{-\rho_1}]^{-1/\rho_1}, \tag{29}$$

$$\mathrm{L} = [\mathrm{LS}^{-\rho_2} + [\mathrm{LD}^{-\rho_1} + \mathrm{LP}^{-\rho_1}]^{+\rho_2/\rho_1}]^{-1/\rho_2}, \tag{30}$$

where ρ_1 and ρ_2 measure, respectively, the degree of mismatch between installed capacities and the composition of the demands for goods and between labor demand and supply at the micro level (whatever the reasons for such inadequacies: qualification, location, etc.).

Instead of estimating directly the CES specification,[4] one might adopt an alternative procedure that makes use of survey information about the constraints met by the firms on their demand for labor and their supply of goods.

Moreover, this alternative procedure will be seen to ease estimation.

The first step is to write down another result of the "smoothing by aggregation" approach, namely the expressions of the proportions of micro-markets in various disequilibrium situations. Under the same distributional hypotheses conducting to the CES transaction curve, one writes

$$\frac{\mathrm{L}}{\mathrm{LS}} = \mathrm{prop}(l^a > l^s)^{1/\rho_2} \text{ and } \frac{\mathrm{L}}{\mathrm{LA}} = \mathrm{prop}(l^s > l^a)^{1/\rho_2}. \tag{31}$$

Applying the same result to (29), one also writes

$$\frac{\mathrm{LA}}{\mathrm{LD}} = \mathrm{prop}(l^p > l^d)^{1/\rho_1} \text{ and } \frac{\mathrm{LA}}{\mathrm{LP}} = \mathrm{prop}(l^d > l^p)^{1/\rho_1}. \tag{32}$$

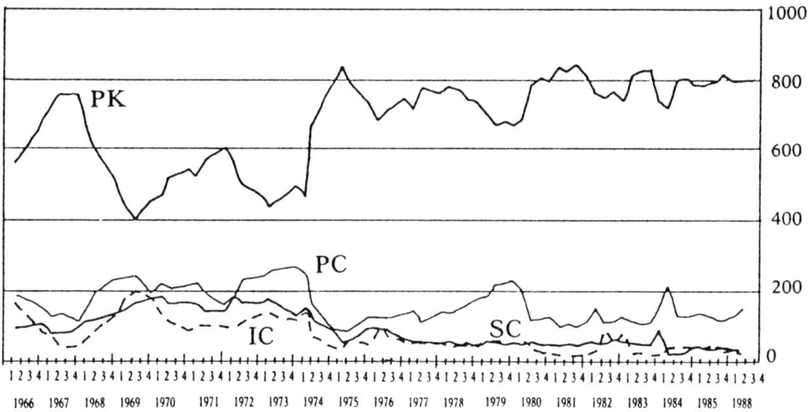

Figure 2.
Regime proportions yielded by the business surveys.

Combining all these equations, one obtains three simultaneous equations:

$$\log(\mathrm{L}) = \log(\mathrm{LS}) + \frac{1}{\rho_2}\log(\mathrm{prop}(l^{\mathrm{a}} > l^{\mathrm{s}})), \tag{33}$$

$$\log(\mathrm{L}) = \log(\mathrm{LP}) + \frac{1}{\rho_2}\log(\mathrm{prop}(l^{\mathrm{s}} > l^{\mathrm{a}})) + \frac{1}{\rho_1}\log(\mathrm{prop}(l^{\mathrm{d}} > l^{\mathrm{p}})), \tag{34}$$

$$\log(\mathrm{L}) = \log(\mathrm{LD}) + \frac{1}{\rho_2}\log(\mathrm{prop}(l^{\mathrm{s}} > l^{\mathrm{a}}) + \frac{1}{\rho_1}\log(\mathrm{prop}(l^{\mathrm{p}} > l^{\mathrm{d}}), \tag{35}$$

which may be estimated as such when the relevant "regime proportions" are available. These proportions may be inferred from the business surveys conducted by INSEE in the industrial sector (see appendix). Here also, as above, we consider that this statistical information may provide reliable indicators, in spite of its limited sectoral coverage.

The survey results allow the firms to be partitioned in three groups. The first one contains the firms that declare not to be able—or at least to experience some problems—to increase their production level because of difficulties met in recruiting new workers. The proportion of firms in this situation is called P_s.

The second group contains the firms that declare to be unable to produce more because of insufficient production capacities; these firms are in proportion P_c. The last group contains all the other firms, which are thus able to meet an increased demand for their products: let us call this proportion P_k. We thus have

$$P_s + P_c + P_k = 1. \tag{36}$$

These three proportions have a direct link with the ones we need to estimate the system of equations (33), (34), (35).

We may state directly

$$\text{Prop}(l^a > l^s) = P_s.$$

The proportion of firms for which the Keynesian labor demand l^d exceeds the potential employment level l^p may be obtained as the share, among all the firms that are not constrained by labor, of the firms that feel constrained by lack of equipment, namely

$$\text{Prop}(l^d > l^p) = \frac{P_c}{P_k + P_c}.$$

Using the proportions inferred from the business surveys, we rewrite the above model as follows:

$$\log \mathrm{L} = \log \mathrm{LS} + \frac{1}{\rho_2}\log(P_s), \tag{37}$$

$$\log \mathrm{L} = \log \mathrm{LD} + \frac{1}{\rho_2}\log(1 - P_s) + \frac{1}{\rho_1}\log\left(\frac{P_k}{P_k + P_c}\right), \tag{38}$$

$$\log \mathrm{L} = \log \mathrm{LP} + \frac{1}{\rho_2}\log(1 - P_s) + \frac{1}{\rho_1}\log\left(\frac{P_c}{P_k + P_c}\right). \tag{39}$$

The functions LS, LD, and LP still have to be specified. For LD and LP, it is important to account for the existence of labor adjustment costs which induce the firms to adjust only progressively their labor force toward "optimal" values.

Assuming a partial adjustment mechanism toward the optimal value ($\widehat{\mathrm{LD}}$, $\widehat{\mathrm{LP}}$) obtained from the first two blocks, one writes

$$\log \mathrm{L} = \lambda_1 \log \widehat{\mathrm{LD}} + (1 - \lambda_1)\log \mathrm{L}_{t-1} + \frac{1}{\rho_2}\log(1 - P_s) + \frac{1}{\rho_1}\log\left(\frac{P_k}{P_k + P_c}\right) + c_1 \tag{38'}$$

and

$$\log L = \lambda_2 \log \widehat{LP} + (1 - \lambda_2) \log L_{t-1} + \frac{1}{\rho_2} \log(1 - P_s) + \frac{1}{\rho_1} \log\left(\frac{P_c}{P_k + P_c}\right) + c_2, \tag{39'}$$

where c_1 and c_2 are intended to account for the fact that LP and LD are only known up to a multiplicative constant. The specification of labor supply LS, which is known as a weak point of existing disequilibrium models (Laroque 1986), is here slightly more refined than usual: labor supply is of course a function of total labor force POPA (defined as the sum of the actual sectoral employment and the unemployed) but depends also on the replacement ratio ALLOC, defined as the ratio of the average unemployment compensation to the average nominal wage:

$$\log LS = \log(c \cdot POPA + d \cdot ALLOC). \tag{40}$$

Estimation of this system of simultaneous equation is performed by the maximum-likelihood method.

Before commenting on the results, let us add two remarks: first, due to convergence problems, we were constrained to impose the equality of the two parameters λ_1 and λ_2 measuring the speed of adjusting labor[5]; second, drawing on previous work, we tested for a trended evolution of the "mismatch" parameters $1/\rho_1$ and $1/\rho_2$. On this second issue, the results obtained suggest that inadequacies might be steadily increasing on the labor market while being stable on the goods market.

The estimated labor supply equation is

$$LS = 0.98\ POPA - 12.7\ ALLOC. \tag{41}$$

The implications of these estimates are the following: a 10% decrease of the average unemployment compensation taking place at mid-1986 would imply, according to our results, an increase of about 30,000 people in the labor supply, which amounts to 0.2% of the total labor force or 1.5% of the unemployed.

Also, equation 41 allows us to get an estimate of frictional unemployment, which accounts for the unemployed who are not ready to accept immediately a job at the ruling wage. The extent of this unemployment component corresponds to the discrepancy between the total labor force and the actual labor supply as estimated by (41).

Frictional unemployment appears to be growing along the observation period. Compared to estimates proposed in other works, our results suggest a lesser extent of frictional unemployment (about 440,000 people at the end of 1978 compared to the 580,000 as estimated by Artus, Laroque, and Michel) which moreover exhibits a tendency toward stabilization at the end of the observation period.

The estimation results of equations (37′) and (38′) shed another light on the unemployment issue, first by providing an estimate of potential employment LP.

Estimates of the Employment Block

c	0.98	(655)
d	-12.7	(-6.1)
$\frac{1}{\rho_1}$	0.010	(13)
$\frac{1}{\rho_2}$	$-0.009 + 0.0007t$	
	(-22)	(26)
λ	0.25	(21)
c_1	0.013	(18)
c_2	0.005	(6.0)

RMSE(eq 37) = 0.008 DW(eq 37) = 0.7
RMSE(eq 38′) = 0.002 DW(eq 38′) = 0.9
RMSE(eq 39′) = 0.003 DW(eq 39′) = 0.8

The discrepancy between the actual employment level and the level of potential employment is conventionally called Keynesian unemployment since it could—in principle—be alleviated through a vigorous and sustained expansionary demand policy. On this particular but important issue, our results differ substantially from those of Artus, Laroque, and Michel (1984), who, for 1978.4, diagnose a Keynesian unemployment level of about 250,000 people against about one million according to our estimates. It might be that our procedure may result in slightly overestimating this component of unemployment: indeed, it relies heavily on an estimate of the potential employment ceiling, which itself is strongly dependent on the business survey answers about the idle capacities. Insofar as the business leaders consider total physically installed capacities instead of the sole profitable capacities, our potential employment (and hence our Keynesian unemployment) might be somewhat overestimated. We tried, of course, to account for this possible bias (see our discussion in section II.1), but our correction might be insufficient. Anyway, we feel more confident in our result about the extent of the Keynesian unemployment component than in the figures presented in Artus et al. 1984—all the more since our diagnosis

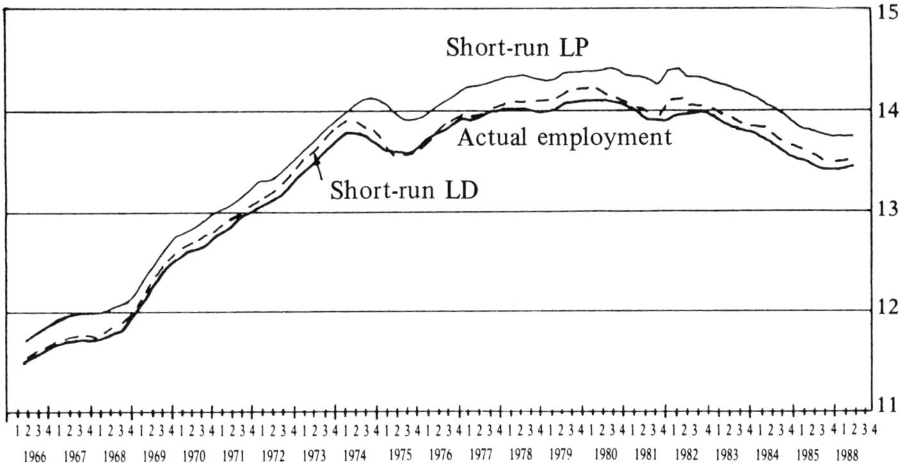

Figure 3.
Short-run labor demand (in millions).

is backed by previous results obtained without reliance on survey data (see Lambert, Lubrano, and Sneessens 1985).

The positive discrepancy, if any, between actual labor supply and the potential employment ceiling represents the component of unemployment, which is not attributable to deficient demand for goods but to the lack of profitable equipment. This represents what is called the "classical unemployment" component. A glance at figure 4 reveals that this component of unemployment is gaining steadily in importance since the early 1980s.

Figure 4 provides indeed an illustrative summary of our results about the unemployment issue: while frictional unemployment appears as a permanent feature along the whole observation period, Keynesian unemployment, which was, until the mid-1970s, almost unexistent became suddenly the prominent feature, only to be supplemented a few years later by a growing classical component. At the end of the period, all three components seem to account roughly for an equal share of total unemployment.

It might also be interesting to comment briefly on the discrepancy between actual employment and the "Keynesian" labor demand: this corresponds to unfilled vacancies which may coexist with massive unemployment in the case of inadequacies at the micro level, either between goods demanded and available capacities or between labor demanded and the available labor force. According to the estimates of the ρ parameters already commented on above, the mismatch on the labor market seems to

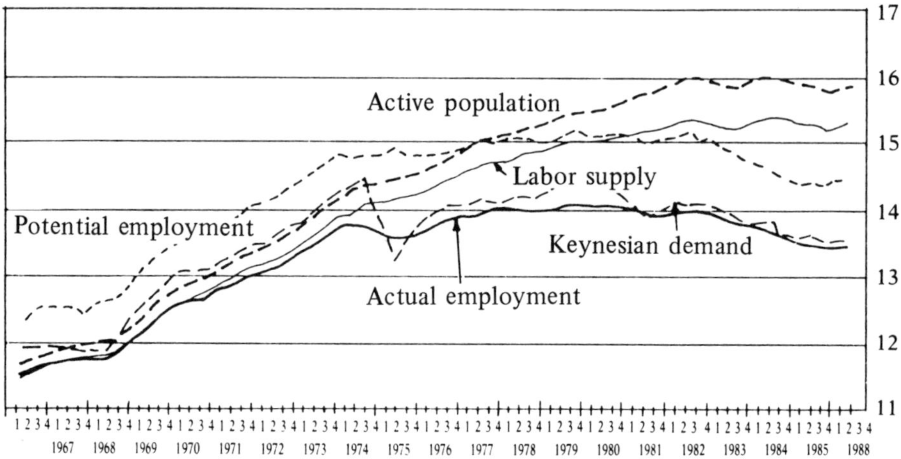

Figure 4.
Long-run labor demand and labor supply (in millions).

be steadily growing in importance. The model as such does not tell us more on how to properly interpret this empirical finding. Available outside information (from business surveys as well as other sources) suggests, however, that growing inadequacies should not be attributed to mounting regional, or sectoral, mismatch but to a qualification problem.

III. Conclusion

The "first-generation" rationing models, characterized by the *minimum* condition, suffered from (sometimes severe) estimation problems, which induced some authors to recommend the "smoothing by aggregation" approach. Such an approach therefore opens the way for more "realistic" specifications.

This paper presents a model developed along these lines, which moreover provides a natural framework for incorporating survey data. The results illustrate the potential of this method to get estimates of the extent of disequilibria, as well on the goods market as on the labor market. The delicate frictional unemployment issue, in particular, could be given a more appropriate treatment, thanks to the availability of an original indicator of the tensions between demand and supply for labor.

The results presented here do not appear contradictory but instead complementary to those presented in earlier works.

As such, they suggest pursuing the effort in the direction indicated here.

Appendix: The Business Survey Data Interpretation and Exploitation

INSEE conducts regular business surveys within firms. The manufacturing sector is the most extensively covered sector: the 3000 firms of the sample are subjected to a variety of surveys among which is a quarterly survey that is of particular interest in our context.

Each firm is asked about its present situation, in particular about the use of its production factors and about possible bottlenecks. The questions are as follows:

1. The Production Constraints

If you registered more orders, could you produce more with the means presently at your disposal?

YES or NO

	If NO, you are presently prevented from increasing your production	If YES, are you nevertheless presently hampered or slowed down
• because of insufficient equipment	......	......
• because of insufficient labor that you find hard to recruit	......	......
• because of lack of raw material or other reasons	......	......

2. The Idle Production Capacities

• By how much could you increase your production with your presently available equipment without hiring additional labor? ABOUT ....%

• Could you still produce more by hiring additional labor? YES or NO

• If YES, by how much could you on the whole increase your production with your presently available equipment? ABOUT ......%

These statistics are used in each part of the model. First, the idle capacity margins are taken into account in section II.1 to estimate the technical coefficients. Such statistics are now conventional in rationing models in order to assess the true values of capital and labor productivity.

It has sometimes been suggested that some firms might consider all their physically available margins, instead of the sole profitable (at prevailing prices and costs) ones, which would result in overestimating the latter. One notices indeed that reported idle capacities remain high, even in periods of severe tensions. This possible bias will be taken into account in the model.

The answers relative to the experienced production constraints are used in sections II.2 and II.3, in the analysis of "notional" demand and of the labor market. These statistics have been extensively discussed by Bouissou, Laffont, and Vuong (1983) and by Lambert and Sneessens (1985). Let us here briefly recall their interpretation.

These answers enable us to partition the firms in four classes, according to their experiencing rationing of their supply of goods and/or of their demand for labor.

By crossing the answers to the two questions "if you registered more orders, could you produce more with the means presently at your disposal?" and "are you prevented, or at least hampered, from increasing your production because of insufficient labor?" one gets the four proportions of firms that receive the following notation:

	Produce more?		
	Yes	No	Total
Recruitment Difficulties?			
Yes	P_U	P_R	P_S
No	P_K	P_C	$1 - P_S$
Total	$1 - P_G$	P_G	1

The proportion P_G will help to assess the extent of the excess demand for goods and hence the level of notional demand. Similarly, the proportions P_S, P_C, and P_K help assess the extent of the excess demand for and supply of labor and hence the level of potential employment, Keynesian labor demand, and labor supply.

The proposed classification is not the only one possible: other, slightly different, interpretations have been proposed, leading to different proportions. However, as shown by comparison with the works mentioned above, the evolutions appear to be similar and the slight differences in level are not expected to alter the estimation results significantly.

More importantly, let us remember that the business survey covers only the industrial sector: our hypothesis that these data might provide reliable indicators of constraints perceived by other sectors may be questionable, although no statistical evidence might be available to enlighten this issue (refer, for example, to Artus et al. 1987 for a recent attempt to estimate a two-sector model).

Notes

1. This value would probably be still "more negative" if the usage cost of capital had received a better specification taking into account an appropriate discount rate (see, for example, Muet and Avouyi-Dovi 1987).

2. Considering inventory changes as exogenous is a simplification, which is no doubt open to criticism: indeed, stocks are used by firms partly as a buffer against demand fluctuations; changes in stocks might hence absorb part of the excess demand.

3. The approximation consists in substituting x for $\log(1 + x)$, where x represents the percentage of consumption, exports, or imports which is rationed.

4. The direct estimation of this functional form meets often with serious numerical difficulties, due notably to the tendency of the parameter ρ to tend to infinity (see Lambert et al. 1985).

5. These convergence problems might be linked with problems met by other authors who report excessively long adjustment lags for labor (see Artus et al. 1985).

References

Artus, P., and Bismut, C. 1980. "Substitution et coût des facteurs: un lien existe-t-il?" *Economie et Statistique* no. 127, November.

Artus, P., Laroque, G., and Michel, G. 1984. "Estimation of a Quarterly Macroeconomic Model with Quantity Rationing." *Econometrica* 52(6), 1387–1414.

Artus, P., Avouyi-Dovi, S., and Laroque, G. 1985. "Estimation d'une maquette macroéconomique trimestrielle avec rationnements quantitatifs." *Annales de l'INSEE*, January–March.

Artus, P., Avouyi-Dovi, S., and Laffargue, J. P. 1987. "Un modèle économétrique de déséquilibre à deux secteurs et son apport à l'analyse des politiques économiques." *Revue de l'OFCE* 21.

Barro, R. J. and Grossman, H. I. 1971. "A General Disequilibrium Model of Income and Employment." *American Economic Review* 61: 82–93.

Benassy, J. P. 1975. "Neokeynesian Disequilibrium in a Monetary Economy." *Review of Economic Studies* 42: 502–523.

Bouissou, M. B., Laffont, J. J., and Vuong, Q. H. 1983. "Econométrie du déséquilibre sur données individuelles." GREMAQ, Cahier No. 8308, Université de Toulouse.

Fair, R. C., and Jaffee, D. M. 1972. "Methods of Estimation for Markets in Disequilibrium." *Econometrica* 40.

Gouriéroux, C., and Laroque, G. 1985. "The Aggregation of Commodities in a Quantity Rationing Model." *International Economic Review* 26(3): 681–699.

Kooiman, P., and Kloek, T. 1980. An Aggregate Two Market Disequilibrium Model With Foreign Trade. Working paper, Econometric Institute, Rotterdam.

Kooiman, P., and Kloek, T. 1985. "An Empirical Two Market Disequilibrium Model for Dutch Manufacturing Sector." *European Economic Review* 29(3): 323–354.

Lambert, J. P. 1984. *Disequilibrium Macromodels Based on Business Survey Data: Theory and Estimation for the Belgian Manufacturing Sector.* Cambridge University Press.

Lambert, J. P., Lubrano, M., and Sneessens, H. R. 1985. "Emploi et chômage en France de 1955 à 1982: un modèle macroéconomique annuel de rationnement." *Annales de l'INSEE* 55–56: 39–75.

Lambert, J. P., and Sneessens, H. R. 1985. Econométrie du rationnement et enquêtes de conjoncture: un essai d'intégration avec application au secteur manufacturier français. CRESGE, Université de Lille.

Laroque, G. 1986. "Le chômage des années 1970 était-il classique?" *L'actualité Economique* 62(3).

Maddala, G. S., and Nelson, F. D. 1974. "Maximum Likelihood Methods for Models of Markets in Disequilibrium." *Econometrica* 42.

Malinvaud, E., 1977. *The Theory of Unemployment Reconsidered.* Blackwell.

Malinvaud, E. 1982. *Essais sur la théorie du chômage.* Calmann-Levy.

Muet, P. A., and Avouyi-Dovi, S. 1987. "L'investissement productif dans les années 80: diagnostic et perspectives." *Revue d'économie industrielle,* No. 40–41.

Sneessens, H. R. 1983. "A Macroeconomic Rationing Model of the Belgian Economy." *European Economic Review* 20: 193–215.

Sneessens, H. R., and Dreze, J. H., 1985. "A Discussion of Belgian Unemployment, Combining Traditional Concepts and Disequilibrium Econometrics," *Economica* 53: S89–S119.

Thelot, C. 1985. "La croissance du chômage depuis vingt ans: interprétation macroéconomique." *Economie et Statistique,* No. 183, December.

28 Wages and Wage Policy

Philippe Nasse

To cope with the problem of unemployment, what economic policy should be applied? What advice can economists give? What guidelines can be provided, in particular for wage policy? Is there any solid economic analysis to support such recommendations, if we consider that the relationship between wages, growth, and employment has been the subject of a long but so far inconclusive debate among the best economists?

Between the acceptance of what one no longer hopes to prevent and the ambition of a general solution, this paper will chart a middle path, focusing on a more modest empirical goal. Rather than proposing an original model or new econometric estimates, we shall seek to derive a few practical, potentially applicable solutions from the impressive corpus of information, analyses, and results published on the subject. From a close, unprejudiced but selective reading of the literature—for this does not pretend to be a survey—we can conclude that there are some directions to be explored that offer a reasonable chance of yielding a worthwhile improvement, however limited and local.

The first part of the paper deals with the empirical determination of wage equations. The rigidity evidenced by these equations indicates, as is well known, that the labor market functions according to rules very far removed from those of a competitive system. This explains the long French tradition of government interventionism—in the form either of direct incomes policies or, as today, of attempts to influence market flexibility. This constant feature of French economic policy seems consistent with a well-established rigidity that appears to be even stronger in France than abroad.

The second part analyzes the consequences of this situation on the gap reportedly introduced between the effective price of labor and the price that would have been appropriate taking into account the general economic situation, notably employment. That is the crucial issue of past and present debates. On this point, the empirical studies are sometimes contradictory or inconclusive but, on the whole, they support the assumption that such a gap did occur in France in the early 1980s. Thus, the wage-restraint policy (*rigueur salariale*) applied at the time seems justified not only by the circumstances then prevailing—such as the anti-inflation drive and foreign competitiveness—but also for deeper reasons related to the nature of the macroeconomic disequilibrium generated during that period by the insufficiency of profits.

Since 1983, the situation has changed considerably. The preservation of a stable purchasing power, combined wih growing productivity and the improvement of the terms of trade in 1986, has narrowed the lead of real wages on available productivity. Is this reduction adequate? Probably yes, if we consider only the immediate short-term inflation targets. Probably no, if we refer to profit rates and compare them with past values or with a suitable target. Definitely no, if we compare profit rates with the interest rates on financial investments competing with real investments.

Using these observations, the third part of the paper examines whether there are ways to reconcile in an empirical manner the necessary reduction of wage rigidity, the continued recovery in profit rates, and a lessening of the purchasing-power constraint. We formulate two proposals. The first, relative to flexibility, concerns the desirability of reviving profit-sharing policies in the light of recent economic work on the issue. Profit-sharing had few attractions when it was seen as a substitute for a seemingly guaranteed increase in purchasing power. Now that the stagnation of purchasing power has become the norm, profit-sharing acquires a new attractiveness if it is seen as the economically bearable means of transferring to employees some of the fruits of their productivity.

Our second proposal is based on the observation of the sharp drop in the equipment-utilization rate due to shorter working hours. This phenomenon accounts for a large share of the fall in profit rates. Taddei (1986) has already raised the question, but we discuss it here from a different angle, taking wage controls and reorganization of working hours as substitutable within a given profit-rate target. Policy, we argue, should seek not to alter the objective—higher profit rates—or to relax the economic effort, but to channel the latter more efficiently by shifting its focus from labor price to work organization. This would create some scope for accommodating purchasing power.

1. Wage Determination

The following section takes some macroeconomic results drawn from recent econometric studies to try and identify the origin of wage-determination rigidity. By comparing these results with estimates relating to longer periods or other countries, we shall attempt to demonstrate the oldness of this rigidity and to determine whether it is specific to France.

1.1. Some Recent Macroeconomic Results

The development of macroeconomic modeling and, more recently, the interest shown for French wage policy since 1982 have led to an estimation of many econometric equations that spell out the major determinants of wage rates. The obvious correlation between nominal wages and prices typically leads econometricians to analyze wage formation in the context of a group of equations—or a dynamic system—in which the two variables are determined simultaneously.

An overview of the available literature rapidly reveals a major common theme: prices are determined in level terms and wages in growth-rate terms. The level/rate price/wage matrix should, in principle, allow four types of configuration; when run simultaneously, these ought to exhibit different theoretical properties (see Debonneuil and Sterdyniak 1983; Morin and Loué 1986).

Despite repeated attempts to obtain level equations, notably for wages, the empirical results converge very strongly on a single one of these configurations. This would indicate that economic reality is particularly constraining on this point. Yet the long-term consequences of this empirical choice are considerable and negative, as a level specification makes it possible to incorporate in the description of past behavior the characteristics favorable to long-term equilibria. In the case of prices, the producer-customer relationship exhibits a long-term norm to which firms seek to adjust, period after period. By contrast, the employer-employee relationship does not seem to exhibit a wage norm playing an analogous role in the long run.

There is no absolute proof that economic reality corresponds to what the models describe. It would be surprising if wage levels were not subjected in the long term to feedback forces typical of an equilibrium situation. The empirical studies, however, do not demonstrate such forces. We may rightly ask, therefore, if they are not unusually weak, or of such a kind as to exert an influence only in the very long run. Be that as it may, the structure of the empirically determined wage equations corroborates the notion that wages could durably depart from an economically adequate level. That assumption legitimates the approach adopted here.

In nearly all the available models—with the exception of COPAIN (1981)—firms set their prices by applying an operating-surplus ratio to variable costs more or less extensively defined. This behavior can be justified either in the context of oligo-political competition rules or by other theoretical considerations (on this point, see P. Artus 1983). In either case, the important point is that price-setting behavior seems to be influenced, empirically, by the sharing of value added between wages and profits, and not by capital profitability. This is indeed a crucial issue, as the insufficiency of capital profitability is one of the salient features of the French economy today. The indexation of prices on variable costs alone would therefore help to explain the persistence of that insufficiency and to justify the exogenous measures designed to reverse the trend.

As regards wages, the available models describe the determination of their growth rate in terms of the enlarged Phillips curve. The rate depends on the rise in consumer prices (present, past, and expected), pressures on the labor market, and, sometimes, the growth rate of productivity. Table 1 gives a succinct summary of some of these results, calculated on quarterly data.

The quarterly estimates reveal two major phenomena. First, the indexation of the wage-rate rise on the price rise is unitary, and even more than unitary. Second, the purchasing-power change persisting after this indexation depends mainly, in the short run, on the changes in the inflation rate, for unitary indexation is lagged; in the long run, it depends on labor-market pressures—to within one constant, which might embody the productivity effect.

By isolating wage purchasing power from the price level, unitary indexation further undermines the possibility of long-term equilibrium, already limited by the level/rate specification of the wage/price system. Indeed, the simultaneous determination of prices and wages implies that the reduced equation describing purchasing power depends on the exogenous variables introduced into the price equation. In the present case, this influence is limited to very-short-term variations. Once the pace of inflation stabilizes, the profit and capacity-margin variables, which are the main exogenous determinants of prices, no longer influence purchasing power.

The effect of pressures on employment seems to be vaguer and more ambiguous than the price effect, as witnessed by the diversity of modeling choices made in these studies. Let us take, for example, the pressure in-

Table 1.
Quarterly Changes in the Wage Rate (All Sectors or Manufacturing Only)

Sources	Constant term	Pressure on employment: Pres.	Pressure on employment: Unemployment rate	Inflation: ST	Inflation: One year	Inflation: LT	Productivity	SEE	DW
METRIC (1981)									
(Manufacturing)	2.32	−0.88[a]	—	0.51	1	1	—	0.29	1.84
1964-II to 1976-IV	(8.9)	(5.8)							
Maarek (1983)									
(Manufacturing)	0.018	−0.0024[b]	—	0.2	1	1	—	0.4	1.01
1970-I to 1980-IV	(11.6)								
Sterdyniak (1984)									
(Manufacturing)	1.86	−0.47[c]	—	0.29	0.86	1	—	0.37	—
1964-III to 1981-IV	(10.5)	(6.6)							
Minczeles and									
Sicsic (1986)	−0.14	—	−0.007	0.21	1.1	1	0.2	0.29	0.9
1970-I to 1983-IV	(7.5)		(11.7)						
Morin (1986)	0.016	—	−0.0017	0.43	0.91	1.04	—	0.43	0.94
1967-I to 1985-IV	(8.3)		(7.9)	(4.0)					
Cling and Meunier									
(1986)	0.52	−0.55[d]	—	0.18	0.57	1.15	0.35	0.22	2.01
1966-I to 1982-II	(3.1)	(9.5)		(2.8)					
Ralle (1987)	1.49	—	−0.36	0.20	1	1	—	0.30	1.3
1971-III to 1982-II	(9.8)		(8.1)						
1971-III to 1986-II	1.28	—	−0.26	0	1	1	—	0.20	1.9
	(7.0)		(5.3)						

Note: Dummy and secondary variables have been omitted from all equations.
[a] TENS: 4-period mean of the log of ratio of demands to unfilled vacancies.
[b] TENS: log of ratio of demands to unfilled vacancies.
[c] TENS: 3-period mean of the log of ratio of job-seeking labor force to unfilled vacancies.
[d] TENS: log of ratio of demands on unfilled vacancies for males aged 25 to 49.

dicator. The inclusion of recent years diminishes the role of the ratio of demands to unfilled vacancies because of the virtual disappearance of job offers. There are no empirical arguments to help us decide between a linear or logarithmic specification of the unemployment rate, despite the grave consequences this choice entails with regard to future changes in purchasing power if unemployment keeps rising. A second example is the inclusion of productivity. The two sharp falls in the productivity rate in 1974 and 1980 make one skeptical as to whether the equation constant term is an adequate proxy for this effect. They justify the direct introduction of the productivity variable. Unfortunately, this inclusion seems to cause an over-indexation on prices—which takes us into another trouble zone.

Morin and Loué (1986) analyze the robustness of these different specifications. The authors are led to the following conclusions: a slightly lagged unitary indexation seems well proven; the role of labor market pressures seems crucial, although no specification emerges as unquestionably superior; the robustness of the other variables is doubtful. The study by Brillet (1985) on annual data and by sector for the "Dynamique Multisectoriel" (DMS) model corroborates the preceding quarterly results.

To sum up, the main findings of the empirical studies are a rapid, total indexation, and a demonstrable but more imprecise effect of unemployment. Accordingly, purchasing power does not respond to prices unless their rates vary continuously. The unemployment level weighs on purchasing power without, however, ensuring its cyclical regulation, because its short-run changes remain small. Finally, there is no demonstrable direct link between purchasing power and available productivity. These findings enable us to distinguish the constituent elements of French wage rigidity. While none of them is sufficient on its own, the rigidity arises from their combination.

Do these empirical models accurately describe reality? That might seem doubtful in view of their limited ability to account properly for the effects of the oil-price collapse of 1986. Yet, if we look more closely, this failure would appear to be due to the fact that reality, in this particular instance, proved even more rigid than the model allowed for. Moreover, that so many different models all describe an extreme wage rigidity argues in favor of the robustness of the diagnosis. Recent history furnishes an additional proof. If, in 1982, the government sought to intervene directly in price and wage regulation, it was indeed because, in reality, adequate adjustment mechanisms were patently missing. The wage policy of the Finance Minister Jacques Delors involved a wage-and-price freeze and, more important, a pre-indexation on a deliberately low price reference. This may be interpreted as the injection of an exogenous flexibility into rigid wage-determination mechanisms whose "perverse effects" were clear.

The efficiency of the Delors policy has been variously judged (Cling and Meunier 1986; Minczeles and Sicsic 1986; Morin 1986). It seems certain that it cut purchasing power and dampened inflation; it may also have lengthened the indexation lags (Ralle 1987). But nothing suggests that it radically altered the system's fundamental rigidity. As a result, the issue is still as topical as ever.

1.2. Long-Term Analysis and International Comparisons

The results reported above concern the last 20 years. They indicate the absence of regulatory elements to counteract inadequate wage movements and to ensure the congruence between long-term changes in purchasing power and in available productivity.

It is well worth investigating whether this rigidity is too recent for the regulatory mechanisms to have already been revealed, or whether it is an old phenomenon—the sign of a chronic, deep-seated problem. Sauvy's (1984) study of the French economy between the wars suggests the second alternative might be correct. In a more detailed manner, Boyer (1978) estimates enlarged Phillips curves specified in identical fashion for various subperiods between 1920 and 1976, excluding the decade 1937–1947. His findings reveal sizable differences in numerical estimation from one subperiod to another, but they corroborate the persistently significant indexation of wages on prices—a strong indexation that does not appear to have become unitary until the most recent period. The effect of unemployment, by contrast, seems more erratic. By and large, wage determination between the wars does not seem to have been very different from what it is today. Wage rigidity therefore seems to be an old issue.

The same study by Boyer for the 1841–1913 period and the work of Lévy-Leboyer and Bourguignon (1985) for the years 1825–1913 show that one has to go back to the nineteenth century in order not to find a significant indexation of wages on prices. Thus, the problem of wage determination in its modern form appears to date from World War I.

The estimation of identically specified wage equations for the main OECD countries allow a comparison between France and the other developed economies. These international comparisons (see especially P. Artus 1983; Coe and Gagliardi 1985) yield results for France consistent with those already cited. They also show that the enlarged Phillips curve provides an adequate description of wage-determination behavior in other countries.

Despite certain analogies, these international comparisons point to a stronger wage *rigidity* in France than in other countries. Using differential simulations, P. Artus (1983) shows that the response of wage purchasing power to a change in the unemployment rate is much weaker in France than in the United States or Japan. Similarly, French real wages adjust much more weakly than elsewhere to a worsening in the terms of trade.

Taking up the approach of Grubb, Jackman, and Layard (1983), Coe and Gagliardi consider another way of measuring wage rigidity by calculating the ratio between the elasticity of nominal wages with respect to prices (in the short or long run) and their elasticity with respect to unemployment. The ratio characterizes the rise in unemployment required to cancel the effects of an exogenous inflationary shock of 1%. It therefore constitutes a synthesis of the two calculations by P. Artus. According to Coe and Gagliardi, France's wage rigidity is very high in the short term—where it is exceeded only by that of Britain—and medium in the long term compared with that of the four other countries.

From this selection of studies on wage formation, two robust results seem to emerge: (1) the enlarged Phillips curve is an adequate representation of wage formation in the leading developed economies; (2) France does not escape this rule, but appears to provide a particularly simple and rigid example of it.

2. The Wage Gap

We now turn to the consequences of the wage-determination mechanism described in section 1 and of the rigidity it induces. A rigid increase in purchasing power can constitute a steady underpinning for growth, provided the production factors are sufficient to guarantee it. But such rigidity can also lead to inadequate wage rates. If these are too weak, Keynesian underemployment will be chronic, for regulation by unemployment will exert a cumulative effect. If the rates are too high, they will generate the classical situation, which may occur at two levels. The inadequacy of supply profitability may be confined to the share of supply directed to international markets: in that case, an exchange-rate adjustment may provide an effective remedy. But if the inadequacy exceeds the level that one may reasonably hope to correct through the exchange rate, then one ought to witness (1) an external disequilibrium impervious to currency depreciation and (2) persistent unemployment. The present French situation makes this analysis plausible. If the latter is accurate, wage regulation through unemployment ought, in the long run, to correct the initial cause; but, as we have seen, this is a weak, slow-moving regulation mechanism, likely to generate a long-run stop-go cycle.

This old debate of the 1930s has gained fresh relevance, but its outcome has barely evolved. The present section seeks only to shed some light on the issue by gathering and comparing the findings of various empirical and theoretical studies on the relationship between wages, unemployment, and growth.

2.1. The "Wages Simulation" of the METRIC Model

A simple way to analyze these questions would be to run the available macroeconomic models. But these are not very helpful: their neo-Keynesian structure makes little allowance for supply behavior, and their investment functions give only limited weight to profit variables. While not amounting to a proof, these common features of the conventional models argue against the predominance of supply effects, at least for their estimation period. However, even their current performance is often poor, especially as regards investment, which impairs their credibility.

Be that as it may, the METRIC (1981) model, to take one example, describes in the following manner the influence of a steady 1% rise in nominal wage levels on French gross domestic product:

	1 year	2 years	3 years	4 years	5 years
Deviation from reference GDP (%)	+0.2	+0.1	−0.1	−0.4	−0.6

(In this simulation, the indexation of social security benefits on prices is not total and the public deficit is unconstrained.)

Contrary to appearances, the depression induced by the wage rise in the third year does not reflect the predominance of classical behavior but the effect of a worsening of external competitiveness due to the wage rise. For lack of a satisfactory modeling of France's complex exchange system, the variant is expressed in fixed rates, which is not very realistic.

Although it would be interesting to incorporate the role of exchange rates in the analysis, we have excluded that factor from the present discussion. Indeed, intuition suggests that external profitability, for a given value of the exchange rate, is secondary and dependent on the domestic-price profitability of the production factors utilized. The fundamental problem is the adequate level of the labor price and its influence on capital profitability.

2.2. Effective Wage and Appropriate Wage

The neo-Keynesian structure of macroeconomic models is too constraining to allow an indication of a negative correlation between labor and its price. Some authors have therefore sought to make a direct test of the statistical long-run existence of a causal link between real wages and employment. Using this approach, Geary and Kenan (1982) find it impossible to rule out the hypothesis of independence in a general manner. Le Cacheux and Szpiro (1984) estimate a model for the manufacturing industries of the six largest OECD countries; explaining employment by the wage share of value added, they obtain "heterogeneous and largely insignificant" results.

The failure of these direct attempts is not truly conclusive, for there are many other variables whose influence could conceal the sought-for relationship. For this reason, P. Artus (1987) adopts a much more systematic approach. The author tries to analyze employment using explanatory variables specified in a manner consistent with a three-factor production function (capital, labor, raw materials) in the matrix of four configurations corresponding to

- the short run (fixed capital);
- the long run (flexible capital);
- the Keynesian regime (constrained demand);
- the classical regime (unconstrained demand).

The desired correlation is virtually absent.

This finding is important, as Artus's study is particularly thorough. It is as if the Phillips-curve correlation between real wages and unemployment ruled out any possibility of a negative correlation between labor and its price. In the observed statistics, the Phillips effect predominates. It is not surprising, therefore, that the attempts to seek an inverse correlation too directly are inconclusive. The failure of even the most careful methods seems to shut this path of investigation for good.

How, then, can we estimate the wage level appropriate to employment needs? Several authors calculate an equilibrium wage consistent with the optimal behavior of the representative firm or compatible with a normal macroeconomic situation. They then show the gap between the effective wage and this appropriate wage.

Continuing his earlier work (Sachs 1979) on the international comparison of the role of wages and profits in macroeconomic adjustment, Sachs (1983) evaluates the wage gap in manufacturing in the six major OECD countries as shown in the following table (the gap is interpreted as the lead of the effective real wage on full-employment productivity adjusted for the terms of trade):

	Wage gap in French manufacturing (%)			
1965–1969	1973	1978	1981	1982
0 (by definition)	−0.3	1.5	1.9	4.4

The realism of this empirical study is fairly convincing. For France, there is a presumption of a wage gap harmful to employment. Yet these figures are contradicted by Le Cacheux and Szpiro (1984), who calculate a wage gap based on slightly different assumptions. The gap's explanatory power with respect to employment does not seem at all significant for the countries studied. The role of statistical application in these studies therefore appears to be very important.

To calculate the wage gap, P. Artus (1987) estimates a function of firms' labor demand that notably includes the wage rate among its arguments. Artus resolves the function in terms of this rate so as to make labor demand equal to labor supply. The result is impressive, since the wage gap soars from an initially low level (in 1963) to about 60% in 1983, whether the production-function regime is classical or Keynesian. Such a finding challenges the very concept of a wage gap, but it obviously reflects the relative insensitivity of labor to its price, as demonstrated earlier.

Another estimate of the wage gap is provided by J. Artus (1984) for the manufacturing sector of the seven largest industrial countries. The gap is measured with reference to a three-factor CES function (labor, capital, energy) adjusted to accommodate full-employment productivity; the function also incorporates exogenous technical progress adjusted to allow for observed discontinuities in the different countries. For France, this estimate tallies with the findings of Dubois (1980). Interestingly, J. Artus shows that, in France, the appropriate-wage share is approximately stable within the limits of the estimate's accuracy. As a result, the fluctuations in the observed wage share may be read as a direct indicator of the wage gap. Moreover, as the following figures show, the gap would seem to have expanded early in France—just after the 1968 crisis—and to have worsened from 1975 under the impact of the oil shocks. The salient features of this study are the quantitative differences with respect to other findings, such as those of Sachs, and the implication that wage formation is an old problem in France.

	Wage gap in French manufacturing (%)			
1965–1969	1973	1978	1981	1982
0 to 5	0	5	10	15

Order of magnitude of overrun with respect to warranted wage, according to Model B.
Source: J. Artus (1984).

2.3. Theoretical Approach and Inclusion of Uncertainty

The attempt to measure the wage gap does not exhaust the subject. We must also try to determine why the gap—if it exists—is as persistent as J. Artus suggests, and what its macroeconomic consequences are. One of the weaknesses of the studies cited is their underemphasis of the link between an inadequate wage-profit distribution and its effect on capital accumulation. Noting this weakness, Malinvaud (1982) seeks to remedy it with a theoretical model (see Malinvaud 1981) that analyzes the conditions in which stationary equilibria arise in an economy where factor costs, wages, and interest rates are taken as given and where investment explicitly depends on these prices. With respect to the modest aim of the present paper, the model's attractiveness is its theoretical yet realistic explanation of the negative effects of the wage gap (or the interest-rate gap) on employment. Malinvaud establishes the link—missing in the earlier studies—between investment and profit, an assumption that is beginning to be tested empirically (Lambert and Mulkay 1987).

Using this model, Malinvaud (1986) takes into account the uncertainty on the future demand for the representative firm's output and tries to determine its impact on the appropriate level of factor remuneration. The author shows that the representative firm's profit maximization—through the choice of its productive capacity and the capital intensity of its production technique—leads to a relationship between the uncertainty's probability distribution P and Tobin's q, defined as the ratio between the expected profit rate and the user cost of capital. (If $P(x)$ is the probability perceived by the firm that demand for its output will be at most equal to x, we get $q = T/(1 - P)$, where T is the mean productive-capacity utilization rate.)

Assuming that, in the long run, the interest rate equals the growth rate, we therefore have a simple rule for determining the profit-rate target consistent with a growth-rate target for a given level of uncertainty. Using an earlier quantification of the profit rate linked to the "steady-state" growth of the years 1962–1972 (Malinvaud 1983), the author determines the profit-rate target compatible with (1) a growth that allows a time spread of the rise in the labor supply (+3%) and (2) a greater uncertainty, characterized by a probability—higher than in the reference period—that demand will at most be equal to productive capacity (+10%). These results are reported in figure 2, where the reader will have a visual indication of their likelihood with respect to the position of the various profit-rate indicators available.

For the present paper, the implications are numerous. First, Malinvaud's study distinctly suggests that the ritual reference to past ratios can be highly misleading. While it is vain to hope to return to the growth rates and "certainties" of the 1960s, it is equally vain to aim for the wage or profit ratios of that period. The study offers us a guide based on a rigorous theoretical approach rather than a mere simplistic reference to the past.

Second, the numerical result obtained does not seem beyond reach, especially after the strong profit-margin recovery of 1986 and its continuation in 1987. However, real interest rates remain very far removed from those of the golden rule. Conversely, a 3% growth is no doubt the lower limit at which one can hope to stabilize the unemployment rate; such growth would not suffice to reduce the rate. It is also very hard to judge whether the measurement of the uncertainty variation is realistic. Yet the form of the profit-target determination rule is such that, the more stringent the assumptions (higher growth, greater uncertainty), the higher the target. By and large, however, the theoretical argument and its quantification seem to provide one of the more useful elements to take into account for setting a reasonable wage-policy objective.

To conclude this analysis of "appropriate wages," three points emerge as fairly indisputable. First, the absence of a clear statistical correlation between labor and its price—with the exception of the Phillips curve, and conversely to the expected sign. From this observed fact, we must conclude that the labor price is surely not the direct controlling variable that permits a cyclical regulation of employment. Cutting the labor price is not the simple solution that would suffice to solve the entire problem.

Second, the available studies bolster the assumption of the emergence of a wage gap unfavorable for growth and ultimately for employment. The distortion of income sharing seems the simplest way to observe the phenomenon. Its effects are apparently long-term, involving a weakening of corporate finances that affects investment. As a result, the correction of the gap becomes a prerequisite within a broader strategy encompassing the interest rate and the demand level. On its own, however, such a correction is incapable of improving employment in the short run.

The third point is the easily misleading nature of the reference to the past. Macroeconomic conditions are no longer those of the 1960s. Defining suitable objectives requires a more synoptic analysis to understand the past and apply its lessons to the new situation in a relevant manner. A few theoretical guides exist to help us look ahead.

Looking ahead also implies making sure we have properly understood the present. The macroeconomic situation, however, is changing fast. The oil-price collapse of 1986—which occurred after the studies cited—greatly modified the relative price of energy and weighed on income distribution. To illustrate the possible consequences of this event on the appropriate wage level, we shall conclude by examining a study by Loué (1986). The author builds a complete model of fixed-price equilibrium with rationing, comprising a short-run supply function estimated in a disequilibrium situation. Loué uses the model to study the effect, in variable terms, of a continuous impact on nominal wages from early 1969 on.

Figure 1 reproduces the effect of this impact on gross domestic product.

The results are significant. Up to 1975, the reaction is Keynesian: the wage rise stimulates GDP, the multiplier reaching 1.1. From 1976 to 1986, by contrast, we observe a classical reaction: wage stimulation depresses economic activity. These findings are by and large consistent with the

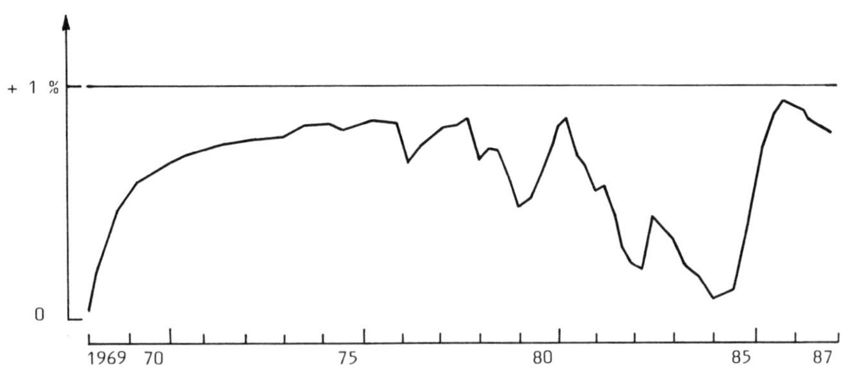

Figure 1.
Effect on GDP of a continuous 1% impact on the wage level.

general conclusions described earlier. This period corresponds to the full-scale emergence of the wage gap. The effect of the oil "countershock" is reflected in the 1986 and 1987 (forecast) upswing. While this curve is not an absolute proof, it suggests that a distinct improvement in the wage gap is under way.

3. Two Wage-Policy Proposals

The econometric studies show that wage-formation behavior is particularly rigid, unemployment being the only apparent long-term regulatory factor. As the empirical analyses suggest, its harsh but slow effects have in all likelihood allowed the creation of a gap between effective and appropriate wage levels. The latter would have enabled firms to respond more effectively to the difficulties inherited from the boom of the 1960s and aggravated by the energy crisis.

The active wage policy implemented since 1982–1983 has introduced an adjustment factor exogenous to empirically determined wage behavior: the purpose has been to close the gap, improve firms' financial positions, and restore their capacity to invest. This policy has unquestionably altered the wage-profit distribution. There is no sign, however, that the root cause of wage rigidity has been affected. Indeed, that is why the government is now recommending a greater microeconomic flexibility in the labor market—in keeping with international recommendations (Klau and Mittelstädt, OECD 1985). By brutally altering the pace of inflation, the energy-price collapse of 1986 caused a short-term boost in purchasing power and triggered a new upswing in profits: this time, the rigidity of wage-price dynamics worked in a virtuous circle.

Given these developments, it would have been useful to update the empirical studies discussed here in order to buttress the analysis of wages. This, unfortunately, is impossible, because the distinctive statistical features of each study are too complex. We are left with the alternative of examining the most recent values of two simple indicators: (1) the wage share in value added and (2) the profit rate. Some of the available studies offer valuable insights into them. In particular, J. Artus (1984) has shown that for an elasticity of substitution between capital and labor slightly smaller than unity (as is probable), the changes in wage share remain a reliable indicator of the gap with appropriate wages. We also know that the profit rate is a key indicator, less with respect to its past value than in terms of the reasonable target we set for it—as suggested by Malinvaud.

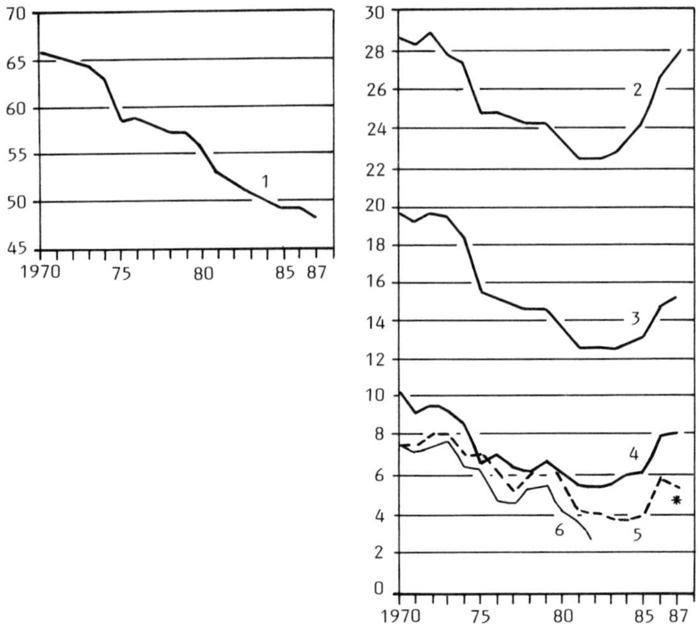

Figure 2.
Operating surplus ratio and profit rate. (1) Apparent yield: value added on capital (real pure capital productivity). (2) Operating surplus ratio: gross operating surplus on value added. (3) Gross return: gross operating surplus on capital. (4) Net return: net return on nonfinancial assets before distribution. (5) Profitability: net profits (corrected for tax inflation of debt) on equity. (6) "Corrected net profit rate" and objective assigned to this rate (*): Malinvaud (1983).

Lastly, it would be unrealistic to formulate wage-policy recommendations without taking into account—as we shall endeavor to do—at least the broad features of the socio-economic reality covered by the term "market" when applied to labor.

Figure 2 provides an overall view of changes in these indicators for all firms excluding public-sector service companies (1970 = 100).

The examination of these graphs shows, in the first place, that the operating-surplus-ratio indicator displays a significant improvement, since it has returned to its pre-oil-crisis level. If we assume a likely correlation between this indicator and the wage gap, the curve seems to corroborate the hypothesis that the gap has narrowed considerably. It is hard to judge, however, if its level is now adequate. According to J. Artus (1984), the wage gap was already very wide in 1973, whereas Loué (1986) suggests that at the time it was generating only a very small probability of classical unemployment. Lastly, we must bear in mind Malinvaud's warning against misleading references to the past.

The examination of profitability ratios requires us to qualify our assessment. Their recovery is weaker than that of value-added sharing. Admittedly, their calculation leaves greater room for approximation as they incorporate sometimes precarious estimates of capital, depreciation, equity, and tax inflation of debt. Nevertheless, the roughly parallel movement of the three profitability ratios suggests that this overall trend corresponds to a basic reality. The breakdown of gross return into operating surplus ratio and capital productivity clearly demonstrates the latter's depressive effect.

The fall in apparent capital productivity seems to be a key factor. As we shall see below, its main cause is apparently the reduction in the equipment-utilization rate, itself linked to the fall in annual working hours. In the production functions studied, it should have been taken into account through a decrease in capital-embodied technical progress and not through the autonomous trend of technical progress. There is a risk, therefore, that this major factor may have been inadequately dealt with.

As the objective is to restore adequate capital profitability, the following question arises: can the weakness of the value added derived from each unit of capital be adequately offset by sharing that value added in a manner consistently favorable to profits and unfavorable to wages?

Moreover, the comparison of the curves for profitability (5) and Malinvaud's "corrected net profit rate" (6) shows a certain closeness of the two values. It is therefore interesting to compare the target equilibrium profit rate (which Malinvaud sets at 5.6%) with current profitability. The optimistic impression we might derive from this should be tempered by the following observation: the real interest rate calculated on the basis of today's inflation rate is a long way from the golden rule; in particular, it exceeds the expected long-term growth rate (3%) consistent with the target equilibrium profit rate.

Although any assessment is necessarily subjective, we can conclude that the present problem seems to hinge as much on an inordinate weakness of capital productivity and an excessively high real interest rate as on the real wage level and its influence on the wage gap—for the recovery in profit margins would be facilitated just as much by a rise in capital productivity as by the continuation of wage restraint. Furthermore, the target of 3% growth does not appear unrealistic in the light of existing production factors. It corresponds to the potential capacity for growth (under full factor employment and 1986 conditions) as calculated by Turner (1987) using the same method as J. Artus (1984).

3.1. A Dual Approach to the Labor Market

In concrete terms, the definition of a wage policy should take account of the main features of the labor market. The models developed by labor economists, however, are very different from the simple macroeconomic wage-formation equation. Without going into this diversity, our discussion must nevertheless take account of a major feature that some of the models allow us to regard as realistic: the market's duality.

According to Doeringer and Piore (for France, see Piore 1978), the labor market comprises two contrasting sectors: a "primary sector" where wages are high, employment is qualified, seniority is significant and well remunerated, and career opportunities are numerous; and a "secondary sector" with the opposite characteristics. This interpretation is more microeconomic and cross-sectional in space than macroeconomic and cross-sectional in time. It greatly enhances the analysis of the labor market (see, for instance, McDonald and Solow 1981, 1985). By incorporating the behavior of trade unions, this approach makes it possible, for example, to reinterpret the employment-unemployment relationship, in particular the Phillips curve (Oswald 1982).

The approach cannot be completely transposed to France, no doubt because French trade unions do not lend themselves to the same modeling as their American counterparts. However, two studies on France show that the approach yields an acceptably realistic description of the French labor market.

The first study is by Glaude (1986). The author performs an econometric analysis of the links between wage-earners' seniority and professional experience on the one hand, and their wage level on the other, according to various characteristics of the employer organization (region, size, sector, etc.). Although the study makes no prior assumption of market duality, its findings point quite strongly to it. Glaude nevertheless remains very cautious, concluding that the dualist theory is rather an "analytical principle" than the means to define a "nomenclature."

In the second study, Reynaud (1986) examines the links between the various wage-remuneration rules and a set of criteria describing the wage earner (qualification, seniority) and the employer (size, industry). An analysis of the main components leads the author to identify two sets of rules for wage formation, work organization, and job management. These rules define a "rigid pole" and a "flexible pole"—in a manner highly reminiscent of the "two-sector" hypothesis. The author describes the flexible pole as characterized by "a high proportion of wage-earners on low wages, young people and unskilled workers. Its economic organization is dominated by small entities that frequently resort to 'economically-motivated' dismissals to adjust their workforce. Shift work is rare." Reynaud also observes that remunerations are variable, personalized, and structured in cycle-sensitive ways. The "rigid pole" exhibits diametrically opposite features.

The two studies above tend to substantiate the hypothesis of a clear-cut segmentation of the French labor market—a hypothesis that can shed light on the rigidity of macroeconomic changes in wages. Indeed, if we look at wages movements rather than wage levels, we can observe that wages grow along fairly parallel lines in all economic sectors. The "primary sector" or "rigid pole" of the labor market may act as the trend-setter for the "secondary sector" in a manner relatively unaffected by the actual macroeconomic situation. To the extent that the "rigid-pole" firms manage to survive, unemployment—under the duality hypothesis—is concentrated in the "flexible pole." However, a high, lasting level of unemployment would be required before a feedback effect on real wages was observed, possibly through starting wages, according to the implicit-contract theory (Garnier 1985).

If the microeconomic functioning of the labor market conforms to this pattern, what practical form should be given to the public-policy recommendation concerning greater flexibility? Should flexibility be increased further in the "secondary sector," where it seems already high, or should it be introduced in the "rigid pole"? But if we attempt to bring the operating rules of the rigid sector in line with those of the flexible sector, are we not deliberately ignoring the reasons for the objective economic and social differences that separate the two poles?

3.2. Developing Employee Profit-Sharing in the Rigid Pole of the Labor Market

The features of the employer-employee relationship in the rigid pole suggest that the development of a wage based on profit-sharing could inject greater flexibility into this sector in an efficient manner. The popularity of Weitzman's views (1985, 1987) has rekindled an interest in profit-sharing schemes, but perhaps to an excessive degree, as some observers see this as a means for a sharp and rapid expansion of employment, in particular thanks to the disinflation such sharing would produce. Without discussing the economic basis and implications of this model (see Saint-Paul 1987), one can arguably question the credibility of a procedure designed to make employees believe that their wages have not suffered, while at the same time convincing employers that the cost of labor has diminished. In this connection, we should mention that, to introduce a reform of this kind on a small scale, the British government was obliged to implement major tax incentives to overcome the common reluctance of employers and employees.

On the other hand, even if the most positive theoretical consequences are unlikely, several arguments militate in favor of such schemes and of their potential success. The first and most crucial argument is the reintroduction of productivity into the formation of the overall wage. The first two parts of this paper have tried to show how the current absence of a direct link between the remuneration of labor and its productivity was prejudicial to a balanced functioning of the economy. Any method of reestablishing that link should be examined attentively.

Second, the "primary sector" effectively appears to be the more rigid, the sector more in need of greater flexibility, whereas the wage flexibility due to a remuneration based on actual hours worked or on productivity is already high in the "secondary sector" of the market.

A third set of arguments pertains to the composition of the "rigid pole." Its firms are larger; its employees are better trained and—most important—they possess greater seniority and experience than their counterparts in the "flexible pole." These features ought, in principle, to foster the development of a more complex system such as *intéressement*, which requires greater stability of the employer and greater maturity of the employee, and becomes meaningful only in the long run.

Lastly, the rigid pole seems to be characterized by high employment stability. Now if the wage is determined by contract, and employment guaranteed de facto, the entrepreneurial risk is entirely borne by the firm so long as it does not go bankrupt. In the flexible pole, instead, the risk is shared between the entrepreneur and the employee, since the latter can always be fired. Therefore, in the flexible pole, a better-guaranteed wage (such as a monthly salary) would counterbalance job insecurity. In the rigid pole, a wage based on profit-sharing would offset high job security. A rebalancing between the two poles would be fairer and compatible with economic efficiency.

The enactment of a profit-sharing wage should be restricted to increases in purchasing power. This limitation would allow a smooth, gradual implementation, while ensuring that substantial effects could be achieved in the long run. Such an arrangement seems suited to the present economic situation. The emergence of distributable profits in a firm would be the sign that the firm could safely relax wage restrictions. This would allow a microeconomic decentralization to take place far more naturally than by applying macroeconomic norms.

A final argument should be mentioned. In France, profit-sharing by employees was introduced by decree in 1959 (*intéressement des salariés aux fruits de l'expansion*). The notion therefore has a well-established historical and national tradition. Its development has suffered, perhaps, from an inadequate examination of the desirable conditions for its application. Most important, profit-sharing has been confused with *participation*, which is designed for the very different purpose of encouraging employees to invest their savings in the company through redeemable nonvoting shares. The time may have come to revive the initial idea.

3.3. Increasing Equipment Productivity

This second proposal may be examined separately from the first. The analysis of the wage gap shows that the crucial question is indeed "how far should wage controls go." An increase in wage purchasing power in parallel with the expansion of available productivity is a prerequisite for steady-state growth, as is a profit rate ensuring that necessary investments will actually be made.

However, the various investigations into the subject have not produced a very clear-cut answer. It is assumed that the wage gap has begun to close, but it is not certain that the reduction is sufficient to generate an adequate recovery of profit rates. An examination of the series in figure 2 clearly shows that the delay in gross-return (3) recovery was mainly due to the fall in capital productivity. This delay also affects net return (5) and profitability (6). There are three possible causes for this decrease: a high substitution of capital for labor, a misguided allocation of investment to declining industries, and a low capital-utilization rate.

Although it generates unemployment, an increase in capital intensity would be an appropriate response to the wage gap, but it hardly seems to constitute the main explanatory factor. Similarly, the problems experienced in certain industries such as steel and heavy chemicals furnish tangible examples of the second cause. But an evaluation by Rouilleault (1987) shows that the fall in productivity cannot be explained by the structural effects of the differences in capital coefficients by industry, combined with the differences in growth rates.

The analysis by Dubois (1985) of the causes of the interruption in growth seems to show that the third explanation predominates. Over a period of 20 years, the hourly productivity of utilized capital does not exhibit any marked trend. Its gap with the hourly productivity of installed capital reproduces the cyclical fluctuations of margins. As the author shows, the reduction in working hours and the decline of shift work account for three-quarters of the 20% fall in installed-capital productivity between 1973 and 1984. Only in Britain can one observe a comparable situation (Chan-Lee and Sutch 1986), and even there the fall in capital productivity was halted in 1981. The other developed economies do not display any significant changes, except for Japan, where the growth of capital productivity has been dramatic.

In these conditions, to prolong wage restraint until profit rates recover despite low capital utilization is equivalent to forcing employees to pay a late bill for the economic cost of two reforms initially perceived as "free": the reduction in annual working hours and the introduction of flexible time.

Taddei (1986) has convincingly demonstrated the economic gain that could result from better capital utilization, but on the assumption that this wealth reserve would be available as a collateral for future improvements. A more realistic view would be to regard it as available to remedy certain consequences of past errors.

To be specific, public policy should seek to slow the rise in the sharing of value added between wages and profits, or to keep it constant at its new-found level. Another desirable aim is a recovery in the capital-utilization rate, accompanied by the recommendation that the growth in purchasing power should be linked to opportunities for flexible arrangements within a given total of working hours. Such a policy could be negotiated case by case at company level, avoiding the drawbacks of overall macroeconomic norms.

For firms, the profit-rate recovery would continue to be fueled by the efforts of their employees, but these efforts would be better directed, as they would focus on the most deteriorated element—capital productivity—and no longer on the primary sharing of income. For employees, the effort would be more acceptable, as it would be offset by a growth of their purchasing power. This increase might once again reach the growth rate of available productivity—a characteristic of stable profit-wage sharing. Lastly, at the macroeconomic level, a small gain in purchasing power would dampen some of the "perverse effects" of slow growth.

The wealth reserve that could be released by better equipment utilization is neither unlimited nor—more importantly—simple to apply. It would be misleading to exaggerate its possible effects; as for the reorganization of working hours, it demands an unquestionable effort on the part of employees. Yet this type of economically better-proportioned effort may be more acceptable socially than the continuation of wage restraint alone.

These two suggestions—developing profit-sharing preferably in the rigid sector of the labor market, and promoting flexible working time to improve the equipment-utilization rate—are not particularly original, nor, of course, can they claim to provide general solutions to the problem of unemployment. Nevertheless, by explaining the rigidities at the root of the wage gap, we have attempted to show why these two measures seem well suited to the special case of France. For lack of a general solution, any local initiative with a reasonable potential for application remains worthy of interest.

These suggestions admittedly concern the world of management-labor relations, an area where economists are "off limits" and must exercise restraint. It is their task, however, to restate a few simple rules that no society, whatever its organization, can afford to ignore: the growth of purchasing power cannot exceed the growth of available productivity for very long; the rate of equipment utilization is a key factor of profitability; the levels and mode of remuneration, as well as the quantity and organization of working hours, are closely interdependent variables that can be determined only simultaneously.

References

Artus, Jacques R. 1984. "The Disequilibrium Real Wage Rate Hypothesis: An Empirical Evaluation." *International Monetary Fund Staff Papers* 31, no. 2.

Artus, Patrick. 1983. "Formation conjointe des prix et des salaires dans cinq grands pays industriels: peut-on comprendre les ecarts entre taux d'inflation?" *Annales de l'INSEE*, no. 49, pp. 5–52.

Artus, Patrick. 1987. "Salaire reel et emploi." *Revue Economique* 38, no. 3, pp. 625–659.

Boyer, Robert. 1978. "Les salaires en longue période." *Economie et Statistique*, no. 103, pp. 27–57.

Brillet, Jean-Louis. 1985. Les salaires. INSEE note no. 320/54, March.

CEPREMAP-Cordes. 1977. Approches de l'inflation. Paris.

Chan-Lee, J. H., and Sutch, H. 1986. "Profits et taux de rendement et investissements dans les industries manufacturières." *Perspectives de l'OCDE*, May.

Cling, Jean-Pierre, and Meunier, François. 1986. "La désinflation en France: le point de vue de l'économètre." *Revue Economique* 37, no. 6, pp. 1093–1125.

Coe, David T., and Gagliardi, Francesco. 1985. Détermination des salaires nominaux dans dix économies de l'OCDE. Document de travail OCDE no. 19, June.

COPAIN. 1981. "Le modèle COPAIN: comportements patrimoniaux et interprétation financière." *Economie et Prévision*, no. 48.

Debonneuil, Michèle, and Sterdyniak, Henry. 1984. "La boucle prix-salaire dans l'inflation." *Revue Economique* 35, no. 2, pp. 267–311.

Dubois, Paul. 1980. "La rupture de 1974." *Economie et Statistique* no. 124, pp. 3–20.

Dubois, Paul. 1985. "Ruptures de croissance et progrès techniques." *Ecconomie et Statistique* no. 181, pp. 3–31.

Garnier, Olivier. 1985. Marchés internes et marché externe du travail: leur rôle dans la formation des salaires. *Unité de recherche, INSEE.*

Geary, Patrick T., and Kennan, John. 1982. "The Employment–Real Wage Relationship: An International Study." *Journal of Political Economy* 90, no. 4, pp. 854–871.

Glaude, Michel. 1986. "Ancienneté, expérience et théorie dualiste du marché du travail: une étude sur données individuelles." *Economie appliquée* 39, no. 4, pp. 847–876.

Grubb, O., Jackman, R., and Layard, R. 1983. "Wage Rigidity and Unemployment in OCDE Countries." *European Economic Review*, March–April, pp. 11–39.

Klau, F., and Mittelstädt, A. 1985. Flexibilité du marché du travail et chocs extérieurs sur les prix. *Documents de travail OCDE* No. 24 (September).

Lambert, J. Paul, and Mulbray, B. 1987. Investment in a Disequilibrium Context, or Does Profitability Really Matter? CORE Discussion Paper No. 8703.

Le Cacheux, Jacques, and Szpiro, Daniel. 1984. "Part salariale et emploi." *Observations et Dianostics Economiques, OFCE*, No. 8 (July), pp. 121–140.

Levy-Leboyer, Maurice, and Bourguignon, François. 1985. *L'économie française du 19°siècle*. Economica.

Loué, Jean-François. 1986. Un modèle d'offre pour l'économie française. Direction de la Prévision, Document de travail no. 14.

Maarek, Gérard. 1983. "ICARE: modèle conjoncturel de l'économie française." *Revue del'IPECODE*, no. 1.

McDonald, Ian M., and Solow, Robert M. 1981. "Wage Bargaining and Employment." *American Economic Review* 71 (December), pp. 896–908.

McDonald, Ian M., and Solow, Robert M. 1985. "Wage and Employment in a Segmented Labor Market." *Quarterly Journal of Economics* 100 (November), pp. 1125–1141.

Malinvaud, Edmond. 1981. *Théorie macroéconomique*. Dunod.

Malinvaud, Edmond. 1982. "Wages and Unemployment." *Economic Journal* no. 92, pp. 1–12.

Malinvaud, Edmond. 1983. *Essais sur la théorie du chômage*. Calmann-Lévy.

Malinvaud, Edmond. 1986. "Jusqu'où la rigueur salariale devrait-elle aller ?" *Revue Economique* 37, no. 2, pp. 181–205.

METRIC. 1981. *Une modélisation de l'économie française*. INSEE.

Minczeles, Alain, and Sicsic, Pierre. 1986. "La désinflation 1982–1985: une analyse variantielle." *Revue Economique* 37, no. 6, pp. 1127–1146.

Morin, Pierre, and Loué, Jean François. 1986. "La boucle prix-salaires des modèles de l'économie française: structure et robustesse." *Revue Economique* 37, no. 6, pp. 1067–1091.

Morin, Pierre. 1986. Une analyse du processus de désinflation. Direction de la Prévision, Document de travail No. 6.

Oswald, Andrew J. 1982. "Trade Unions, Wages And Unemployment: What Can Simple Models Tell Us?" *Oxford Economic Papers* (November), pp. 526–545.

Piore, Michael J. 1978. "Dualism in the Labor Market: A Response to Uncertainty and Flux. The Case of France." *Revue Economique* 19, no. 11, pp. 26–48.

Ralle, Pierre. 1987. Les déterminants macroéconomiques du taux de salaire ont-ils changé depuis 1982? Les enseignements d'une analyse économétrique. INSEE Note No. 71/341, 1 (April).

Rapport sur les Comptes de la Nation 1987. 1988. Les collections de l'INSEE, Série C No. 147–148—Tome 1: le Rapport.

Reynaud, Bénédicte. 1986. "Règles et logique des relations salariales." *Economie et Statistiques* No. 192, pp. 43–63.

Rouilleault, Henry. 1987. La baisse de la productivité du capital dans l'industrie concurrentielle. Note Direction de la Prévision, 129/87, No. 24 (April).

Sachs, Jeffrey D. 1979. "Wages, Profits and Macroeconomic Adjustment." *Brookings Papers on Economic Activity* 2, pp. 269–319.

Sachs, Jeffrey D. 1983. "Real Wages and Unemployment in the OECD Countries." *Brookings Papers on Economic Activity* 1, pp. 225–304.

Saint-Paul, Gilles. 1987. Analyse économique des formules d'intéressement. Direction de la Prévision, Document de travail No. 4.

Sauvy, Alfred. 1984. *Histoire économique de la France entre les deux guerres*. Economica.

Sterdyniak, Henry. 1984. "Le modèle trimestriel de l'OFCE." *Observation et Diagnostics Economiques, OFCE* No. 9 (October).

Taddei, Dominique. 1986. "Des machines et des hommes pour l'emploi par une meilleure utilisation des équipements." La Documentation Française, Paris.

Turner, Anthony G. 1987. Potential Output In Manufacturing For Ten Industrial Countries: Revised Estimates 1965, 1986. International Monetary Fund Working Paper 87/2.

Weitzman, M. 1985. "The Simple Macroeconomics of Profit-Sharing." *American Economic Review* 75 (December), pp. 137–953.

Weitzman, M. 1987. "Steady-State Unemployment under Profit-Sharing." *Economic Journal* 97 (March), pp. 86–105.

II

Statistical Methods and Econometrics

29

The Adjustment of Contingency Tables: Two New Approaches

Yacine Aït-Sahalia,
Michel Balinski, and
Gabrielle Demange

The phrase "the adjustment of contingency tables with given marginals" has been used to refer to a host of statistical problems—for example, the adjustment of a sampled frequency table when expected marginal totals are known, or the estimation and projection of trade flows among countries. An entire issue of the *Annales de l'INSEE* was devoted to the subject and its applications. Roughly speaking, the generic problem may be described as follows. Given are two types of data: a matrix and constraints on marginal totals. For example, the matrix represents sampled data whereas the marginal totals are the result of a complete enumeration. One then wishes to find a table that satisfies the marginal constraints but reflects the information contained in the sampled data. The usual approach is to choose some measure of distance between tables and then to find a table nearest to the given matrix that verifies the known marginal constraints. The question that at once presents itself is: what measure of distance should be taken? In fact, many different measures have been used and the specific application may naturally call for the choice of a particular measure. The aim of this paper is to justify, via two different approaches, the choice of Kullback's information function, which gives rise to what we will call the entropy method.

The first approach consists in formulating precise axioms concerning the properties a method "should" enjoy, thereby permitting a better appreciation for the nature of the implicit assumptions made when one or another measure is chosen, and then deriving the class of methods that meets the axioms. Specifically, we propose a set of properties that are intuitively convincing or many concrete instances of the problem, and show that the entropy method is the only one that verifies them all. It would be interesting to extend the analysis to characterizing other methods by other axioms, for each concrete situation may well suggest a different set of axioms. The axiomatic approach could then be used as a mean of choosing among the several possible methods.

The second justification is statistical in nature and depends on the information function of Kullback and the theory of large deviations. We show in what sense the entropy method yields a most likely solution.

The first section defines the problem, outlines several applications, and gives the methods most frequently used. The second section explains the entropy method, sketches the RAS algorithm that converges to the entropy solution when the marginal constraints are equations, and presents a generalization of the method for inequality marginal constraints. The final two sections develop the two justifications for the entropy method, one axiomatic and the other statistical. The proofs of the assertions made are relegated to the appendix.

I. The problem

1. Notation and Definition

The rows of the matrices considered in this paper are all indexed by $M = \{1, \ldots, m\}$ with typical element i, and the columns by $N = \{1, \ldots, n\}$ with typical element j.

If $\mathbf{a} = (a_{ij})$ is a matrix, $a_{i.}$ designates the sum of the entries in row i; and $a_{.j}$ and $a_{..}$ are defined analogously. If $\mathbf{l} = (l_i)$ is a vector, $l_.$ is the sum of its entries.

Given a matrix $\mathbf{a} = (a_{ij})$, $a_{ij} > 0$, and given marginal constraints on rows $\mathbf{l}^- = (l_i^-)$ and $l^+ = (l_i^+)$ for $i \in M$, on columns $\mathbf{c}^- = (c_j^-)$ and $\mathbf{c}^+ = (c_j^+)$ for $j \in N$, and a constraint on the sum t of all entries of the matrix, one seeks a method that associates with $\mathbf{a}$ a matrix that belongs to the set

$$A = \{\mathbf{b} = (b_{ij}),\ b_{ij} > 0\colon l_i^- \leqslant b_{i.} \leqslant l_i^+,\ i \in M,$$
$$c_j^- \leqslant b_{.j} \leqslant b_{.j}\ j \in N \text{ and } b_{..} = t\}.$$

This gives rise to the following definitions.

A *problem* is specified by the data $\mathbf{p} = (\mathbf{a}, \mathbf{l}^-, \mathbf{l}^+, \mathbf{c}^-, \mathbf{c}^+, t)$.

A matrix belonging to the corresponding set A is said to be *admissible*. It will be assumed that the data $\mathbf{p}$ are such that the set A always contains a strictly positive matrix. This is equivalent to supposing that $l_.^- \leqslant t \leqslant l_.^+$ and $\Sigma_{i \in I}\, l_i^- < t$ for every proper subset I of M and $l_i^+ > 0$ for all i, and the same for columns.

If C is a class of problems, a *method on* C is a function S that associates to every problem of C at least one admissible matrix.

A problem is *equality constrained* if $\mathbf{l}^- = \mathbf{l}^+ = \mathbf{l}$ and $\mathbf{c}^- = \mathbf{c}^+ = \mathbf{c}$. It is a *vector problem* if m or n is equal to 1.

2. Examples

Example 1. The adjustment of sampled frequency data.

Suppose the matrix **a** is a table of estimates of distribution of a population classified according to two characteristics, and that an exhaustive survey provides relatively precise bounds on the incidence of each characteristic type of the population, so yielding constraints $(\mathbf{l}^-, \mathbf{l}^+, \mathbf{c}^-, \mathbf{c}^+, t)$. The problem is then to find a two-way frequency table reflecting as closely as possible the results of the sample estimates. A table that is proportional to **a** is the natural candidate: but when, due to omissions or commissions of the sampling procedure or other noise, the proportional solution is not admissible, what solution should be chosen?

Example 2. Passenger flows in the Paris métro.

The administration of the Paris métro wishes to know the number of passengers using each of the parts of its network between 7:00 and 8:00 in the morning. To obtain an estimate it subdivides the Paris region into zones that are primarily residential $(i = 1, \ldots, m)$ and primarily non-residential $(j = 1, \ldots, n)$. It seeks to obtain a tableau **b** where b_{ij} is the number going from zone i to zone j. For various technical reasons, it is very costly to attempt a direct count. However, from the number of inhabitants in each residential zone i an estimate l_i of the number leaving for work by métro can be estimated and from the number of workers in each non-residential zone j a similar estimate c_j of the number arriving for work by métro can be obtained.

By another process, the number of passengers going from i to j is evaluated a priori by $a_{ij} = l_i f(d_{ij}) c_j$, where d_{ij} is a generalized cost of transportation (taking into account such factors as cost and direction of trip, number of changes, etc.) and f is a decreasing function.

Here again, if a matrix **b** proportional to **a** is admissible it is a reasonable candidate for a solution. But if not, then what?

Example 3. Projected tables.

Margins imposed: Consider the world market for some raw material, organized into importing countries and exporting countries. Suppose that the value of exports from country i to country j in year y is estimated to be a_{ij} (typically based on the known figures for year $y - 1$) but not yet known precisely, whereas the value of total imports and exports is already known for each country. One wishes a best estimate of international trade for year y that satisfies the known marginal totals.

Margins planned: Consider the problem of how to assign incoming students to Parisian universities according to the subject matters of their interests. Let a_{ij} be an estimate of the number of students to be enrolled in discipline i at university j, obtained from the data of past years and current samples (e.g., RAVEL, a census of the preferences of lycée students instituted in 1987). In addition, both the total number of students per university and the total number of graduates of a given discipline must satisfy planning objectives. The a priori affectation of students to universities has little chance of satisfying the marginal constraints: students in Parisian universities prefer those situated within the city limits, they do not take sufficient account of future professional opportunities in their choice of discipline, etc.

Example 4. Apportioning seats in a legislature.

The 518 seats of the European Parliament are shared by the nations that are members of the EEC. An equitable distribution requires an apportionment of seats that is proportional to the distribution of the populations of the respective countries but that assures a minimal representation to each country (in particular to the two smallest, Luxembourg and Ireland). This gives rise to a vector problem where $\mathbf{a}$ is the vector of populations, $\mathbf{c}^-$ the vector of minima (with $\min_j c_j^- = 6$ today) and t the total number of seats. This is in fact a problem that has an additional constraint: an answer in integers is required. How to approach it has been analyzed by Balinski and Young (1982) for vector problems and generalized to matrix problems by Balinski and Demange (1987).

3. Methods in Current Use

We mention only the predominant approach, which consists in minimizing the "distance" between two matrices, $\boldsymbol{\lambda} = (\lambda_{ij})$ that must be admissible, and $\boldsymbol{\mu} = (\mu_{ij})$ that is given.

Several "distances" have been suggested in the literature, as follows:

- Kullback's information function (or "entropy"):

$$I(\lambda/\mu) = \Sigma_{i,j}\lambda_{ij}\log\frac{\lambda_{ij}}{\mu_{ij}}.$$

• Pearson's chi-square:

$$\chi_1^2 = \Sigma_{i,j} \frac{(\lambda_{ij} - \mu_{ij})^2}{\mu_{ij}},$$

whose minimization subject to $\boldsymbol{\lambda}$ being admissible leads to a system of linear equations.

• Neyman's chi-square:

$$\chi_2^2 = \Sigma_{ij} \frac{(\lambda_{ij} - \mu_{ij})^2}{\lambda_{ij}},$$

whose minimization does not lead to a linear system.

• Quadratic programming:

$$d_2(\lambda, \mu) = \Sigma_{i,j} \alpha_{i,j} (\lambda_{ij} - \mu_{ij})^2,$$

where α_{ij} are positive coefficients.

• $d_1(\lambda, \mu) = \Sigma_{i,j} \alpha_{ij} (\lambda_{ij} - \mu_{ij})$, whose minimization leads to the solution of a linear program.

The question that must immediately be raised is what distance concept is to be taken. One approach is to do a historical comparison. For example, in the international trade problem one can take the estimate found by using each of the different methods for each year y, based on the actual known data of year $y - 1$ and margins of year y, and see how they compare with the actual data of year y. An econometric study using this idea was done and concluded that the entropy method was best. Our aim is to show there exist other justifications for the choice of the entropy method over others.

II. The Entropy Method

We begin with a proposition that permits a proper definition.

Proposition. Given a problem $(\mathbf{a}, \mathbf{l}^-, \mathbf{l}^+, \mathbf{c}^-, \mathbf{c}^+, t)$, there exists one any only one admissible matrix $\mathbf{b}^*$ that minimizes entropy $\Sigma_{M \times N} b_{ij} \log(b_{ij}/a_{ij})$. Moreover, $\mathbf{b}^*$ is the unique admissible matrix for which there exist multipliers $\delta > 0$, $\boldsymbol{\lambda} = (\lambda_i) > \mathbf{0}$, $i \in M$, $\boldsymbol{\mu} = (\mu_j) > \mathbf{0}$, $j \in N$, satisfying

$$b_{ij}^* = \delta \lambda_i a_{ij} \mu_j \qquad \text{for all } i \text{ and } j$$

$$\lambda_i > 1 \Rightarrow b_{i.}^* = l_i^-, \ \lambda_i < 1 \Rightarrow b_{i.}^* = l_i^+ \qquad \text{for all } i$$

$$\mu_j > 1 \Rightarrow b_{.j}^* = c_j^-, \ \mu_j < 1 \Rightarrow b_{.j}^* = c_j^+ \qquad \text{for all } j$$

The matrix $\mathbf{b}^*$ so defined is called the entropy solution to the problem. The method that associates to every problem its entropy solution is called the *entropy method.*

In words, the entropy solution of a problem is obtained from a matrix proportional to $\mathbf{a}$ by multiplying each row and column by an appropriate factor. The multiplier associated with a row is greater (respectively, less) than 1 only if it must be to satisfy the lower (respectively, upper) margin.

In the case of an equality-constrained problem, the conditions on the multipliers are automatically satisfied and $\mathbf{b}^*$ is the unique admissible matrix obtained from $\mathbf{a}$ by multiplying its rows and columns. It is easily found by the RAS algorithm: multiply each row of $\mathbf{a}$ by a scalar so that the sum of the entries in the resulting row sums to its prescribed margin; then, do the same thing but to the columns of the matrix just obtained; and continue alternating from rows to columns. This process is easily generalized to the case of inequalities (as proposed in Balinski and Demange 1987, where its convergence is proven).

To begin, consider a vector problem $(\mathbf{a}, \mathbf{c}^-, \mathbf{c}^+, t)$ where the admissible set is

$$A = \{\mathbf{b} = (b_j), j \in N: b_j > 0 \text{ and } c_j^- \leqslant b_j \leqslant c_j^+ \text{ for } j \in N, b_. = t\}.$$

Given three unordered real numbers x, y, z, let $\text{mid}(x, y, z) = y$ if $x \leqslant y \leqslant z$, and define the real function $\sigma(\delta) = \Sigma_N \text{mid}(c_j^-, \delta a_j, c_j^+)$. The entropy solution is obtained by finding a positive root δ of the equation $\sigma(\delta) = t$. For then

$$\mu_j = \text{mid}(c_j^-, \delta a_j, c_j^+)/\delta a_j \quad \text{and} \quad b_j^* = \delta \mu_j a_j,$$

so the conditions of the proposition are verified.

A positive root δ must exist because A is assumed to be nonvoid. In the algorithm given below for the general problem it will be assumed that the multipliers μ_j satisfy a supplementary condition, namely, $\min \mu_j \leqslant 1 \leqslant \max_j \mu_j$. It is easily shown that such a choice is always possible.

Each step of the *general algorithm* is the solution of a vector problem:

Step 0. $\lambda_i = 1 = \mu_j$ for all i and j.

Step $2k + 1$. Compute the solution of the vector problem $((\Sigma_j a_{ij} \mu_j^{2k}), \mathbf{l}^-, \mathbf{l}^+, t)$. Let δ^{2k+1} and λ^{2k+1} be the multipliers associated with this solution, and set $\boldsymbol{\mu}^{2k+1} = \boldsymbol{\mu}^{2k}$.

Step $2k + 2$. Compute the solution to the vector problem $((\Sigma_i \lambda_i^{2k+1} a_{ij}), \mathbf{c}^-, \mathbf{c}^+, t)$. Let δ^{2k+2} and μ^{2k+2} be the multipliers associated with this solution and set $\lambda^{2k+2} = \lambda^{2k+1}$.

Thus each matrix $(b_{ij}^k) = (\delta^k \lambda_i^k a_{ij} \mu_j^k)$ sums to t and satisfies the row constraints when k is odd and the column constraints when k is even (see

Balinski and Demange 1987 for a proof of convergence to the entropy solution).

III. Axiomatic Approach

We characterize the entropy method first for equality constrained problems, next for vector problems, and finally for the general problem.

1. Equality-Constrained Problems

An equality-constrained problem may be written $(\mathbf{a}, \mathbf{l}, \mathbf{c})$, since $t = l_{.} = c_{..}$.

Let S be any method defined on the set of equality-constrained problems. The characterization is given in terms of three axioms: exactness, homogeneity, and uniformity.

> *Exactness.* S is exact if, for all problems $\mathbf{p} = (\mathbf{a}, \mathbf{l}, \mathbf{c})$, $(t/a_{..})\mathbf{a}$ admissible implies $S(\mathbf{p}) = \{(t/a_{..})\mathbf{a}\}$.

The axiom requires that if the matrix proportional to $\mathbf{a}$ and summing to t verifies the constraints, then it is the unique solution to the problem.

> *Homogeneity.* S is homogeneous if, for all problems $\mathbf{p} = (\mathbf{a}, \mathbf{l}, \mathbf{c})$ such that the rows i and k are proportional and the margins l_i and l_k are equal, rows i and k of $\mathbf{b}$ are identical for all $\mathbf{b}$ in $S(\mathbf{p})$. And the same property holds for columns.

If $\mathbf{d}$ is an $m \times n$ matrix and I and J are nonempty subsets of M and N, $\mathbf{d}_{I \times J}$ represents the submatrix of $\mathbf{d}$ defined on rows I and columns J. Given $\mathbf{b}$ in $S(\mathbf{p})$ one can associate to every pair of nonempty subsets I of M and J of N the *subproblem* $\mathbf{p}' = (\mathbf{a}_{I \times J}, \mathbf{l}'_I, \mathbf{c}'_J)$ where $l'_i = l_i - \Sigma_{j \notin J} b_{ij}$ for $i \in I$ and $c'_j = c_j - \Sigma_{i \notin I} b_{ij}$ for $j \in J$.

> *Uniformity.* S is uniform if, for all problems $\mathbf{p} = (\mathbf{a}, \mathbf{l}, \mathbf{c})$ and all subsets $I \subset M$ and $J \subset N$, $\mathbf{b}$ in $S(\mathbf{p})$ implies
> (i) $\mathbf{b}_{I \times J} \in S(\mathbf{p}')$, and
> (ii) if $\mathbf{b}'_{I \times J} \in S(\mathbf{p}')$, then the matrix $\mathbf{b}'$ equal to $\mathbf{b}'_{I \times J}$ for $(i, j) \in I \times J$ and otherwise equal to $\mathbf{b}$, also belongs to $S(\mathbf{p})$.

Uniformity imposes that (i) any part of a solution is a solution to the corresponding subproblem and (ii) replacing this part of a solution by an alternate solution to the subproblem provides an alternate solution to the problem itself.

In all of the examples exactness appears to be an indispensable property.

Consider the meaning of homogeneity for example 1, the adjustment of samples frequency data. Suppose the table gave the results of a poll on the voting preferences of the inhabitants of different cities. If the samples of two different committees of the same size gave the same percentages of voting preferences, then it is natural to foresee that each political party or candidate would obtain the same total vote in each of the two committees. This is precisely what the axiom of homogeneity demands.

To illustrate the ramifications of uniformity we consider the two examples that concern projected tables. In the case of tables of values of international trade in a raw material, suppose that the analysis was restricted to a projection of the trade between two importing and two exporting countries, the margins for this partial table being given by those projected by the global solution. The axiom of uniformity imposes a consistency on the projections: if an econometrician confines his study to the submarket, he obtains the same projected estimates. As for the second example that concerns a planning problem, note first that any method that optimizes an objective must be uniform. But even if the objectives of a plan are not subsumed in specifying a function that is to be maximized uniformity is essential since otherwise it would be possible in certain cases to find improved "local" solutions, that is, improved solutions to one or more subproblems.

Theorem 1. The entropy method is the unique method that satisfies exactness, homogeneity, and uniformity over the set of equality problems.

2. Vector Problems

The entropy method for vector problems $\mathbf{p} = (\mathbf{a}, \mathbf{l}^-, \mathbf{l}^+, t)$ is characterized by axioms of exactness, uniformity, and monotonicity. The first two have the same meaning and interpretation as above. In this section S is any method defined on the set of vector problems.

> *Exactness.* S is exact if, for all problems $\mathbf{p} = (\mathbf{a}, \mathbf{l}^-, \mathbf{l}^+, t)$, $(t/a_.)\mathbf{a}$ admissible implies $S(\mathbf{p}) = \{(t/a_.)\mathbf{a}\}$.

Given $\mathbf{b} \in S(\mathbf{p})$ and $J \subset N$, define the *subproblem* $\mathbf{p}' = (\mathbf{a}, \mathbf{l}^-, \mathbf{l}^+, t')$ where $t' = t - \Sigma_{i \notin I} b_i$.

> *Uniformity.* S is uniform if, for all problems $\mathbf{p} = (\mathbf{a}, \mathbf{l}^-, \mathbf{l}^+, t)$ and all subsets $I \subset M$, $\mathbf{b}$ in $S(\mathbf{p})$ implies
> (i) $\mathbf{b}_I \in S(\mathbf{p}')$ and

(ii) if $\mathbf{b}'_I \in S(\mathbf{p}')$ then the vector $\mathbf{b}'$ equal to $\mathbf{b}'_I$ for $i \in I$ and otherwise equal to $\mathbf{b}$, also belongs to $S(\mathbf{p})$.

Monotonicity. S is monotonic if, for all vector $\mathbf{a}$, $\mathbf{a}'$ with $a_k < a'_k$ for some one $k \in M$ and $a_i = a'_i$ otherwise, $\mathbf{b}$ in $S(\mathbf{a}, \mathbf{l}^-, \mathbf{l}^+, t)$ and $\mathbf{b}'$ in $S(\mathbf{a}', \mathbf{l}^-, \mathbf{l}^+, t)$ implies $b_k \leqslant b'_k$.

Monotonicity asks that an increase in one entry of the vector $\mathbf{a}$ cannot result in a decrease in the corresponding entry of the solution. In example 4, the apportionment of seats in a legislative, uniformity is a guarantee of stability: if a subset of countries were to redistribute among themselves their total allocation of seats, they would find the same solution. Monotonicity ensures that if the population of one single nation increased, its representation could not decrease.

Theorem 2. The entropy method is the unique method that satisfies exactness, uniformity, and monotonicity over the set of vector problems.

3. The General Problem

To characterize the entropy method in the general, inequality constrained problem an additional axiom called relevance is introduced and uniformity is generalized. In this section S is any method defined on the set of all problems (as defined in I.1).

Given $\mathbf{b} \in S(\mathbf{p})$ and $I \subset M$, $J \subset N$ define the *subproblem* $\mathbf{p}' = (\mathbf{a}_{I \times J}, \mathbf{l}'^-, \mathbf{l}'^+, \mathbf{c}'^-, \mathbf{c}'^+, t')$, where $l'^-_i = l^-_i - \Sigma_{i \notin J} b_{ij}$ and similarly for the other row and column constraints, and $t' = t - \sum_{i \notin I, j \notin J} b_{ij}$.

Uniformity. S is uniform if, for all problems $\mathbf{p} = (\mathbf{a}, \mathbf{l}^-, \mathbf{l}^+, \mathbf{c}^-, \mathbf{c}^+, t)$ and all subsets $I \subset M$, $J \subset N$, $\mathbf{b}$ in $S(\mathbf{p})$ implies
(i) $\mathbf{b}_{I \times J} \in S(\mathbf{p}')$
(ii) if $\mathbf{b}_{I \times J} \in S(\mathbf{p}')$ then the matrix $\mathbf{b}'$ equal to $\mathbf{b}'_{I \times J}$ for $i \in I$, $j \in J$, and otherwise equal to $\mathbf{b}$, also belongs to $S(\mathbf{p})$.

Given $\mathbf{b}$ in $S(\mathbf{p})$, with $\mathbf{p} = (\mathbf{a}, \mathbf{l}^-, \mathbf{l}^+, \mathbf{c}^-, \mathbf{c}^+, t)$, the induced *equality constrained problem* of $\mathbf{b}$ for $\mathbf{p}$ is the problem $\mathbf{p}' = (\mathbf{a}, \mathbf{l}, \mathbf{c})$ where $l_i = b_{i.}$ for $i \in M$ and $c_j = b_{.j}$ for $j \in N$.

Relevance. S is relevant if, for all problems $\mathbf{p}$, $\mathbf{b} \in S(\mathbf{p})$ implies that $\mathbf{b} \in S(\mathbf{p}')$, where $\mathbf{p}'$ is the induced equality constrained problem of $\mathbf{b}$ for $\mathbf{p}$.

In words, a projection obtained as a solution to a general inequality constrained problem determines marginal totals. If one then obtains a projection with the same method but for the equality problem with these fixed marginal totals then it should be exactly the same.

Theorem 3. The entropy method is the unique method over the class of general problems that satisfies

- uniformity and relevance,
- exactness and homogeneity over the subset of equality constrained problems, and
- monotonicity over the subset of vector problems.

IV. Statistical Approach

We propose now to use the mathematical theory of large deviations to establish a statistical justification for the choice of the entropy measure.

To begin, recall the example concerning international trade of a raw material (example 3.a): the problem is to estimate the matrix of imports for the current year on the basis of

- **a**, an a priori estimate of the matrix (typically the known import matrix of the preceding year modified in some appropriate way), and
- partial information concerning **b**, namely upper and lower bounds on the sums of its rows and columns, that determine the admissible set A to which **b** must belong.

We show that the maximum-likelihood estimate of the matrix **b** is the solution of the program to minimize the entropy function over the constraint set A.

Each franc paid in the market for the raw material in question may be viewed as having the probability μ_{ij} of being received by producer i in payment of deliveries to consumer j: the t francs (the total of all transactions in the market) are distributed independently by a multinomial distribution having probabilities (μ_{ij}). The a priori estimate **a** can thus be normalized to $\mu = (1/t)\mathbf{a}$. Given the distribution based on (μ_{ij}) and the admissible set A, the theory of large deviations produces an estimate of **b** in A. We confine our discussion to the results necessary for our particular purposes.

1. Situating the Empirical Distribution Associated with a Sample

Let X be the set $M \times N$, and $P(X)$ the set of probabilities on $M \times N$ having the usual topology on $\mathbb{R}^{m \times n}$.

If μ is in $P(X)$ and X_k is a sequence of independent, identically distributed random variables with common distribution μ then for all trial sequences w in $X^{\mathbb{N}}$, let $X_k(w)$ be the index (i, j) found at the kth trial.

Let $\hat{\mu}_k$ be the function that associates to each sequence of trials w the empirical distribution $\hat{\mu}_k(w)$ defined by

$$\hat{\mu}_k(w) = (\delta_{X_1(w)} + \cdots + \delta_{X_k(w)})/k,$$

where $\delta_{(i,j)}$ is Dirac's measure at the point (i, j), that is, $\delta_{(i,j)}$ is the measure having value 1 for index (i, j) and 0 otherwise.

For example, suppose that $m = n = 2$ and μ is given by

1/2	1/8
1/4	1/8

.

If one has obtained, in 1000 trials, the index (1, 1) 505 times, the index (1, 2) 123 times, the index (2, 1) 252 times, and the index (2, 2) 120 times, then the empirical distribution is the probability given by

1/1000

505	123
252	120

.

The distribution $\hat{\mu}_k(w)$ converges to the common distribution μ as $k \to +\infty$ by the weak law of large numbers and, moreover, satisfies the theorem of Glivenko-Cantelli which, like the central limit theorem, establishes the convergence of $\sqrt{k}(\hat{\mu}_k - \mu)$.

The theory of large deviations studies the properties of the convergent sequence $\hat{\mu}_k - \mu$. It gives the asymptotic behavior of $P_\mu(\hat{\mu}_k \in G)$, where G is a subset of $P(X)$ the set of probability measures on X. The information function of Kullback is defined by

$$I(\lambda/\mu) = \Sigma_{M \times N}\, \lambda_{ij} \log\left(\frac{\lambda_{ij}}{\mu_{ij}}\right).$$

We let $I(G/\mu) = \inf\{I(\lambda/\mu) \colon \lambda \in G\}$.

Theorem of large deviations (see, for example, Bretagnolle 1979). Let μ be a probability distribution on $M \times N$ with $\mu_{ij} > 0$ for all (i, j). If $\hat{\mu}_k$ is the empirical distribution of a sequence of independent random variables with common distribution μ then (1) for all closed subsets G of $P(X)$

$$\limsup_{k \to \infty} \left(\frac{1}{k} \log_{\mu} (\hat{\mu}_k \in G) \right) \leqslant -I(G/\mu);$$

(2) for all open subsets G of $P(X)$

$$\liminf_{k \to \infty} \left(\frac{1}{k} \log P_{\mu} (\hat{\mu}_k \in G) \right) \geqslant -I(G/\mu).$$

Corollary 1. Under the same hypotheses as in the theorem of large deviations, if G is a closed convex subset of $P(X)$ with nonempty interior, then

$$P_{\mu}(\hat{\mu}_k \in G) \underset{k \to \infty}{\sim} \exp\{-kI(G/\mu)\}.$$

The information function of Kullback $I(\lambda/\mu)$ is positive, strictly convex in λ and zero only when $\lambda = \mu$. Thus, when G is a closed convex nonempty subset of $P(X)$ there exists a unique probability λ^* in G that minimizes $I(\lambda/\mu)$ for given μ. Therefore, $I(G/\mu) = I(\lambda^*/\mu) \geqslant 0$ and $I(G/\mu) > 0$ when μ is not in G.

If μ belongs to G, then one obtains the weak law of large numbers: the probability that $\hat{\mu}_k$ belongs to G tends to 1.

But if μ does not belong to G, the event $\{\hat{\mu}_k \in G\}$ is very unlikely since $I(G/\mu)$ strictly positive implies $e^{-kI(G/\mu)}$ is very small. Nevertheless, if one knows that this event was in fact realized, that is if one knows that the empirical distribution belongs to G, then it can be situated more precisely. This is the goal of Corollary 2 below.

If λ belongs to G let $\overline{B}(\lambda, \varepsilon)$ be a closed ball with center λ and radius $\varepsilon > 0$ (for any norm). If G is closed, convex, and has a nonvoid interior then $G(\lambda/\varepsilon) = G \cap \overline{B}(\lambda, \varepsilon)$ has the same properties. Applying Corollary 1 to $G(\lambda/\varepsilon)$ one deduces:

Corollary 2. With the same hypotheses as in the theorem of large deviations, G a closed convex subset of $P(X)$ with nonvoid interior implies that for all λ of G and $\varepsilon > 0$

$$P_{\mu}(\hat{\mu}_k \in G(\lambda, \varepsilon)/\hat{\mu}_k \in G) \underset{k \to \infty}{\sim} \exp\{-k[I(G(\lambda, \varepsilon))/\mu - I(G/\mu)]\}.$$

In particular, for $\lambda = \lambda^*$,

$$\forall \varepsilon > 0, \quad \lim_{k \to \infty} P_\mu(\hat{\mu}_k \in G(\lambda^*, \varepsilon)/\hat{\mu}_k \in G) = 1.$$

2. Application to the Adjustment of Contingency Tables

The matrix **a**, an a priori estimate of **b**, provides after normalization the probability distribution $\mu = (1/t)\mathbf{a}$. Similarly, the set A may be normalized by defining G to be set satisfying $\mathbf{b} \in A$ if and only if $(1/t)\mathbf{b} \in G$. Then the solution to the program $\mathrm{Min}\{I(\lambda/\mu)\colon \lambda \in G\}$ gives the distribution λ^*, the entropy solution. The empirical distribution $\hat{\mu}_k$ if in G is the natural estimate of $(1/t)\mathbf{b}$. Indeed, Corollary 2 shows that this estimate is in probability asymptotically in the ball centered at λ^* with radius arbitrarily small. In other words, choosing λ^* as the estimate for $(1/t)\mathbf{b}$ (or choosing $t\lambda^*$ as the estimate for **b**) means choosing the most likely estimate, in the sense that the asymptotic equivalent given in Corollary 2 is maximized.

This approach is easily generalized to take into account other information concerning the sample: in fact, we have only introduced as constraints margins within certain intervals. But it is also possible to impose fixed values on certain entries of the matrices or any other constraints so long as the set G remains closed, convex, and with a nonempty interior (a hypothesis of Corollary 1).

Conclusion

The use of the entropy method to adjust contingency tables with given marginal constraints thus presents, in our view, two advantages:

- One can "reconstruct" it by a characterization depending on intuitively necessary axioms.
- The entropy method solution constitutes the maximum likelihood point estimate of the adjusted table relative to a multinomial sample distribution.

Appendix

Proof of Corollary 2. If G is a closed convex set with nonempty interior $\mathring{G}$ then it is equal to the closure of $\mathring{G}$ and so $I(G/\mu) = I(\mathring{G}/\mu)$. By the theorem on large deviations,

$$-I(G/\mu) \leqslant \liminf_k \left\{\frac{1}{k}\log P_\mu(\hat{\mu}_k \in G)\right\}$$

$$\leqslant \limsup_k \left\{\frac{1}{k}\log P_\mu(\hat{\mu}_k \in G)\right\} \leqslant I(G/\mu).$$

We now establish Theorems 1, 2, and 3.

Given an $m \times n$ matrix $\mathbf{a}$ and an n-vector $\tilde{y}$, $\mathbf{a} \otimes \mathbf{y}$ is defined to be the matrix obtained by multiplying the jth column of $\mathbf{a}$ by y_j, and similarly $\mathbf{x} \otimes \mathbf{a}$ is obtained by multiplying the ith row of $\mathbf{a}$ by x_i.

Proof of Theorem 1. Let S be an exact, uniform, and homogeneous method over the set of equality constrained problems. Given one such problem $\mathbf{p} = (\mathbf{a}, \mathbf{l}, \mathbf{c})$ and an n-vector $\mathbf{y} > \mathbf{0}$, consider the problem $\mathbf{p}' = ((\mathbf{a}, \mathbf{a} \otimes \mathbf{y}), 2\mathbf{l}, (\mathbf{c}, \mathbf{c}))$. Here column $n + j$ of $\mathbf{a}' = (\mathbf{a}, \mathbf{a} \otimes \mathbf{y})$ is proportional to column j and the sum imposed on column j is the same as that imposed on column $n + j$. Therefore, S homogeneous implies that every matrix in $S(\mathbf{p}')$ is of form $(\mathbf{b}, \mathbf{b})$. By uniformity of S, $\mathbf{b}$ belongs to $S(\mathbf{p})$ and also to $S(\mathbf{a} \otimes \mathbf{y}, \mathbf{l}, \mathbf{c})$. If, on the other hand, another matrix $\mathbf{b}'$ also belongs to $S(\mathbf{p})$ then $(\mathbf{b}, \mathbf{b}')$ belongs to $S(\mathbf{p}')$. $\mathbf{b} \neq \mathbf{b}'$ contradicts homogeneity, so $S(\mathbf{p})$ contains a unique matrix $\mathbf{b}$. Similarly, if $\mathbf{b}''$ belongs to $S(\mathbf{a} \otimes \mathbf{y}, \mathbf{l}, \mathbf{c})$ then $\mathbf{b}'' = \mathbf{b}$. Therefore $S(\mathbf{a} \otimes \mathbf{y}, \mathbf{l}, \mathbf{c})$ is also reduced to the unique matrix $\mathbf{b}$ for all $\mathbf{y} > \mathbf{0}$. By an analogous argument on the problem $(\mathbf{a} \otimes \mathbf{y}, \mathbf{l}, \mathbf{c})$ one obtains $\{\mathbf{b}\} = S(\mathbf{x} \otimes \mathbf{a} \otimes \mathbf{y}), \mathbf{l}, \mathbf{c})$ for all m-vectors $\mathbf{x} > \mathbf{0}$ and n-vectors $\mathbf{y} > \mathbf{0}$. Choose $\mathbf{x}$ and $\mathbf{y}$ to be the vectors $\delta\lambda$ and μ where δ, λ, and μ are the multipliers associated with the entropy solution (see Proposition 1). For this choice the matrix $\mathbf{b}^* = (\mathbf{x} \otimes \mathbf{a} \otimes \mathbf{y})$ is admissible and, S being exact, it must be the unique element of $S(\mathbf{x} \otimes \mathbf{a} \otimes \mathbf{y}, \mathbf{l}, \mathbf{c})$ and therefore of $S(\mathbf{p})$. So S is the entropy method.

It is a simple exercise to verify that the entropy method satisfies the three axioms.

Proof of Theorem 2. Let S be an exact, uniform, and monotone method over the set of vector problems. Suppose $\mathbf{b}^* = (\delta a_j \mu_j)$, $j \in N$ is the entropy method solution to problem $\mathbf{p} = (\mathbf{a}, \mathbf{c}^-, \mathbf{c}^+, t)$. By exactness, $\mathbf{b}^*$ is the unique element of $S((a_1\mu_1, \ldots, a_n\mu_n), \mathbf{c}^-, \mathbf{c}^+, t)$. If $\mu_1 \neq 1$, say $\mu_1 < 1$, consider any $\mathbf{b}'$ in $S((a_1, a_2\mu_2, \ldots, a_n\mu_n), \mathbf{c}^-, \mathbf{c}^+, t)$. S monotonic implies $b_1' \geqslant b_1^*$; but $\mu_1 < 1$ implies $b_1^* = c_1^+$ and so $b_1^* = b_1' = c_1^+$. Now, by the uniformity of S, $(b_2^*, \ldots, b_n^*)$ and $(b_2', \ldots, b_n')$ are both elements of $S((a_2\mu_2, \ldots, a_n\mu_n), (c_2^-, \ldots, c_n^-), (c_2^+, \ldots, c_n^+), t - c_1^+)$, and so S exact implies $(b_2^*, \ldots, b_n^*) = (b_2', \ldots, b_n')$, and thus $\mathbf{b}^* = \mathbf{b}'$.

Repeating this same argument for each $\mu_j \neq 1$ one concludes $S(\mathbf{p}) = \{\mathbf{b}^*\}$. The proof of necessity is immediate.

Lemma. Suppose that $\mathbf{b} = (x_i a_{ij} y_j)$, $(i, j) \in M \times N$, $\mathbf{x} > \mathbf{0}$, $\mathbf{y} > \mathbf{0}$ is admissible for problem $\mathbf{p} = (\mathbf{a}, \mathbf{l}, \mathbf{l}^+, \mathbf{c}^-, \mathbf{c}^+, t)$ and satisfies $x_i > x_k$ implies $b_{i.} = l_i^-$ or $b_{k.} = l_k^+$ for all $i, k \in M$, and $y_j > y_l$ implies $b_{.j} = c_j^-$ or $b_{.l} = c_l^+$ for all $j, l \in N$. Then $\mathbf{b}$ is the entropy solution to problem $\mathbf{p}$.

Proof. Suppose $\mathbf{b}$ satisfies the conditions of the lemma. Then there exists an $\alpha > 0$ with $x_i \leqslant \alpha \leqslant x_k$ for all $i, k \in M$ for which $b_{i.} > l_i^-$ and $b_{k.} < l_k^+$. For if $b_{k.} = l_k^+$ for all $k \in M$ then take $\alpha = \max\{x_k, k \in M\}$. Otherwise, there exists k with $b_{k.} < l_k^+$ and one can take $\alpha = \min\{x_k\colon b_{k.} < l_k^+\}$. α is strictly positive for otherwise $x_k = 0$ and $b_{k.} < l_k^+$ for some k would imply that for every index i with $x_i > 0$, $b_{i.} = l_i^-$. But then $t = \Sigma_{i \neq k} l_i^-$ and the admissible set A contains no matrices whose entries are all positive, a contradiction. A similar choice $\beta > 0$ can be made for columns. Then taking $\delta = \alpha\beta$, $\lambda_i = x_i/\alpha$, and $\mu_j = y_j/\beta$ shows that $\mathbf{b}$ is the entropy solution.

Proof of Theorem 3. Let S be a method that is exact and homogeneous over equality constrained problems, monotone over vector problems, and uniform and relevant over all problems. Suppose $\mathbf{b}$ belongs to $S(\mathbf{p})$ for $\mathbf{p} = (\mathbf{a}, \mathbf{l}^-, \mathbf{l}^+, \mathbf{c}^-, \mathbf{c}^+, t)$ a general problem, and consider the equality problem $\mathbf{p}' = (\mathbf{a}, (b_{i.})$ for $i \in M$, $(b_{.j})$ for $j \in N, t)$. S relevant implies $\mathbf{b}$ belongs to $S(\mathbf{p}')$. Theorem 1 shows $\mathbf{b} = \mathbf{x} \otimes \mathbf{a} \otimes \mathbf{y}$ for some multipliers $\mathbf{x} > \mathbf{0}$, $\mathbf{y} > \mathbf{0}$. We show that these multipliers satisfy the conditions of the lemma. Suppose $b_{.j} > c_j^-$ and $b_{.l} < c_l^+$ for some two column indices j and l. If i is some row index then S uniform implies (b_{ij}, b_{il}) is a solution to the vector problem $((a_{ij}, a_{il}), (c_j'^-, c_l'^-), (c_j'^+, c_j'^+), (b_{ij} + b_{il}))$, where $c_k'^- = c_k^- - b_{.k} + b_{ik}$, $c_k'^+ = c_k^+ - b_{.k} + b_{ik}$ for $k = j, l$. By Theorem 2 (b_{ij}, b_{il}) is the entropy solution to this vector problem. But $b_{il} < c_l'^+$ and $b_{ij} > c_j'^-$ implies $b_{ij}/a_{ij} \leqslant b_{il}/a_{il}$ and so $y_j \leqslant y_l$. Using the analogous argument for rows one concludes that $\mathbf{x}$ and $\mathbf{y}$ satisfy the conditions of the lemma and that $\mathbf{b}$ is the entropy solution to problem $\mathbf{p}$.

Once again the necessity part of the proof is immediate.

References

Y. Aït-Sahalia. 1987. Entropie et Equité. Undergraduate memoir, Ecole Polytechnique.

Annales de l'INSEE. 1976. "Annales et ajustement de tableaux statistiques." (April–September)

M. L. Balinski and G. Demange. 1987. "An Axiomatic Approach to Proportionality between Matrices." Laboratoire d'Econométrie of the Ecole Polytechnique, August; to appear in *Mathematics of Operations Research*.

M. L. Balinski and G. Demange. 1987. "Algorithms for Proportional matrices in reals and integers." Laboratoire d'Econométrie of the Ecole Polytechnique, April; to appear in *Mathematical Programming Series B*.

M. L. Balinski and H. P. Young. 1982. *Fair Representation: Meeting the Ideal of One Man, One Vote*. Yale University Press.

J. Bretagnolle. 1979. "Formule de Chernoff pour les lois empiriques de variables à valeurs dans des espaces généraux." In *Astérisque*, no. 68 (Séminaire Orsay, Société Mathématique de France, Paris).

S. Kullback. 1959. *Information Theory and Statistics*. Wiley.

P. Nijkamp and J. H. P. Paelink. 1976. "Some Methods for Updating Input-Output Tables." *Revue Belge de Statistique, d'Informatique et de Recherche Opérationnelle* 6, no. 4.

30 Parametric Sufficiency and Model Encompassing

Jean-Pierre Florens

One of the main subjects in recent econometric literature consists in formalizing and examining empirical search procedures for model specification, as shown by the number of publications concerning, for instance, "specification tests," "nonnested hypothesis test," procedures of "model's choice," and so on. In the heart of this abundant literature, the concept of "encompassing" appeared, and it seems to be now well introduced in the vocabulary of econometricians, despite the inaccuracy spoiling its definitions in several papers.

The main scope for using the notion of encompassing is the comparison between two statistical models, which explain how the same observations are generated but are different with regard to the choice of parameter spaces and sampling probabilities.

The intuition behind the notion of encompassing is the following: a model will be preferred to another if, on the basis of its own results, it can explain its competition's results and if it encompasses the second model. This intuitive definition appeared, only in the particular case of regression models, in Hendry and Anderson 1977 and Davidson et al. 1978. A definition is presented in Hendry and Richard 1982 and has two kinds of extensions in Mizon 1984 and Mizon and Richard 1986 on the one hand (see also Govaerts 1987) and in Florens et al. 1983 and Florens and Mouchart 1985 on the other.

Some notations are necessary in order to clarify the two accepted types of formalizing. A statistical model is defined by a sample space S provided with a σ-field $\mathscr{S}$ and a family P^a of sampling probabilities. P^a is indexed by elements a of A, the latter being the parameter space of the model. The choice of the term "parameter space" obviously does not exclude a nonparametric or semiparametric approach. As a matter of fact, no structure at this stage is imposed on A, which may be or may contain a distribution or function space.

If one wishes to take into account the notion of sample size, particularly in adopting an asymptotic point of view, the model can be further enriched with a filtration $\mathscr{S}_T$ $(T = 1, 2, 3, \ldots)$ of sub-σ-fields of $\mathscr{S}$ satisfying $\mathscr{S}_T \subset \mathscr{S}_{T'}$ if $T < T'$.

We assume the union of $\mathscr{S}_T$ generates $\mathscr{S}$. $\mathscr{S}_T$ then represents the available information due a sample of size T and $\mathscr{S}$ represents the "asymptotically" available information.

P_T^a denotes the trace of the sampling probability on $\mathscr{S}_T$, and in practice the model specifies the P_T^a series (satisfying $P_{T'}^a$ limited to $\mathscr{S}_T$ equals P_T^a if $T' \geqslant T$), whose limit P^a is deduced. A usual example is given by a dominated model, i.e., where P_T^a is defined by its density $p_T(s/a)$ with respect to a measure that is independent of a.

Let Θ be a family of real-valued functions defined over A. In the model whose sample size is not specified, an estimation procedure for Θ consists of an application $\mathscr{M}$ of Θ over the space of real $\mathscr{S}$-measurable functions. For example, if A is a subset of $\mathbb{R}^k$, $\mathscr{M}$ can be defined with help of on estimator $\hat{a}$ from S to A, by the relation $\mathscr{M}(f) = f_0\hat{a}$ for every measurable function f of A over $\mathbb{R}$. As our point of view will be essentially a Bayesian one, we have to consider subsequently an estimation procedure of a different nature (the transition from a function to its posterior expectation) and we cannot be limited to usual estimations. The roundabout means consisting of the notion of estimation procedure allows us to simultaneously deal with classical and Bayesian points of view. In a model where the sample size is introduced, the estimation procedure will naturally be extended to a sequence $\mathscr{M}_T$ of applications of Θ over the set of random variables defined over S such that, for every $f \in \Theta\mathscr{M}_T(f)$ is $\mathscr{S}_T$ measurable.

Consider two models $\mathscr{E} = ((S, \mathscr{S}), A, P^a)$ and $\mathscr{F} = ((S, \mathscr{S}), B, Q^b)$ and suppose they are provided with estimation procedures $\mathscr{M}$ and $\mathscr{N}$, respectively, defined over Θ and Ω. Θ is a set of real functions defined over A and Ω a set of real functions defined over B. $\mathscr{M}$ and $\mathscr{N}$ formalize the intuitive notion of "results" from models $\mathscr{E}$ and $\mathscr{F}$.

To say that results of model $\mathscr{E}$ contain or explain results of $\mathscr{F}$ will be formalized by assuming the existence of a mapping $\mathscr{D}$ which is called pseudotrue value of Ω in Θ such that $\mathscr{N}$ is equal to (or almost surely equal to, or nonsignificantly different from) $\mathscr{M} \circ \mathscr{D}$. In other words, a real function g of parameters $b \in B$ of $\mathscr{F}$ can be equally well estimated in $\mathscr{F}$ by $\mathscr{N}(g)$ or transformed by $\mathscr{D}$ in a function of parameters $a \in A$ of $\mathscr{E}$ and then estimated in $\mathscr{E}$ by $\mathscr{M}(\mathscr{D}(g))$. This then shows that model $\mathscr{E}$ is richer than $\mathscr{F}$, to which it must be preferred. This definition will be fully clarified in the case of Bayesian models.

Several extensions are possible in the scope of models specifying a sample size and within which two sequences $\mathcal{M}_T$ and $\mathcal{N}_T$ can be pointed out. $\mathcal{D}$ may be replaced by a sequence $\mathcal{D}_T$ such that $\mathcal{N}_T$ is close or equal to $\mathcal{M}_T \circ \mathcal{D}_T$, or $\mathcal{D}$ can be held constant. One's attention can be focused on the limit of the difference between $\mathcal{N}_T$ and $\mathcal{M}_T \circ \mathcal{D}_T$ when T increases indefinitely. This principle is common to all definitions but these are differentiated by the way $\mathcal{D}$ is chosen.

The first viewpoint relies upon examining a sampling property in the sense of $\mathscr{E}$ of procedure $\mathcal{N}_T$. Let us confine ourselves, for the sake of simplicity, to the case where $\mathcal{N}_T$ is defined by an estimator $\hat{b}_T$ belonging to B, assumed to be a subset of $\mathbb{R}^q$. It is possible for instance to construct $\mathcal{D}_T$ by means of the function $\delta_T(a) = E^{\mathscr{E}}(\hat{b}_T/a)$, where $E^{\mathscr{E}}$ represents the sampling mathematical expectation (thus conditional upon a) over $\mathscr{E}$.

One obviously assumes this expectation exists and δ_T is therefore a function of A over $\mathbb{R}$, from which the mapping $\mathcal{D}_T$ will be constructed by the relation $\mathcal{D}_T(g) = g \circ \delta_T$, where g is a function of B over $\mathbb{R}$, and $\mathcal{D}_T(g)$ consequently is a function of A over $\mathbb{R}$.

This construction makes use of sample properties, leading to a sequence $\mathcal{D}_T$. An asymptotic argument yields the definition of a $\mathcal{D}$ independent of T: $\mathcal{D}(g)$ is defined by $\mathcal{D}(g) = g \circ \delta$, where $\delta(a)$ is the limit (a probability limit in the sense of P^a or a P^a = almost sure limit) of $\hat{b}_T$. With $\mathcal{D}$ characterized this way, the comparison between $\mathcal{M}_T$ and $\mathcal{N}_T \circ \mathcal{D}$ is reduced in this framework to a comparison between $\hat{b}_T$ and $\delta(\hat{a}_T)$. One can use for instance $(\hat{b}_T - \delta(\hat{a}_T))' H(\hat{b}_T - \delta(\hat{a}_T))$, where H is a generalized inverse of the variance of $(\hat{b}_T - \delta(\hat{a}_T))$. Such a statistic is called "Wald Encompassing Test Statistic" (WET) by Mizon and Richard (1986). One can see that in both definitions of the pseudotrue values and in the analysis of the encompassing property, only the model $\mathscr{E}$ (provided with its estimation procedure) and the estimation procedure of the second model enter. It is therefore quite improper to talk about the comparison of models whereas the procedure is based on the comparison between a model and an estimation procedure. This point can be illustrated in the following elementary example:

Example 1. Consider two regression models: $\mathscr{E}$ is defined by the relation $y_t = \beta x_t + u_t$ and $\mathscr{F}$ by $y_t = \gamma z_t + v_t$ $(t = 1, \ldots, T)$. β in $\mathscr{E}$ is estimated by ordinary least squares $(\hat{\beta}_T = \sum x_t y_t / \sum x_t^2)$ and for $\mathscr{F}$ two estimators are considered: the ordinary least-squares estimator $(\hat{\gamma}_T = \sum z_t y_t / \sum z_t^2)$ and the generalized least-squares one, which is derived from a heteroscedastic specification of $v_t(\text{Var } v_t = \tau^2 z_t^2)$, i.e.,

$$\gamma_t^* = \frac{1}{T}\sum \frac{y_t}{z_t}.$$

To confine oneself to a small sample size argument, we notice that $\hat{\gamma}$ and γ^* are both unbiased estimators of γ in the model $\mathscr{F}$ if v_t has zero mean for every t. The sampling expectation of $\hat{\gamma}_T$ and γ_T^* in $\mathscr{E}$ are, however, different and lead to the functions

$$\delta_T(\beta) = \left(\frac{\sum z_t x_t}{\sum z_t^2}\right)\beta$$

and

$$\lambda_T(\beta) = \left(\frac{1}{T}\sum \frac{x_t}{z_t}\right)\beta$$

as soon as u_t has zero mean for every t. Under the usual assumptions, the asymptotic argument leads here to different choices of δ and λ, as probability limits in the $\mathscr{E}$ sense of $\hat{\gamma}$ and γ_T^*, and such limits are equal to limits of δ_T and λ_T. One notices that in the $\mathscr{F}$ sense, $\hat{\gamma}_T$ and γ_T^* are both consistent estimators of γ. All this requires sound assumptions on the exogenous variables. In order not to make the example any longer, these are not detailed here. □

This approach of the encompassing analysis, although important in its applications, is reduced to being only the successor of a long series of statistical works concerning properties of an estimator in a misspecified model. Examples are the works of Cox (1961, 1962), Huber (1967), and, for an asymptotic Bayesian version, those of Berk (1966, 1970), which were directly inspired by Le Cam (1953).

These results were the subject of new presentations in the recent econometric literature by White (1982), Gouriéroux et al. (1983, 1984), and Holly (1987). Some specification tests have been proposed in these works.

Note. In the case when models $\mathscr{E}$ and $\mathscr{F}$ are characterized by their likelihood functions, and under the assumption of an estimation procedure in $\mathscr{F}$ which is built from the maximum-likelihood estimate $\hat{b}_T$, the pseudo-true value defined by the probability limit in $\mathscr{E}$ of $\hat{b}$ also has a characterization based upon observation densities. Under reasonable regularity condition (see for example White 1982, $\delta(a)$ is then equal to the value of b that minimizes

$$\lim \frac{1}{T} \int \ln \frac{p_T(s/a)}{q_T(s/b)} p_T(s/a)\, ds,$$

where p_T and q_T are the densities of $\mathscr{E}$ and $\mathscr{F}$ for a sample size T. This magnitude appearing as a measure of the spread between $\mathscr{E}$ and $\mathscr{F}$, it may seem that δ is intrinsically defined without defining estimation procedures. This is of course incorrect insofar as another estimator of parameters in $\mathscr{F}$, even convergent, asymptotically normal and efficient, may not converge in probability to $\delta(a)$, in the $\mathscr{E}$ sense. The so-constructed pseudotrue value hence is of interest only for the maximum likelihood estimator. In a more general way, Amemya (1985) and Holly (1987) show that if $\hat{b}_T$ is obtained by maximizing a criterion such as $1/T \sum h(x_t, b)$ with $s = (x_1, \ldots, x_T)$, $\hat{b}_T$ converges in the $\mathscr{E}$ sense to the maximum of $E^{\mathscr{E}}[h(x_t, b)]$ as soon as the x_t's satisfy a law of large numbers in $\mathscr{E}$, and as regularity conditions are satisfied (for instance, local uniformity of the criterion convergence).

This approach stresses the relation between maximum likelihood and the Kullback quantity of information, but it also shows that another estimation procedure should be connected to another measure of the spread between $\mathscr{E}$ and $\mathscr{F}$.

The second viewpoint leading to the construction of a pseudotrue value will be the subject of this paper. It suggests choosing $\mathscr{D}$ using an optimization argument, so as to bring closer in the best way (in a sense we will clarify later) the estimation defined by $\mathscr{N}$ in the model $\mathscr{F}$, and $\mathscr{M} \circ \mathscr{D}$, the estimation in model $\mathscr{E}$ of real functions of parameters in model $\mathscr{F}$, which one transformed by $\mathscr{D}$ into functions of model $\mathscr{E}$ parameters. This approach is straightforward is the Bayesien framework; it has been introduced by Florens et al. (1983) and Florens and Mouchart (1985). A systematic exposition can be found in Florens et al. 1989, and a presentation of the recent synthesis in Hendry and Richard 1990.

The object of the present paper is mainly to provide a synthesis of these works (same of them only forthcoming), with an attempt to justify the adopted definitions. The second approach has been favored (contrary to Hendry and Richard 1987); its main interest is the relation with the sufficiency concept. However, we display its relations with the first approach, at least with some examples. This paper is divided into three sections devoted, respectively, to the definition of exact encompassing, the study of specificity in relation with the theory of tests between models, and the comparison between encompassing and sufficiency.

I. Exact Encompassing

We present a Bayesian definition of exact encompassing between models without conditioning variables in a first step. This definition will be extended to conditional models in a second step.

Let us first recall the definition of a Bayesian model. It is generally built up from a sampling model, introduced in the introduction, noted $\{A(S, S'), P^a\}$. One then assumes A to be provided with a σ-field $\mathscr{A}$ such that $P^a(X)$ is $\mathscr{A}$ measurable for every X in $\mathscr{S}$; P^a is therefore a transition probability from $\mathscr{A}$ to $\mathscr{S}$. Further, a prior probability M over $(A, \mathscr{A})$ is assumed, which enables a joint probability Π to be constructed by extending to $\mathscr{A} \otimes \mathscr{S}$ the set function defined by

$$\Pi(E \times X) = \int P^a(X)\, dM, \qquad E \in \mathscr{A}, X \in \mathscr{S}. \tag{1.1}$$

The marginal probability P, deduced from Π on $(S, \mathscr{S})$, is called a predictive probability. We assume there exists a transition probability $M^s(E)$ $(s \in \mathscr{S}, E \in \mathscr{A})$, which is called a posterior probability, satisfying

$$\Pi(E \times X) = \int_E M^s(X)\, dP, \qquad E \in \mathscr{A}, X \in \mathscr{S}. \tag{1.2}$$

M^s then appears as a regular version of the probability on $\mathscr{A}$ conditional on $\mathscr{S}$; the twin decomposition (1.1), (1.2) will be denoted

$$\Pi = M \otimes P^a = P \otimes M^s. \tag{1.3}$$

If P^a is defined by its density $p(s/a)$ with respect to a dominating measure ν such that p is $\mathscr{A} \otimes \mathscr{S}$ measurable, one verifies that P is dominated by ν, which has density $\int_A p(s/a)\, dM$, and that M^s is dominated by M with the density

$$\frac{dM^s}{dM} = \frac{p(s/a)}{\int p(s/a)\, dM}, \qquad \Pi\text{—almost surely.} \tag{1.4}$$

Details on this presentation of the Bayesian model can be found in Florens and Mouchart 1986 or in Florens et al. 1990 (the latter is denoted EBS in the remainder of this paper).

In a Bayesian model, the most natural estimation procedure $\mathscr{M}$ consists in associating to a function of parameters its posterior expectation. In order to avoid problems of integrability, we confine ourselves to positive numerical functions.

If f is a positive and $\mathscr{A}$-measurable random variable, we write

$$\mathscr{M}(f) = \int_A f\, dM^s = E(f/\mathscr{S}), \tag{1.5}$$

which is an $\mathscr{S}$-measurable, positive (or zero) and defined P—almost surely random variable. $\mathscr{M}$ can be considered as the extension of the posterior probability of events to random variables. This choice of $\mathscr{M}$ is of course not a necessity and different Bayesian estimation procedures can be considered (median, posterior mode, etc.), particularly in the presence of specified loss functions.

This model without sample size extends to the sequential case by providing $\mathscr{S}$ with a filtration $(\mathscr{S}_T)_{T \geqslant i}$. The different elements of the model can then be considered asymptotically or in the limited-sample-size case.

Consider two Bayesian models,

$$\mathscr{E} = \{A \times S, \mathscr{A} \otimes \mathscr{S}, \Pi = M \otimes P^a = P \otimes M^s\}$$

and

$$\mathscr{F} = \{B \times S, \mathscr{B} \otimes \mathscr{S}, \chi = N \otimes Q^b = Q \otimes N^s\},$$

provided with their estimation procedures $\mathscr{M}$ and $\mathscr{N}$, respectively defined in (1.5).

We then propose the following definition:

Definition 1.1. The model $\mathscr{E}$ exactly encompasses model $\mathscr{F}$ if
(a) Q dominates P,
(b) $\exists \Delta^a(F)$, transition probability defined on $A \times \mathscr{B}$, such that $\forall F \in \mathscr{B}$,

$$N^s(F) = \int_A \Delta^a(F)\, dM^s, \qquad P\text{—almost surely.}$$

The role of assumption (a) is the following. The posterior transition N^s is not unique and $N^s(F)$ is only Q—almost surely defined (since the zero measure set over which two versions of the posterior probability differ generally varies with F). The domination condition then leads to condition (b) not depending on the choice of the posterior probability version in $\mathscr{F}$. Assumption (a) may well not be introduced; in that case the equality in condition (b) becomes a condition of existence of an element contained both in the $N^s(F)$ class and in the class of $\int_A \Delta^a(F)$ obtained by considering all versions of M^s. Such a more complex presentation will not be accepted here but is detailed in EBS. We nevertheless point out that the domination condition, little constraining in small samples, is in general not satisfied asymptotically. The actual asymptotic situation is the one where P and Q are, on the contrary, mutually singular ($\exists X \in \mathscr{S} / P(X) = 1$ and $Q(X) = 0$), but in that case the true model is known with certainty and the specification is not problematic. The encompassing problem is essentially a small sample one, even if it is necessary to study asymptotic properties of procedures coming from such an approach.

Condition (b) is obviously the principal one. Intuitively, it can be interpreted as the possibility of evaluating the posterior probability in $\mathscr{F}$, from the posterior probability in $\mathscr{E}$ without the sample being manipulated. The constraining assumption is here that Δ^a must not depend on s, because condition (1.6) is generally satisfied for a transition defined over $(A \times S) \times \mathscr{B}$. To interpret (1.6) better, we extend it to estimation procedures and particularize it to the dominated models case.

In this framework, the sets Θ and Ω of numerical functions defined over A and B, respectively, represent the nonnegative random variables. A usual argument of monotonic classes (see, for example, Dellacherie and Meyer 1975) allows extension of (1.6).

Notice first that Δ^a defines a mapping $\mathscr{D}$ of Ω over Θ by

$$\forall g \in \Omega, \qquad \mathscr{D}(g) = \int_B g \, d\Delta^a. \tag{1.7}$$

Condition (b) then implies

$$\forall g \in \Omega \int_B g \, dN^s = \int_A dM^s \int_B g \, d\Delta^a, \qquad P\text{—almost surely} \tag{1.8}$$

or

$$\mathscr{N}(g) = [\mathscr{M} \circ \mathscr{D}](g). \tag{1.9}$$

The encompassing condition presented in the introduction is therefore satisfied. Let us stress nevertheless that estimation procedures and the mapping $\mathscr{D}$ are not any mappings but are constructed from transition probabilities, and thus possess specific linearity and continuity properties for instance.

The encompassing condition admits a more familiar form in dominated models. If $n(b/s)$ and $m(a/s)$ are posterior densities of $\mathscr{F}$ and $\mathscr{E}$, and if Δ^a admits a density $\delta(b/a)$, 1.6 then becomes

$$n(b/s) = \int_A \delta(b/a) \, m(a/s) \, da, \qquad \text{almost surely.} \tag{1.10}$$

The "almost surely" of (1.10) is related to the product of the dominating measure on A and the predictive measure of $\mathscr{E}$. The exact encompassing property is obviously rarely satisfied and it is used as a reference. We nevertheless given two artificial but simple examples.

Example 1.1. In the case of models with finite sample and parametric spaces, it is easy to construct examples of exact encompassing. If S, A, and B are sets of cardinal n, p, and q, respectively, posterior transitions of $\mathscr{E}$ and $\mathscr{F}$ are described by matrices $\bar{N}$ and $\overline{M}$, respectively, of dimension $n \times p$ and $n \times q$. These matrices have positive or zero coefficients, whose sum in line equals 1. A transition probability of A over B is also a matrix $\bar{\Delta}$ of dimension $p \times q$, satisfying the same properties. Condition (1.6) in the definition then becomes the matrix equality $\bar{N} = \overline{M}\bar{\Delta}$ and numerical examples satisfying this condition are easily constructed. □

The second example introduces conditioning variables and thus necessitates extending definition (1.1) to conditional models.

A Bayesian conditional model is essentially characterized by a transition probability of $(Z, \mathscr{Z})$ over $(A \times S, \mathscr{A} \otimes \mathscr{S})$ devoted by Π^z. Z is interpreted here as a conditioning variable space, and Π^z as the probability over $\mathscr{A} \otimes \mathscr{S}$ conditional on $\mathscr{Z}$ deduced from a joint probability over Π on $(A \times S \times Z, \mathscr{A} \otimes \mathscr{S} \otimes \mathscr{Z})$. The analysis of such models avoids using properties of Π, which are generally not specified, but tries to concentrate on those of Π^z. However, it cannot be entirely eliminated, and one has to refer to it, at least in order to define almost surely relations containing z. A more general, detailed presentation is found in EBS (chapter 1).

Consider thus two conditional models $\mathscr{E}^z = [A \times S, \mathscr{A} \otimes \mathscr{S}, \Pi^z]$ and $\mathscr{F}^z = [B \times S, \mathscr{B} \otimes \mathscr{S}, \chi^2]$ in which conditioning variables are identical. $\mathscr{E}^z$ and $\mathscr{F}^z$ are deduced from nonreduced models, respectively equal to

$$\mathscr{E} = \{A \times S \times Z, \mathscr{A} \otimes \mathscr{S} \otimes \mathscr{Z}, \Pi\}$$

and

$$\mathscr{F} = \{B \times S \times Z, \mathscr{B} \otimes \mathscr{Y} \otimes \mathscr{Z}, \chi\}.$$

Definition 1.2. The model $\mathscr{E}$ encompasses the model $\mathscr{F}$ conditionally on $(Z, \mathscr{Z})$ (or $\mathscr{E}^z$ encompasses $\mathscr{F}^z$) if

(a) $Q_{\mathscr{S} \otimes \mathscr{Z}}$ dominates $P_{\mathscr{S} \otimes \mathscr{Z}}$

(b) $\exists \Delta^{a,z}(F)$, a transition probability defined over $(A \times Z) \times \mathscr{B}$ such that

$$\forall F \in \mathscr{B}, \qquad N^{s,z}(F) = \int_A \Delta^{a,z}(F)\, dM^{s,z}, \qquad P_{\mathscr{S}\otimes\mathscr{Z}} \text{ almost surely.} \quad (1.11)$$

Notations naturally extend those previously defined: $M^{s,z}$ is the posterior of $\mathscr{E}^z$ (and $\mathscr{E}$), and $P_{\mathscr{S}\otimes\mathscr{Z}}$ is the marginal probability over $\mathscr{S} \otimes \mathscr{Z}$ of Π.

This definition, considered a notion of encompassing of $\mathscr{F}$ by $\mathscr{E}$, is a weakening of definition (1.1), in the sense that it allows Δ to depend upon a part of the sample, this part however being formed by conditioning variables. Notice that in practice, two models to be compared will apparently have different conditioning variables. Such a comparison, however, makes sense only if models are considered conditional upon the same variables but the specification of each model contains a conditional independence assumption which in turn implies eliminating some conditioning variables. This point is illustrated in the following example.

Example 1.2. Consider two regression models: $y = X\beta + u$ and $y = Z\gamma + v$. To use the previously defined concept, it is necessary to consider both of these models conditional on (X, Z). The first one assumes y independent in the sampling sense of Z given X, whereas the second one assumes independence in the sampling sense of y and X conditional on Z. In other words, sampling probabilities are

(1) $y|X, Z, \beta \sim N(X\beta, \sigma^2 I)$, over $\mathscr{E}^{x,z}$

and

(2) $y|X, Z, \gamma \sim N(Z\gamma, \tau^2 I)$, over $\mathscr{F}^{x,z}$.

σ^2 and τ^2 are supposed to be given, for the sake of simplicity. When we confine ourselves to uniform prior measures, the following posterior transitions are achieved:

(1) $\beta|y, X, Z \sim N((X'X)^{-1}X'y, \sigma^2(X'X)^{-1}$ over $\mathscr{E}^{x,z}$

and

(2) $\gamma|y, X, Z \sim N((Z'Z)^{-1}Z'y, \tau^2(Z'Z)^{-1})$ over $\mathscr{F}^{x,z}$.

Assuming $\tau^2 \geqslant \sigma^2$, if the space generated by Z is contained in the X_s' one, i.e., if

$(I - X(X'X)^{-1}X')Z = 0,$

$\mathscr{E}^{x,z}$ encompasses exactly $\mathscr{F}^{x,z}$ and the transition $\Delta^{a,x,z}$ is normal with expectation $(Z'Z)^{-1}Z'X\beta$ and variance $(\tau^2 - \sigma^2)(Z'Z)^{-1}$.

Note. In the preceding example, the search for simple results led us to choose prior uniform measures, therefore taking away a lot of interest from a Bayesian approach. It can easily be verified in this example that, in the case of normal prior probabilities with arbitrary moments, the property of exact encompassing remains satisfied, and that transition Δ then depends upon moments of both priors. A coherence problem then appears between the second model prior specification and the encompassing property. Two probabilities on $\mathscr{B}$ are in fact available: the one specified on $\mathscr{F}$ and the image by Δ of the prior on A over $\mathscr{E}$. Imposing the equality between these two priors leads to the concept of consistent encompassing, which is a slightly richer property than ordinary encompassing, at least in the small sample case.

We conclude this section with a remark concerning Δ^a. It is natural to call this transition a pseudotrue value, though this definition diverges from usual definitions of this concept based upon the limit of estimators or on the proximity of sampling probabilities. Δ^a generalizes the concept of pseudotrue value, defined as a function, by using the notion of probability transition. It leads to a Bayesian interpretation of parameters of $\mathscr{F}$ over $\mathscr{E}$.

Various problems arise from our definition; they will not be dealt with in this brief introductory paper. Examples are the study of properties of the partial order introduced over the class of models by this comparison, factorizing properties of likelihood functions which are equivalent to the encompassing, the study of properties of encompassing relating a model to its reductions by marginalization on conditioning, and so on. Some of these properties are analyzed in Florens, Hendry, and Richard 1989.

II. Specificity and Tests

The exact encompassing situation is of course rarely encountered. The obvious extension at this notion consists in looking for the transition probability Δ^a which brings close as much as possible $\mathscr{N}$ and $\mathscr{M} \circ \mathscr{D}$ (see equality 1.9) for a given family of functions g. Such a transition is therefore the one that best allows model $\mathscr{E}$ to explain results of $\mathscr{F}$. Thus, the remaining distance between $\mathscr{N}$ and $\mathscr{M} \circ \mathscr{D}$ for this optimal Δ^a gives a measure of the specificity of $\mathscr{F}$ with regard to $\mathscr{E}$. This magnitude is a real number, but it will appear as the expectation (relative to the predictive of

$\mathscr{E}$) of a statistic that can be interpreted as the specificity of $\mathscr{F}$, conditional on a particular sample realization. This statistic is then used as the test statistic of model $\mathscr{E}$ versus $\mathscr{F}$.

The realization of this program is somewhat difficult. The first difficulty consists in choosing a definition for the measure of the distance between N^s and $M^s \circ \Delta^a$, knowing that the transition that minimizes this spread depends generally on this choice. Therefore, asymptotic properties of the procedure, in particular, may well differ according to the adopted measure. The second problem is more practical. It comes from the difficulty of computing an optimal Δ^a. Once the transition is underscored, analysis of the properties regarding tests of associated encompassing is easy in simple models only. Finally, it may be necessary for the sake of theoretical relevance, to relate this approach to the classical theory of pseudotrue values and to the asymptotic properties of misspecified Bayesian models.

In the present state of theoretical works on encompassing, it is not possible with own knowledge to answer all of these questions. We, however, point out that they are of a standard nature in statistics. It is so that, for instance, outside the framework of iid models studied by Berk (1966, 1970), general results are not known on asymptotic behavior of a sequence of expectations conditional on a probability different from the one used in their construction. We have, moreover, developed, in some papers that are not yet published, some results relative to the case in which $\mathscr{F}$ can be obtained by mean of $\mathscr{E}$, using a mapping of $A \times S$ over $B \times S$, which transforms Π into χ.

To keep this paper introductory, we confine ourselves to presenting two examples in which these various problems are dealt with.

Example 2.1. Here, we deal with the classic problem of comparing two regression models whose variances are known and which are not necessarily nested. The hypothesis of known variances is adopted only for the sake of simplicity; the problem can be solved analytically when they are unknown.

Let $\mathscr{E}$ have a sampling probability $N(X, \beta, \sigma^2 I)$ (equivalently, y/X, Z, $\beta\mathscr{E} \sim N(X, \beta, \sigma^2 I)$ and β a priori is normal $N(\beta_0, \sigma^2 H_0^{-1})$). We know that the predictive is described by y/X, Z, $\mathscr{E}$, which is normal $N(X\beta_0, \sigma^2(I + XH_0^{-1}X'))$ and that the posterior probability satisfies $\beta/y, X, Z, \mathscr{E} \sim N(\beta_*, \sigma^2 H_*^{-1})$, with $H_* = H_0 + X'X$ and $\beta_* H_*^{-1}(X'y + H_0\beta_0)$. Equivalently, $\mathscr{F}$ is described by $y/X, Z, \gamma, \mathscr{F} \sim N(Z\gamma, \tau^2 I)$, $\gamma/y, X, Z \sim N(\gamma_0, \tau^2 K_0^{-1})$. Then y/X, Z, γ, $\mathscr{F} \sim N(Z\gamma_0, \tau^2(I + ZK_0^{-1}Z'))$ and γ/X, Z, γ, $\mathscr{F} \sim$

$N(\gamma_*, \tau^2 K_*^{-1})$, with $K_* = K_0 + ZZ$ and $\gamma_* = K_*^{-1}(Z'y + K_0\gamma_0)$. Dimensions are $y \in \mathbb{R}^n$, $\beta \in \mathbb{R}^k$, and $\gamma \in \mathbb{R}^p$.

The search for transition $\Delta^{\beta,x,z}$ is limited to homoscedastic normal distributions and linear regression. Δ will be a probability over $\mathbb{R}^p$ conditional on $\beta \in \mathbb{R}^k$ (and on X and Z) of the form γ/β, X, $Z \sim N(C\beta + c, V)$. The posterior probability distribution on γ, deducted from $\mathscr{E}$ using $\Delta^{\beta,x,z}$, is then γ/y, X, Z, $\mathscr{E} \sim N(C\beta + c, V + \tau^2 CH_*^{-1}C')$. One still has to compare the two probability distributions on γ generated from $\mathscr{E}$ and $\mathscr{F}$, and to minimize this distance wih respect to C, c, and V.

A measure of the spread between these two distributions, which allows simple calculations, is then

$$\xi = \int_{\mathbb{R}^n} p(y/x, z, \mathscr{E})\, dy \int_{\mathbb{R}^p} \ln \frac{m(\gamma/s, \mathscr{E})}{n(\gamma/s, \mathscr{F})} m(\gamma/s, \mathscr{E})\, d\gamma, \tag{2.1}$$

where $p(y/x, z, \mathscr{E})$ is the predictive density of y over $\mathscr{E}$, $m(\gamma/s, \mathscr{E})$ and $n(\gamma/s, \mathscr{F})$ are the posterior densities of γ, as deducted from model $\mathscr{E}$ and obtained in $\mathscr{F}$, respectively ($s = (y, X, Z)$). Equation 2.1 is in fact the predictive expectation of the Kullback quantity of information between the two posterior on γ. Calculation of 2.1 is lengthy but not particularly difficult; it leads to the result (see Florens, Hendry, and Richard 1987b):

$$\begin{aligned} C &= K_*^{-1} Z'X(X'X)^{-1} H_*, \\ c &= K_*^{-1}[K_0\gamma_0 - Z'X(X'X)^{-1} H_0 \beta_0], \\ V &= K_*^{-1}[\sigma^2 Z'(I - X(X'X)^{-1}X')Z + K_* \\ &\quad - \sigma^2 Z'X(X'X)^{-1} H_* (X'X)^{-1} X'Z] K_*^{-1}. \end{aligned} \tag{2.2}$$

Existence of the transition implies that σ^2 and τ^2 are such that V is positive semidefinite. One verifies that if the prior measures degenerate into a Lebesgue measure, expectation of $\Delta^{\beta,x,z}$ is identical to the usual pseudotrue value $(ZZ)^{-1}Z'X\beta$. Equivalently, if sample size tends to infinity, expectation of $\Delta^{\beta,x,z}$ has the same limit as $(Z'Z)^{-1}Z'X\beta$, and its variance tends to zero under usual conditions on the behavior of explanatory variables.

The optimal $\Delta^{\beta,x,z}$ being chosen, the magnitude in (1.1) then measures the specificity of $\mathscr{F}$ relative to $\mathscr{E}$; this specificity is the predictive expectation of the specificity conditional on y, as measured by the Kullback quantity of information between the two posterior on γ. If one wishes to adopt a strategy of hypothesis testing within a Bayesian framework, the conditional specificity gives an encompassing test statistic whose analytic formulation can be obtained in this example. The nature of this statistic enables us to study its distribution relative to $\mathscr{E}$ and $\mathscr{F}$. Details on such a calculation are found in Florens, Hendry, and Richard 1987b, and a presentation of hypothesis tests in a Bayesian approach can be found in Florens and Mouchart 1990.

Example 2.2. In the case of iid models with finite parametric spaces, an analytic solution can be found to the problem of searching for an optimal transition Δ_T^a for a sample of size T. It is also straightforward in this case to study the asymptotic behavior of Δ_T^a, as well as its relation with the classical approach of pseudotrue values.

Assume $A = \{a_1, \ldots, a_K\}$; P_T^a is a sampling probability on $S = X^T$ (where X is an arbitrary measurable space) which has density

$$p_T(s/a) = \prod_{t=1}^{T} f(x_t/a)\,(a \in A,\, s = (x_1, \ldots, x_T) \in S)$$

with respect to a measure ν, such that this notation characterizes an identically distributed process. The prior probability measure is described by real numbers $m(a_k) > 0$ satisfying $\sum_{k=1}^{K} m(a_k) = 1$. It will be assumed that the so-described model $\mathscr{E}$ is identified

$(a_K \neq a_{K'} \Rightarrow f(x_t/a_K) \neq f(x_t/a_{K'})$ almost surely).

Model $\mathscr{F}$ is its counterpart: $B = \{b_1, \ldots, b_L\}$, and Q_T^b over X^T has density $\prod_{t=1}^{T} g(x_t/b)$ with respect to ν. The prior probability is defined by numbers $n(b_1) > 0$, and it will be assumed that the predictive P on $\mathscr{E}$ is dominated by this of $\mathscr{F}$. It is, however, not necessary to assume identification of $\mathscr{F}$.

A transition Δ_T^a on A over B is defined by $\delta_T(b_1/a_k)$ (satisfying $\delta_T(b_1/a_k) \geqslant 0$ and $\sum_l \delta_T(b_l/a_k) = 1$) and we denote also by $\bar{\Delta}_T$ the $(L \times K)$ matrix of generic element $\delta_T(b_l/a_k)$. If $m_T^s \in \mathbb{R}^k$ denotes the vector of posterior probabilities of the a_k's over $\mathscr{E}$, $\Delta_T m_T^s$ is then the probability on B, deduced from $\mathscr{E}$ by $\bar{\Delta}_T$. Furthermore, $n_T^s \in \mathbb{R}^L$ is the posterior probability on B over $\mathscr{F}$ and one has to compare n_T^s and $\bar{\Delta}_T m_T^s$.

A quite straightforward measure of distance between these two probabilities in this context is

$$\xi = \int_S (n_T^s - \bar{\Delta}_T m_T^s)'(n_T^s - \bar{\Delta}_T m_T^s)\, dP_T.$$

This magnitude is interpreted as follows. Let g_l be a random variable defined on B and equaling 1 for b_l and 0 otherwise. The above expression is the sum over l ($l = 1, \ldots, L$) of squared distances (in the $\mathscr{L}_2$ sense) between the a posteriori expectation of g_l in $\mathscr{F}$ and the a posteriori expectation in $\mathscr{E}$ of the image $\Delta_T^a(g_l)$ in the set of random variables defined over A. In order to locate on optimal Δ_T, one has to minimize ξ constraints to $\delta_T(b_l/a_k) \geqslant 0$ and $\sum_l \delta_T(b_l/a_k) = 1$.

To simplify notation, we implement minimization under the last constraint only, and thus we implicity assume positivity constraints to be satisfied. The result is then described by the matrix

$$\Delta_T^* = \left(I - \frac{s}{T}ii'\right) E(n_T^s m_T^{s'})\, E(m_T^s m_T^{s'})^{-1} + \frac{1}{T}ii', \tag{2.3}$$

where I and i, respectively, denote unity matrix $T \times T$ and the vector of $\mathbb{R}^T$ whose elements are all equal to 1, and where E denotes the expectation relative to the predictive P_T. We denote by $\delta_T^*(b_l/a_k)$ the generic element of Δ_T^*.

The specificity measure of $\mathscr{F}$ with respect to $\mathscr{E}$ equals

$$E(n_T^s - \Delta_T^* m_T^s)'(n_T^s - \Delta_T^* m_T^s),$$

with Δ_T^* given by (2.3). The quantity $(n_T^s - \Delta_T^* m_T^s)'(n_T^s - \Delta_T^* m_T^s)$ is the conditional specificity defining the test statistic of $\mathscr{E}$ against $\mathscr{F}$.

We now define a transition Δ^a by a more usual argument, arising from a comparison of sampling probabilities.

We write

$$D(a_k) = \left\{ b_l \in B \text{ minimizing} \int \ln \frac{f(x_t/a_k)}{g(x_t/b_1)} f(x_t/a_k)\, dv \right\}. \tag{2.4}$$

Notice that we do not assume $D(a_k)$ is a singleton; in general, several points of B are "equidistant" from a_k for the measure defined in (2.4). As the comparison is not a distance, quotes are necessary.

Consider the prior probability over B, conditional upon event $D(a_k)$:

$$\begin{aligned} \delta^0(b_l/a_k) &= 0 \qquad \text{if } b_l \notin D(a_k) \\ &= \frac{n(b_l)}{\sum_{b_l \in D(a_k)} n(b_l)} \end{aligned} \tag{2.5}$$

which degenerates into a Dirac measure if $D(a_k)$ is a singleton. Let Δ^0 be the $(L \times K)$ matrix with generic element $\delta^0(b_l/a_k)$.

We have the following asymptotic results:

Proposition 2.1.

(1) $m_T^s(a_k) \to 1\ P^{a_k}$-almost surely, hence $m_T^s(a'_k) \to 0\ P^{a_k}$-almost surely if $a'_k \neq a_k$.

(2) $n_T^s(b_l) \to 0\ P^{a_k}$-almost surely, $\forall b_l \notin D(a_k)$ and then $n_T^s(D(a_k)) \to 1$ P^{a_k}-almost surely.

(3) Under the assumption $a'_k \in D(a_k) \Rightarrow g(x_t/a'_k) = g(x_t/a_k)$ one has $n_T^s(b_l) \to \delta^0(b_l/a_k)\ P^{a_k}$-almost surely.

(4) Under the same assumption $\delta_T(b_l/a_k) \to \delta^0(b_l/a_k)$ and the specificity $\mathscr{F}$ with respect to $\mathscr{E}$ has a zero limit if $\mathscr{E}$ is the true model. □

Point 1 is truly classic, and its proof is found, for example, in De Groot 1970. Extensions of this result are found in the literature, for instance in EBS on convergence in a well-specified model. Point 2 is in fact a special case of the result of Berk (1966) concerning iid models with arbitrary parameter space. The finite case allows a much more simple proof with the style of De Groot (1970), and is given in Florens et al. 1989. Point 3 is not contained in Berk 1966.

This proposition in fact shows the asymptotic equivalence of the three definitions of pseudotrue values: Δ_T^*, Δ^0, and the one based on the limit of the second model's estimators relative to the first model.

Without considering examples of this kind, it is still true that the search for Δ can be quite complex; it can be worth confirming transitions that are nonoptimal but easily computable, and have equivalent properties at least asymptotically. We point out only two possible directions in this respect.

The first possibility is to evaluate Δ^a without using a minimization argument; a natural solution consists in choosing

$$\Delta^a(F) = \int_S N^s(F)\, dP^a, \tag{2.6}$$

i.e., the sampling expectation in $\mathscr{E}$ of the a posteriori transition in $\mathscr{F}$. Such a choice is clearly suboptimal. Assume $\mathscr{E}$ and $\mathscr{F}$ are identical. The optimal transition is obviously the one that connects every point of A to the Dirac measure in a whereas (2.6) usually is not of this kind. The pseudotrue value defined by (2.6), however, has the same asymptotic properties as the optimal transition. In example 2.1, (2.6) becomes a normal distribution with expectation $N_*^{-1}(Z'X\beta + N_0\gamma_0)$ and variance $\sigma^2 N_*^{-1}(Z'ZN_*^{-1} + \tau^2 N_*^{-1})$. The expectation has the same limit as $(X'X)^{-1}Z'X\beta$, and the variance tends to 0. In example 2.2, (2.6) defines a transition whose general term is equal to

$$\delta_T(b_l/a_k) = \int_{X^T} n_T^s(b_l) \prod f(x_t/a_k)\, dv$$

for a sample of size T. It can be verified that this term converges to $\delta^0(b_l/a_k)$ by making use of the fact that in proposition 2.1, convergences in (1) and (2) are also satisfied in the sense of the $\mathscr{L}_p$ norms for every p.

Another solution for getting rid of difficulties in searching for Δ^a is to restrict the analysis to transitions satisfying a linearity condition with respect to a given finite system of functions of A in $\mathbb{R}$. In this case, we do not deal with estimation of all functions of B, but with a finite number of functions.

Consider, for instance, a real-valued function g defined over B, and $f = (f_1, \ldots, k_k)'$ a vector of real functions defined over A. We try to find Δ^a such that $\Delta^a(g) = \sum_{k=1}^{K} \lambda_k f_k$, the optimization being done with respect to the λ_k's only. A simple criterion is the $\mathscr{L}_2$ norm one, and $\lambda = (\lambda_k)_k$ has to minimize $\|\mathscr{N}(g) - \lambda' \mathscr{M}(f)\|$, recalling that $\mathscr{N}(g)$ is the posterior expectation of g in $\mathscr{F}$, and $\mathscr{M}(f)$ is the vector of posterior expectations of f in $\mathscr{E}$. The norm is in the sense of $\mathscr{L}_2(S, \mathscr{S}, P)$, assuming that f and g are such that all expectations present in this calculation are finites.

One finds then

$$\lambda = [E(\mathscr{M}(f)\mathscr{M}(f)']^{-1}\, E[(\mathscr{M}(f)\mathscr{N}(g)].$$

(E is the expectation relative to P.) Analysis of asymptotic properties of λ depends on the choice of the f_k's and will not be dealt with. This approach is located in the context of Bayesian analysis mean square approximations, which are developed by Mouchart and Simar (1983).

Let us now return to implications of our approach for a Bayesian theory of tests between models. We just showed how to construct a pseudotrue value Δ^a, and how a measure of the specificity conditional on s of $\mathscr{F}$ with respect to $\mathscr{E}$ is associated with Δ^a. Such a measure can, for instance, be defined as the Kullback quantity of information between the posterior probability over B of $\mathscr{F}$, and the image by Δ^a of the posterior probability of $\mathscr{E}$. We are therefore provided with a statistic, in the usual sense of this term. The intuitive underlying argument consists in accepting the encompassing property if this statistic is "small" and rejecting it if the statistic is "large." A more classic point of view could also be supported. It consists in investigating sampling properties (in $\mathscr{E}$ on $\mathscr{F}$) of the test statistic. In the common models, these two points of view diverge in the small sample case, but meet again asymptotically.

The second problem consists in creating the use of hypothesis testing in Bayesian statistics. A detailed exposition of this point is found in Florens and Mouchart 1990; we only recall some of its elements here. The use of hypothesis tests is justified only when the Bayesian specification is not complete, in the sense that some parameters are not provided with a prior probability. It is here the case of the implicit parameter consisting of the label of the model (which equals 1 if we have model $\mathscr{E}$, and 2 if we have model $\mathscr{F}$). It is therefore straightforward to incorporate in the sampling probability, relative to the prior probability, parameters for which this information is specified, and to proceed to usual tests between sampling probabilities marginalized this way. In our case, as a and b are provided with prior measures, the choice between models is in fact a choice between the two predictive probabilities. The construction of the encompassing test statistic corresponds to a particular mode of comparison, which we justified in the introduction.

Notice finally that the second model is introduced entirely, as soon as the test procedure under the alternative hypothesis is examined: if the a posteriori probability only is necessary to search for the pseudotrue value and to conduct the test, the predictive of $\mathscr{F}$ is also required as an alternative to this of $\mathscr{E}$. We point out that in the analysis the specification is not crucial. Tests are often searched for, whose alternative hypothesis is specified as little as possible—for instance, the White (1982) test of the information matrix.

III. Sufficiency and Encompassing

We now intend to justify the title of our paper by showing that the concept of encompassing can be viewed as a concept of (exact or approximate) sufficiency, and the concept of encompassing is formally analogous to the concept of sufficiency on the sample space, by permuting the role of both spaces defining the model.

We therefore briefly recall the definition of sufficiency, as stated from the works of Blackwell (1951, 1953) and Le Cam (1964). Consider two sampling models $\mathscr{E} = (A, (S, \mathscr{S}), P^a)$ and $\mathscr{F} = (A, (V, \mathscr{V}), Q^a)$ with the same parameter space with different sample space. $\mathscr{E}$ is sufficient for $\mathscr{F}$ if there exists a transition $A^s(Z)$ $(s \in S, Z \in \mathscr{V})$ such that

$$\forall Z \in \mathscr{V} \; Q^a(Z) = \int_S A^s(Z)\, dP^a. \tag{3.1}$$

This equality extends to every a in classic theory, and, almost surely, relative to the prior measure on A in $\mathscr{E}$, in Bayesien analysis.

It extends from events Z to real positive function:

$$\int_V \varphi \, dQ^a = \int_V dQ^a \int_S \varphi \, dA^s. \tag{3.2}$$

The concept of approximate sufficiency, proposed by Le Cam (1964), is based on the comparison between Q^a and P^a_*, which is the probability on $(V, \mathscr{V})$ defined by

$$P^a_*(Z) = \int_S A^s(Z) \, dP^a.$$

Le Cam suggests a comparison based on the distance in variation, the deficiency of $\mathscr{F}$ with respect to $\mathscr{E}$ being measured by

$$\mathrm{Sup}|Q^a(Z) - P^a_*(Z)| = 1/2 \int_T |q(t/a) - p^*(t/a)| \, dv^a, \tag{3.3}$$

where q and p^* denote, respectively, densities of Q^a and P^a_* with respect to a dominating common measure v^a, possibly independent of a. Independently of Le Cam's works, approximate sufficiency has been studied by Csizar (1967, 1975), who makes use of a comparison based on a Kullback information measure. The so-measured deficiency is a function of the parameter. In the Bayesian analysis, one constructs from the deficiency conditional on a, a global deficiency measure by integrating the parameter with respect to the prior probability in $\mathscr{E}$.

Comparison between this construction and encompassing now becomes obvious. It suffices to permute sample and parameter spaces by making use of the formal symmetry in the Bayesian model and by substituting sampling transitions and posterior probabilities, respectively.

One can also point out that the exact encompassing extends the definition of a parameter's sufficiency. Recall that if $\mathscr{E} = \{A \times S, \mathscr{A} \otimes \mathscr{S}, \Pi\}$ is a Bayesian model, a sub-σ-field $\mathscr{A}_0$ of $\mathscr{A}$ is sufficient if $P^a(X)$ is $\mathscr{A}_0$-measurable for every X of $\mathscr{S}$. This can be expressed as the conditional independence of $\mathscr{A}$ and $\mathscr{S}$, given $\mathscr{A}_0$ (see Florens and Mouchart 1986 and EBS). This independence is equivalent to the property that the posterior probability on $\mathscr{A}$ conditional upon $\mathscr{A}_0$ does not depend (P—almost surely) on the sample, and therefore can be set equal to the prior probability.

Let us then consider a model $\mathscr{E} = \{A \times S, \mathscr{A} \otimes \mathscr{S}, \Pi\}$ and a model $\mathscr{E}_0$ obtained by restricting Π on $\mathscr{A}_0 \otimes \mathscr{S}$, where $\mathscr{A}_0$ is a sub-σ-field of $\mathscr{A}$. $\mathscr{E}_0$

is defined over $(\{A \otimes S, \mathscr{A}_0 \otimes \mathscr{S}\})$. It is easily verified that $\mathscr{E}_0$ encompasses $\mathscr{E}$ if and only if $\mathscr{A}_0$ is a sufficient σ-field of $\mathscr{A}$ in $\mathscr{E}$. In that case, the pseudotrue value is the prior probability on $\mathscr{A}$, conditional on $\mathscr{A}_0$. Exact encompassing therefore reduces to sufficiency when the first model is a marginalization of the second. The investigation of approximate encompassing of $\mathscr{E}$ by $\mathscr{E}_0$, when sufficiency is not satisfied, is the basis of "parsimonious" encompassing tests. They extend the approach of specification tests in the Hausman sense (see Florens, Hendry, and Richard 1987 and Florens and Mouchart 1990 on that particular matter).

Furthermore, the exact encompassing situation determines sufficiency property which can be described as follows. To say that $\mathscr{E}$ exactly encompasses $\mathscr{F}$ with the transition Δ^a allows us to enlarge $\mathscr{E}$ to $\mathscr{E}^*$, which is defined over $(A \times B \times S, \mathscr{A} \otimes \mathscr{B} \otimes \mathscr{S})$ by the unique extension of Π:

$$\Pi^*(E \times F \times X) = \int_{E \times X} \Delta^a(F)\, d\Pi, \qquad E \in \mathscr{A}, F \in \mathscr{B}, X \in \mathscr{S} \tag{3.4}$$

regarding this probability Π^* (identified as belonging to the σ-field of cylinders $\{E \times B | E \in \mathscr{A}\}$) is a sufficient σ-field of $\mathscr{A} \otimes \mathscr{B}$, because $\mathscr{S}$ and $\mathscr{B}$ are independent, conditionally, on $\mathscr{A}$. In this extended experiment, Δ^a then plays the role both of a priori and a posteriori on $\mathscr{B}$, conditional on $\mathscr{A}$. The encompassing property is thus expressed as the equality (P—almost surely) between the posterior probability on $\mathscr{B}$ (not conditional upon $\mathscr{A}$) in $\mathscr{E}^*$ and in $\mathscr{F}$. The fact that $\mathscr{E}$ encompasses $\mathscr{F}$ can be summarized by saying that there exists an extension of Π over $\mathscr{A} \otimes \mathscr{B} \otimes \mathscr{S}$ such that $\mathscr{A}$ is exhaustive and that this extension allows us to retrieve the posterior probability on $\mathscr{B}$ coming from $\mathscr{F}$. This justifies therefore our exposition of encompassing as being related to parametric sufficiency.

Acknowledgments

The present paper synthesizes a collection of works made in collaboration with D. Hendry, M. Mouchart, and J. F. Richard, whom I greatly acknowledge for our numerous discussions on this subject.

References

Amemya, T. 1985. *Advanced Econometrics.* Blackwell.

Berk, R. H. 1966. "Limiting Behavior of Posterior Distributions When the Model Is Incorrect." *Annals of Mathematical Statistics* 37: 51–58.

Berk, R. H. 1970. "Consistency A Posteriori." *Annals of Mathematical Statistics* 41: 894–906.

Blackwell, D. 1951. "Comparison of Experiments." In *Proceedings of the Second Berkeley Symposium of Mathematical Statistics and Probability* (University of California Press).

Blackwell, D. 1953. "Equivalent Comparison of Experiments." *Annals of Mathematical Statistics* 24: 265–272.

Cox, D. R. 1961. "Tests of Separate Families of Hypotheses." In *Proceedings of the Fourth Berkeley Symposium on Mathematical Statistics and Probability*, volume 1.

Cox, D. R. 1962. "Further Results on Tests of Separate Families of Hypotheses." *Journal of the Royal Statistical Society* B 24: 406–424.

Csizar, I. 1967. "On Information Type Measures of Difference of Probability Distributions and Indirect Observations." *Studia Sci. Math. Hungar.* 2: 329–339.

Csizar, I. 1975. "I Divergence Geometry of Probability Distributions and Minimization Problems." *Ann. Probab.* 3: 146–158.

Davidson, J. E. H., D. F. Hendry, F. Srba, and J. S. Yeo. 1978. "Econometric Modelling of the Aggregate Time-Series Relationship between Consumers Expenditure and Income in the United Kingdom." *Economic Journal* 88: 661–692.

DeGroot, M. H. 1970. *Optimal Statistical Decisions*. McGraw-Hill.

Dellacherie, C., and P. A. Meyer. 1975. *Probabilité et Potentiel*. Hermann.

Florens, J. P., and M. Mouchart. 1985. "Model Selection: Some Remarks from a Bayesian Viewpoint." In *Model Choice*, ed. J. P. Florens, M. Mouchart, J. P. Raoult, and L. Simar (Publication des Facultés Universitaires Saint-Louis, Brussels).

Florens, J. P., and M. Mouchart. 1986. "Exhaustivité, ancillarité et identification en statistique bayésienne." *Annales d'Economie et de Statistique* 4: 63–93.

Florens, J. P., and M. Mouchart. 1990. "Bayesian Tests and Model Specification." In *Contributions to Operations Research and Economics*, ed. B. Cornet and H. Tulkens (MIT Press).

Florens, J. P., M. Mouchart, and S. Scotto. 1983. "Approximate Sufficiency on the Parameter Space and Model Selection." In *Actes du 44ème congrés de I.S.I., Madrid.*

Florens, J. P., M. Mouchart, and J. M. Rolin. 1990. *Elements of Bayesian Statistics*. Dekker.

Florens, J. P., D. F. Hendry, and J. F. Richard. 1987. An information Matrix Approach to Parsimony. Duke University.

Florens, J. P., D. F. Hendry, and J. F. Richard. 1990. Encompassing and Specificity. Duke University.

Gouriéroux, C., A. Monfort, and A. Trognon. 1983. "Testing Nested or Non-Nested Hypotheses." *Journal of Econometrics* 21: 83–115.

Gouriéroux, C., A. Monfort, and A. Trognon. 1984. "Pseudo-Maximum Likelihood Methods: Theory." *Econometrica* 52: 681–700.

Govaerts, B. 1987. Application of the Encompassing Principle to Linear Dynamic Models. Ph. D. dissertation, Université Catholique de Louvain.

Hendry, D. F., and G. J. Anderson. 1977. "Testing Dynamic Specification in Small Simultaneous Systems: An Application to a Model of Building Society Behavior in the United Kingdom." In *Frontiers in Quantitative Economics*, ed. M. D. Intriligator, volume 3A (North-Holland).

Hendry, D. F., and J. F. Richard. 1982. "On the Formulation of Empirical Models in Dynamic Econometrics." *Journal of Econometrics* 20: 3–33.

Hendry, D. F., and J. F. Richard. 1990. "Recent Developments in the Theory of Encompassing." In *Contributions to Operations Research and Economics*, ed. B. Cornet and H. Tulkens (MIT Press).

Holly, A. 1987. "Specification Tests: An Overview." *Advances in Econometrics*, ed. T. Bewley (Cambridge University Press).

Huber, P. J. 1967. "The Behavior of Maximum Likelihood Estimates under Non Standard Conditions." In *Proceedings of the Fifth Berkeley Symposium in Mathematical Statistics and Probability* (University of California Press).

Le Cam, L. 1953. "On Some Asymptotic Properties of Maximum Likelihood Estimates and Related Bayes' Estimates." *University of California Publications in Statistics* 1: 23–53.

Le Cam, L. 1964. "Sufficiency and Approximate Sufficiency." *Annals of Mathematical Statistics* 35: 1419–1455.

Mizon, G. E. 1984. "The Encompassing Approach in Econometrics." In *Econometrics and Quantitative Economics*, ed. D. F. Hendry and K. F. Wallis (Blackwell).

Mizon, G. E., and J. F. Richard. 1986. "The Encompassing Principle and Its Application to Testing Non-Nested Hypotheses." *Econometrica* 54: 657–678.

Mouchart, M., and L. Simar. 1983. "Theory and Applications of Least Squares Approximation in Bayesian Analysis." In *Specifying Statistical Models*, ed. J. P. Florens et al. (Springer-Verlag).

White, H. 1982. "Maximum Likelihood Estimation of Misspecified Models." *Econometrica* 50: 1–26.

31

Estimating Short-Run and Long-Run Parameters in a Homogeneous Markovian Process

Claude Fourgeaud,
Christian Gouriéroux, and
Jacqueline Pradel

I. Introduction

Recently the practice in specifying dynamic macroeconometric models is to distinguish the long-run component from the adjustment process toward this limit path. For instance, the approach of error correction models is essentially based on this idea (see Davidson et al. 1978). Such a decomposition appears also to be useful for the estimation of structural parameters. Various authors discussed a recursive estimation of the parameters, estimating first the long-run parameters, then the short-run parameters (see Engle and Granger 1987; Gouriéroux et al. 1987). These approaches are not specific of macroeconomic models and may also be introduced in some microeconomic context, as soon as the temporal aspect of the problem is kept. In such a case the data are doubly indexed, by individual and dates.

In this paper we analyze this problem for duration data models (see Cox and Oakes 1984; Kalbfleisch and Prentice 1980). In section II we describe a model giving the evolution of the rates of employment and of unemployment in a homogeneous population. The usual parameters, i.e., the instantaneous probabilities of losing (respectively obtaining) a job are replaced by a first parameter giving the long-run equilibrium of the model and by a second one, which may be interpreted as the rate of adjustment toward this equilibrium.

In section III, we discuss the estimation of these two parameters from individual observations collected in two waves. After a description of the asymptotic properties of the maximum likelihood (M.L.) estimators of the short- and long-run parameters, we study how the precision of these estimators depends on the time period between the two sampling waves and on the initial structure of the population. This study gives a lot of information concerning the choice of an adapted survey design. Several difficulties linked to nonidentifiability appear when the time period between the sampling waves tends to zero or tends to infinity. This identifiability problem is examined in section IV. We fully use the possibility to develop an asymptotic theory for the two indices: individual and time and extend to panel data the usual asymptotic theory.

The results of this paper have to be compared with the results given by De Stavola (1986). This author introduces several survey designs and evaluates the associated effects on the precision of the estimators of the instantaneous rates. The results presented in our paper are different at least for the two following points: first, we are mainly interested in the short- and long-run parameters and not in the initial rates; second, the identifiability problem is fully investigated.

II. The Model

We first describe the renewal process (see, e.g., Cox and Miller 1965) and we introduce the main notation. We consider a homogeneous population of individuals, who can be employed or unemployed and we study the evolution of employment in this population. Let us denote $S(t)$ the probability for one individual to be unemployed at time t, $\lambda(t)$ the instantaneous rate of obtaining a job for an unemployed individual, and $\mu(t)$ the instantaneous rate of losing a job for an employed one.

The rates $\lambda(t)$ and $\mu(t)$ are the basis for computing the instantaneous flows between the subpopulations of unemployed individuals and employed individuals. Between two close dates t and $t + dt$, the proportion of people finding a job is approximately given by $\lambda(t)S(t)\,dt$; the proportion of people losing their job is $\mu(t)(1 - S(t))\,dt$.

We deduce the evolution of the survival function $S(t)$ from these flows. The function S satisfies a first-order linear equation:

$$\begin{aligned}\frac{d}{dt}S(t) &= -\lambda(t)S(t) + \mu(t)(1 - S(t)) \\ &= -(\lambda(t) + \mu(t))S(t) + \mu(t). \qquad (1)\end{aligned}$$

The solution of this equation is

$$S(t) = \left(S(0) + \int_0^t \frac{\mu(v)}{D(v)}\,dv\right)D(t), \qquad (2)$$

where

$$D(t) = \exp\left[-\int_0^t (\lambda(u) + \mu(u))\,du\right].$$

In the homogeneous case $\lambda(t) = \lambda$ and $\mu(t) = \mu$ are time independent and the solution takes the simple form

$$S(t) - c = (S(0) - c) \exp - \delta t, \tag{3}$$

where

$$c = \frac{\mu}{\lambda + \mu} \quad \text{and} \quad \delta = \lambda + \mu. \tag{4}$$

The ratio $\mu/(\lambda + \mu)$ is the limit of the probability $S(t)$, when t tends to infinity. It gives the long-run value of the proportion of unemployment in the population. This long-run value depends on the two rates λ and μ. The rate of convergence toward the stationary state increases with the sum $\lambda + \mu$. Therefore two natural parameters for describing the evolution of the proportion of unemployment are c and δ, defined by equations 4. Let us note that parameter c does not depend on the time unit, while δ depends on this unit.

Relation 3 gives the probability $S(t)$ in terms of the initial probability $S(0)$. It may be used to evaluate the probability $S_1(t)$ to be unemployed at time t, when unemployed at time 0 ($S(0) = 1$):

$$S_1(t) = c + (1 - c) \exp(-\delta t) \tag{5}$$

and the probability $S_0(t)$ to be unemployed at time t, when employed at time 0 ($S(0) = 0$):

$$S_0(t) = c - c \exp(-\delta t). \tag{6}$$

Equations 5 and 6 will be used in the next section to estimate the structural parameters c and δ (figure 1).

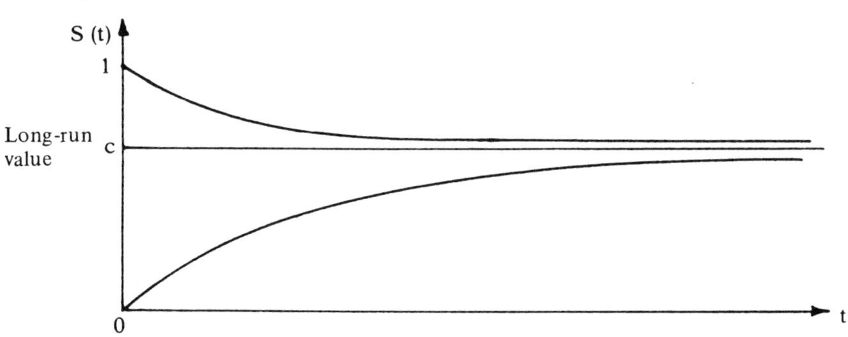

Figure 1.

III. Estimation of the Structural Parameters

We consider a population with n individuals, a proportion k of them (k different from 0 and 1) is unemployed at the initial date $t = 0$ and we examine the state of the system at another date t. $Y(t)$ denotes the random variable taking the value 1 if the individual is unemployed, 0 otherwise; $Y(t)$ is the indicator of unemployment. $\mathfrak{J}_0$ and $\mathfrak{J}_1$ are the sets of indices of people, respectively, employed and unemployed at time $t = 0$.

1. M.L. Estimators

The likelihood associated with the observation $(y_{1,t}, \ldots, y_{n,t})$ of the indicator variables $Y_i(t)$, $i = 1, \ldots, n$ can be expressed in terms of the probabilities $S_0(t)$ and $S_1(t)$ defined in equations 5 and 6:

$$L(c, \delta; y_{1,t}, \ldots, y_{n,t})$$

$$= \prod_{\mathfrak{J}_0} S_0(t)^{y_{i,t}}(1 - S_0(t))^{1-y_{i,t}} \prod_{\mathfrak{J}_1} S_1(t)^{y_{i,t}}(1 - S_1(t))^{1-y_{i,t}}.$$

We deduce the M.L. estimators of c and δ.

Property 1. Let $f_{0,t}$(respectively $f_{1,t}$) denote the observed proportion of unemployed at time t among the employed (respectively unemployed) people at $t = 0$. The M.L. estimators of c and δ exist if and only if $0 < f_{0,t} + f_{1,t} < 1$.

Under these inequalities they are given by

$$c_t^* = \frac{f_{0,t}}{f_{0,t} + f_{1,t}}$$

and

$$\delta_t^* = -\frac{1}{t}\log(1 - f_{0,t} - f_{1,t}).$$

The different notations are summarized in figure 2.

Proof of Property 1. The statistics $f_{0,t}, f_{1,t}$ are the M.L. estimators of $p_{0,t} = S_0(t)$ and $p_{1,t} = 1 - S_1(t)$. From the expressions of $S_0(t)$ and $S_1(t)$ we deduce

$$p_{0,t} = c(1 - \exp(-\delta t)),$$
$$p_{1,t} = (1 - c)(1 - \exp(-\delta t)). \quad (7)$$

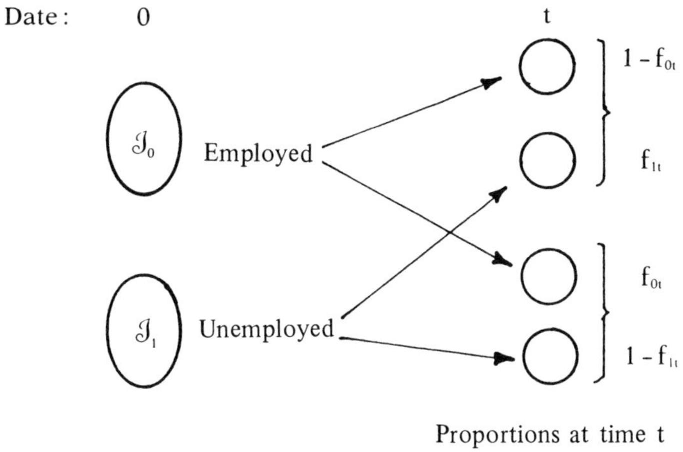

Figure 2.

The parameters $p_{0,t}$ and $p_{1,t}$ satisfy the inequality

$$p_{0,t} + p_{1,t} = 1 - \exp(-\delta t) < 1.$$

Conversely, as soon as $p_{0,t} + p_{1,t}$ is strictly positive and strictly smaller than 1, we have

$$c = \frac{p_{0,t}}{p_{0,t} + p_{1,t}},$$
$$\delta = -\frac{1}{t}\ln(1 - p_{0,t} - p_{1,t}). \tag{8}$$

The M.L. estimators of c and δ are obtained from $f_{0,t}$ and $f_{1,t}$ using relations 8, if $0 < f_{0,t} + f_{1,t} < 1$, and they do not exist otherwise. Q.E.D.

Let us consider the case in which u tends to infinity, the initial structure k being fixed. For a given date t, $f_{0,t}$ and $f_{1,t}$ converge almost surely (a.s) to $p_{0,t}$ and $p_{1,t}$. Thus, the estimators c_t^* and δ_t^* exist a.s asymptotically and converge a.s to c and δ.

The estimation errors on c and δ can be written from the errors $u_{0,t} = f_{0,t} - p_{0,t}$ and $u_{1,t} = f_{1,t} - p_{1,t}$:

$$c_t^* - c = \frac{(1-c)u_{0,t} - cu_{1,t}}{1 - \exp(-\delta t) + u_{0,t} + u_{1,t}}, \tag{9}$$

$$\delta_t^* - \delta = -(1/t)\log[1 - (u_{0,t} + u_{1,t})\exp(\delta t)]. \tag{10}$$

Since $u_{0,t}$ and $u_{1,t}$ are asymptotically normal and c_t^*, δ_t^* are differentiable functions of $u_{0,t}$ and $u_{1,t}$, c_t^* and δ_t^* are also asymptotically normal. Moreover, equations 9 and 10 can be used for determining the asymptotic variance and covariance of c_t^*, δ_t^* (when t is fixed and u tends to infinity).

Property 2. For a given initial structure k and a given date t, the asymptotic second-order moments when n tends to infinity are

$$V_{\text{as}}\left(\sqrt{n}(c_t^* - c)\right) = \frac{c(1-c)}{1-\exp(-\delta t)}\left(\frac{(1-c)^2}{(1-k)} + \frac{c^2}{k} + \frac{c(1-c)}{k(1-k)}\exp(-\delta t)\right),$$

$$V_{\text{as}}\left(\sqrt{n}(\delta_t^* - \delta)\right) = \frac{\exp(\delta t) - 1}{t^2}\left(\frac{c(1-c)}{k(1-k)}\exp(\delta t) + \frac{c^2}{1-k} + \frac{(1-c)^2}{k}\right),$$

$$\text{Cov}_{\text{as}}\left(\sqrt{n}(c_t^* - c), \sqrt{n}(\delta_t^* - \delta)\right)$$

$$= \frac{c(1-c)\exp(\delta t)}{t}\left[\frac{k-c}{k(1-k)} + \left(\frac{c}{1-k} - \frac{1-c}{k}\right)\exp(-\delta t)\right].$$

These results are proved in Appendix 1, and the evolutions of these moments are studied in the next sections.

2. Evolution of the Asymptotic Variance of c_t^*

The study of the variance $V_{c^*}(t)$ gives the following results.

Property 3.

(i) $V_{c^*}(t)$ is a decreasing function of t on $]0, +\infty[$.

(ii) When t tends to 0

$$V_{c^*}(t) \sim \frac{c(1-c)}{\delta t}\left(\frac{1-c}{1-k} + \frac{c}{k}\right).$$

(iii) When t tends to infinity,

$$\lim_{t\to\infty} V_{c^*}(t) = c(1-c)\left(\frac{(1-c)^2}{1-k} + \frac{c^2}{k}\right).$$

Proof. See Appendix 2.

The estimation of the long-run value c is asymptotically more precise when the observations are collected at two farer dates. Moreover, when t

tends to zero, the asymptotic variance of c^* tends to infinity; this means that the long-run parameter is likely not identifiable for $t = 0$.

These properties may be explained if we remember that c is a long-run parameter: it cannot be correctly determined from short-run observations and it becomes more precise if the evolution is observed for a large date t.

3. Evolution of the Asymptotic Variance of δ_t^*

In a similar way, it is possible to analyze the variance $V_{\delta^*}(t)$.

Property 4.

(i) $V_{\delta^*}(t)$ has a unique minimum on the interval $]0, +\infty[$. This minimum is determined for a value t such that $\alpha = \delta t$ is the unique solution of the equation

$$\alpha\left(\frac{a-1}{2} + \exp\alpha\right) = [1 - \exp(-\alpha)]\,(a + \exp\alpha),$$

where

$$a = k\frac{c}{1-c} + (1-k)\frac{1-c}{c}.$$

(ii) As t tends to zero,

$$V_{\delta^*}(t) \sim \frac{\delta}{t}\left(\frac{c}{1-k} + \frac{1-c}{k}\right).$$

(iii) As t tends to infinity,

$$V_{\delta^*}(t) \sim \frac{\exp 2\delta t}{t^2}\,\frac{c(1-c)}{k(1-k)}.$$

Proof. See Appendix 3.

The parameter δ characterizes the rate of convergence toward the long-run equilibrium and from property 4 it seems to be unidentifiable for $t = 0$ and $t = \infty$. When the observations are available for two close dates, it cannot be identified since a too small number of people have a change of state. On the other hand, if the dates of sampling are distant, the system is close to its asymptotic behavior and the rate of convergence is approximated by zero.

Since parameter δ cannot be estimated precisely if the sampling dates are too close or too far from each other property (i) gives an optimal finite sampling date; this optimal date depends on the initial structure k and on the structural parameters.

It is now natural to look for the initial structure k giving asymptotically optimal estimators.

4. Optimal Structure of the Population

In practice the n observed individuals are selected by the statistician from a larger population. The statistician can control the initial structure of the sample, its size, and the date of resampling. He may look for optimal values of these controls in order to improve the estimations. For a given resampling date t, the following property is obtained.

Property 5. For a given t:

(i) the minimum of $V_{c^*}(t)$ is obtained for the unique initial structure k_c, defined by

$$\left(\frac{k_c}{1-k_c}\right)^2 = \left(\frac{c}{1-c}\right)^2 \frac{\exp(\delta t) + (1-c)/c}{\exp(\delta t) + c/(1-c)};$$

(ii) the minimum of $V_{\delta^*}(t)$ is obtained for the unique initial structure k_δ, defined by

$$\left(\frac{k_\delta}{1-k_\delta}\right)^2 = \frac{\exp(\delta t) + (1-c)/c}{\exp(\delta t) + c/(1-c)}.$$

These optimal structures differ and it is not possible to optimize simultaneously the estimations of c and δ, except when $c = \frac{1}{2}$; in this particular case, the optimal structure is $k = c = \frac{1}{2}$. This case corresponds to the equality of the two rates λ and μ.

For large values of t, the optimal structures are c and $\frac{1}{2}$, respectively, for $V_{c^*}(t)$ and $V_{\delta^*}(t)$; the structure is equal to the long-run structure for the estimation of c and it is independent on the structural parameters giving the same weight to employed and unemployed people for the estimation of δ.

When t is small, the optimal structures k_t and k_δ are, respectively, determined through

$$\left(\frac{k_c}{1-k_c}\right)^2 = \frac{c}{1-c} = \frac{\mu}{\lambda}$$

and

$$\left(\frac{k_\delta}{1 - k_\delta}\right)^2 = \frac{1 - c}{c} = \frac{\lambda}{\mu}.$$

When the rate λ of obtaining a job is larger than the rate μ of losing it, the optimal initial short-run structure to estimate the long-run parameter c gives a larger weight to unemployed people. This structure has the same ordering as the asymptotic, but is not equal to it.

The opposite situation occurs concerning the estimation of δ; for a small resampling date, the adjustment parameter is better estimated if the proportion of unemployed in the sample is large.

IV. Asymptotic Study in a Neighborhood of the Nonidentifiability

In the previous section, we have studied the asymptotic variances of the estimators of c and δ for a given date t. We have seen that the variances tend to infinity, when the resampling date t tends to zero or to infinity, which seems to reveal a nonidentifiability problem in the neighborhood of these particular values of t.

In order to study this problem in a systematic way, we now develop an asymptotic theory taking simultaneously into account the evolutions of n and t. Intuitively it is possible to balance the loss of information when t tends to zero or to infinity by an increase of the spatial component n. We determine the sample size n_t associated with the exact balance and for this size we give the asymptotic distribution of the estimate. As in the previous section, the initial structure is k (proportion of unemployed people). The observations are summarized by the two frequencies $f_{0,t}$ and $f_{1,t}$. The distribution of the frequencies in finite sample are the same as before, i.e.,

$$(1 - k)nf_{0,t} \sim> \mathfrak{B}[(1 - k)n, p_{0,t}],$$

$$knf_{1,t} \sim> \mathfrak{B}[kn, p_{1,t}],$$

where the theoretical proportion are given by equation 7.

The asymptotic distributions of the frequencies $f_{0,t}$ and $f_{1,t}$, when the number n tends to infinity and the difference between the sampling dates tends to zero or infinity have to be reexamined (see Appendix 4, Lemmas 1 and 2). When t tends to zero, different limit distributions are obtained, depending on the relative rates of explosion of $1/t$ and n. In the case, in which t tends to infinity, the asymptotic distributions are normal distributions, with moments depending on the relative rates of explosion of t and $\log n/2\delta$.

From these asymptotic results it is possible to deduce the asymptotic behavior of the M.L. estimators c_t^* of the long-run parameter and δ_t^* of the adjustment speed.

We give successively the limit cases where t tends to zero and t tends to infinity.

The first point that is examined concerns the existence of the estimators. The M.L. estimator of c: $c_t^* = f_{0,t}/(f_{0,t} + f_{1,t})$ exists iff $f_{0,t} + f_{1,t} \neq 0$ (see property 1), i.e. iff $f_{0,t} \neq 0$ or $f_{1,t} = 0$. The M.L. estimator of δ: $\delta_t^* = -(1/t)\log(1 - f_{0,t} - f_{1,t})$ exists iff $f_{0,t} + f_{1,t} < 1$. The existence of c_t^* and δ_t^* is directly deduced from the asymptotic properties of the frequencies $f_{0,t}$, $f_{1,t}$. The probabilities of existence of c_t^* and δ_t^* are, respectively, denoted by $P_c(t, n)$ and $P_\delta(t, n)$.

1. Asymptotic Study When t Is Close to Zero

The probabilities $P_c(t; n)$ and $P_\delta(t; n)$ have the following behaviors:

Property 6. When t tends to zero and n tends to infinity

(a) (i) $\lim P_c(t, n) = 0$, if $nt \to 0$,
(ii) $\lim P_c(t, n) = 1 - \exp(-\delta M)[c(1 - k) + (1 - c)k]$, if $nt \to M$,
(iii) $\lim P_c(t, n) = 1$, if $nt \to \infty$.
(b) $\lim P_\delta(t, n) = 1$, for any relative evolution of n and t.

Proof. See Appendix 4.

We can see in Property 3 that the asymptotic variance of c_t^*, computed for fixed t, tends to infinity when t tends to zero. Now we note that this apparent nonidentifiability of the long-run parameter likely disappears if the sample size increases sufficiently fast. The balance is obtained when n tends to infinity at a rate greater than to $1/t$. If the rate of divergence of n is below this balance value, the estimator does not exist asymptotically with probability 1 and therefore it cannot be consistent. On the other hand, the estimator of the adjustment speed δ always exists asymptotically.

These results can be made precise by discussing the asymptotic distributions of the estimators. For this purpose it is important to also distinguish the rate of divergence of n and $1/t$ for the estimation of parameter δ.

Property 7. When t tends to zero and n tends to infinity:

(a) (i) If $nt \to \infty$, $\sqrt{nt}(c_t^* - c) \xrightarrow{d} N\left[0, \frac{c(1-c)}{\delta}\left\{\frac{c}{k} + \frac{1-c}{1-k}\right\}\right]$.

(ii) If $nt \to M$, we have on the existence domain

$$c_t^* - c \xrightarrow{d} \frac{(1-c)\dfrac{Z_0}{1-k} - c\dfrac{Z_1}{k}}{\dfrac{Z_0}{1-k} + \dfrac{Z_1}{k}},$$

where Z_0 and Z_1 are independent, with Poisson distributions with respective parameters

$m_0 = c\delta(1-k)M, \quad m_1 = (1-c)\delta kM.$

(b) (i) When $nt \to 0$, the estimator δ_t^* tends to zero.
(ii) When $nt \to M$, the estimator converges in distribution to

$$\frac{1}{M}\left(\frac{Z_0}{1-k} + \frac{Z_1}{k}\right).$$

(iii) When nt tends to infinity, δ_t^* converges to δ.
(iv) When consistency holds $[nt \to \infty]$, we have, if $\lim t^5 n = A^2$,

$$\sqrt{nt}(\delta_t^* - \delta) \xrightarrow{d} N\left[-\delta^3\frac{A}{2}; \frac{c\delta}{1-k} + \frac{(1-c)\delta}{k}\right],$$

and, if $\lim (t^5 n)^{-1} = 0$,

$$\frac{1}{t^2}(\delta_t^* - \delta) \xrightarrow{P} -\frac{\delta^3}{2}.$$

Proof. See Appendix 4.

While the existence conditions are not the same for both estimators c_t^* and δ_t^* (in particular δ_t^* is always defined asymptotically), these estimations are consistent under the same conditions. For consistency to be satisfied, the sample size has to be large enough, i.e., asymptotically larger than $1/t$.

In the special case in which nt tends to a constant M, we may note that, even if the estimators are not consistent, the true values of the parameters appear in an interesting way inside the limit distributions. For instance the limit distribution of δ_t^* has a mean given by

$$E\left[\frac{1}{M}\left(\frac{Z_0}{1-k}+\frac{Z_1}{k}\right)\right] = c\delta + (1-c)\delta = \delta.$$

The nonconsistent estimator is asymptotically unbiased.

When consistency holds, we obtain the usual asymptotic normality of the estimator c_t^*. However, this usual result does not apply to the other estimate.

2. Asymptotic Study When t Is Close to Infinity

The property of existence is similar to the one given for the case where t is close to zero.

Property 8. When t and n tend to infinity:

(a) $\lim P_c(t, n) = 1$, for any relative evolution of n and t.

(b) (i) If n is large enough compared to $\exp(2\delta t)$,

$\lim P_\delta(t, n) = 1.$

(ii) If $\lim \sqrt{n}\exp(-\delta t) = A$,

$\lim P_\delta(t, n) = \Phi[A\sqrt{k(1-k)/c(1-c)}]$,

where Φ is the cumulative distribution function of the standard normal.

(iii) If n is negligible with respect to $\exp(2\delta t)$,

$\lim P_\delta(t, n) = \frac{1}{2}.$

Therefore the M.L. estimator of c always exists asymptotically, which is coherent with the absence of identifiability problems for this parameter when t is close to infinity. At the opposite, the nonidentifiability of δ when t is close to infinity explains why the estimator is not computable with probability one, when the sample size is not large enough. However, it is notable that the probability of existence is always larger than 1/2. The limit distributions of the estimation are all deduced from normal distributions.

Property 9. When t and n tend to infinity:

(a) For any relative evolution of n and t,

$$\sqrt{n}(c_t^* - c) \xrightarrow{d} N\left[0; c(1-c)\left[\frac{(1-c)^2}{1-k}+\frac{c^2}{k}\right]\right].$$

(b) (i) If n is large enough compared to $\exp 2\delta t$:

$$\sqrt{n}\exp(-\delta t)\, t(\delta_t^* - \delta) \xrightarrow{d} N\left[0; \frac{c(1-c)}{k(1-k)}\right].$$

(ii) If $\lim \sqrt{n}\exp(-\delta t) = A$:

$$\exp(-t(\delta_t^* - \delta)) = \exp(\delta t)\exp(-\delta_t^* \cdot t) \xrightarrow{d} N^+\left(1; \frac{c(1-c)}{A^2 k(1-k)}\right)$$

on the asymptotic existence domain of δ_t^*.
(iii) If n is negligible with respect to $\exp(2\delta t)$:

$$\sqrt{n}\exp(-\delta_t^* \cdot t) \xrightarrow{d} N^+\left(0; \frac{c(1-c)}{k(1-k)}\right)$$

on the asymptotic existence domain of δ_t^*.

($N^+(m, \sigma^2)$ is the normal distribution $N(m, \sigma^2)$ restricted to the positive real line.)

Proof. See Appendix 4.

Concerning the long-run parameter, for which no identifiability problem occurs when t is close to infinity, we obtain the following results: consistency of the estimator, asymptotic normality, asymptotic variance equal to the limit of the variance computed for fixed t (see Property 3iii).

The results are more surprising for the other parameter, since the properties are not directly obtained by taking the limit of the results with fixed t.

The estimator is consistent, asymptotically normal, when n is large enough compared to t (case i).

It remains consistent on the existence domain, when $\lim \sqrt{n}\exp(-\delta t) = A \neq 0$. Nevertheless, the limit distribution on the domain is "exponential normal."

Finally, if $\lim \sqrt{n}\exp(-\delta t) = 0$, i.e., if n increases too slowly, $\log \sqrt{n} - \delta t$ tends to $-\infty$ and asymptotically $\log \sqrt{n}/t < \delta$. We deduce that, even on the existence domain, the estimator is not necessarily consistent (since we do not know if $\log \sqrt{n}/t$ has a limit); moreover it is such that $\delta_t^* < \delta$ asymptotically. When it exists, the estimator underestimates the unknown value of the parameter.

V. Concluding Remarks

The previous results have been described for a simple sampling model with only two parameters. Nevertheless this model allows a joint study of the spatial and temporal aspects outside the usual linear context.

When the classical regularity conditions are not satisfied, the M.L. estimators may have very strange asymptotic properties: partial or global existence of estimators, possibility of asymptotic biases, and asymptotic nonnormality.

These various results are summarized in tables 1 and 2.

These atypical results have surely to be compared with some others obtained for the case of qualitative models estimated from panel data (see Chamberlain 1980).

From a practical point of view, it would be necessary to extend the previous results to the case of nonhomogeneous processes, for which the instantaneous rates would depend on individual and/or temporal characteristics. This generalization is strongly linked with the heterogeneity phenomenon (see Fourgeaud et al. 1987) and will be presented in a subsequent paper.

Appendix 1: Asymptotic Variance of (c_t^*, δ_t^*)

The proof is given conditionally to the initial state. At time $t = 0$, we have nk unemployed and $n(1 - k)$ employed. Since the two subpopulations are independently considered, the frequencies $f_{0,t}$ and $f_{i,t}$ are independent variables. Moreover, we obtain from the binomial scheme and the Central Limit Theorem:

(i) $$\sqrt{n}u_{0,t} = \sqrt{n}(f_{0,t} - p_{0,t}) \xrightarrow{d} N\left[0, \frac{p_{0,t}(1 - p_{0,t})}{1 - k}\right],$$

$$\sqrt{n}u_{1,t} = \sqrt{n}(f_{1,t} - p_{1,t}) \xrightarrow{d} N\left[0, \frac{p_{1,t}(1 - p_{1,t})}{k}\right].$$

(ii) The asymptotic moments of the estimators c_t^* and δ_t^* are then derived from the moments of $u_{0,t}$ and $u_{1,t}$ by limited expansions and the small increases formula.

(iii) For example, we shall derive the asymptotic variance of $\sqrt{n}(c_t^* - c)$. We have

Table 1.
t Close to Infinity

Relative evolutions of n and t	Long-run parameter			Adjustment parameter		
	Probability of existence	Limit distribution	Consistency	Probability of existence	Limit distribution	Consistency
$\lim \sqrt{n} \exp(-\delta t) = \infty$	1	Normal	Yes	1	Normal	Yes
$\lim \sqrt{n} \exp(-\delta t) = A$, $A = 0$	1	Normal	Yes	Between 1/2 and 1	Exponential normal	Partial
$\lim \sqrt{n} \exp(-\delta t) = 0$	1	Normal	Yes	1/2	Exponential normal	No

Table 2.
t Close to Zero

	Long-run parameter			Adjustment parameter		
Relative evolutions of n and t	Probability of existence	Limit distribution	Consistency	Probability of existence	Limit distribution	Consistency
$\lim nt = 0$	0	—	No	1	Convergence to zero	No
$\lim nt = M = 0$	Strictly between 0 and 1	Deduced from Poisson distributions	No	1	Deduced from Poisson distributions	No
$\lim nt = \infty$	1	Normal	No	1	Normal, even degenerate	Yes

$$\sqrt{n}(c_t^* - c) = \frac{(1-c)\sqrt{n}u_{0,t} - c\sqrt{n}u_{1,t}}{1-\exp(-\delta t)} + o_P(1),$$

where the probability limit of $o_P(1)$ is 0.

Moreover, we have

$$p_{0,t}(1-p_{0,t}) = c[1-\exp(-\delta t)]\{1 - c[1-\exp(-\delta t)]\}$$
$$= c[1-\exp(-\delta t)][1 - c + c\exp(-\delta t)],$$
$$p_{1,t}(1-p_{1,t}) = (1-c)[1-\exp(-\delta t)]\{1-(1-c)[1-\exp(-\delta t)]\}$$
$$= (1-c)[1-\exp(-\delta t)][c + (1-c)\exp(-\delta t)].$$

Then we deduce that

$$V_{\text{as}}\left[\sqrt{n}(c_t^* - c)\right]$$
$$= \frac{\dfrac{(1-c)^2}{1-k}p_{0,t}(1-p_{0,t}) + \dfrac{c^2}{k}p_{1,t}(1-p_{1,t})}{[1-\exp(-\delta t)]^2}$$
$$= \left(\frac{(1-c)^2}{1-k}c[1-\exp(-\delta t)][1-c+c\exp(-\delta t)]\right.$$
$$\left. + \frac{c^2}{k}(1-c)[1-\exp(-\delta t)][c+(1-c)\exp(-\delta t)]\right)\Big/[1-\exp(-\delta t)]^2$$
$$= \frac{c(1-c)}{1-\exp(-\delta t)}\left\{\frac{1-c}{1-k}[1-c+c\exp(-\delta t)]\right.$$
$$\left. + \frac{c}{k}[c+(1-c)\exp(-\delta t)]\right\}$$
$$= \frac{c(1-c)}{1-\exp-\delta t}\left\{\frac{(1-c)^2}{1-k} + \frac{c^2}{k} + \frac{c(1-c)}{k(1-k)}\exp(-\delta t)\right\}$$

The derivation of the asymptotic variance of $\sqrt{n}(\delta_t^* - \delta)$ and of the asymptotic covariance of the two estimators is similar.

Appendix 2: Evolution of the Asymptotic Variance of c_t^*

(i) The asymptotic variance of c_t^* is a homographic function of $\exp(-\delta t)$, and thus it is monotonic.

(ii) When t tends to zero, we have

$$V_{c^*}(t) \sim \frac{c(1-c)}{\delta t}\left[\frac{(1-c)^2}{1-k} + \frac{c^2}{k} + \frac{c(1-c)}{k(1-k)}\right]$$

$$= \frac{c(1-c)}{\delta t}\left[\frac{1-c}{1-k} + \frac{c}{k}\right].$$

In particular, the limit of $V_{c^*}(t)$ as tends to 0^+ is infinite. This result shows that $V_{c^*}(t)$ is a decreasing function on t.

(iii) When t tends to infinity, the result is immediate.

Appendix 3: Evolution of the Asymptotic Variance of δ_t^*

(i) We deduce from Property 2 that the function we have to study can be written as

$$f(x) = \frac{(-1 + \exp x)(\mathrm{a} + \exp x)}{x^2}$$

with

$$a = k\frac{c}{1-c} + (1-k)\frac{1-c}{c} \text{ and } x = \delta t \geqslant 0.$$

The logarithmic derivative of f is

$$\frac{d \log f(x)}{dx} = -\frac{2}{x} + \frac{\exp x}{-1 + \exp x} + \frac{\exp x}{a + \exp x}$$

$$= -\frac{2}{x} + \frac{1}{1 - \exp(-x)} + \frac{1}{1 + a\exp(-x)}$$

$$= -\frac{2}{x} + \frac{2 + (a-1)\exp(-x)}{[1 - \exp(-x)][1 + a\exp(-x)]}.$$

The function f is increasing when this derivative is positive, that is, when

$$x > \frac{[1 - \exp(-x)][1 + a\exp(-x)]}{1 + \frac{a-1}{2}\exp(-x)}.$$

(ii) Then denote

$$u(x) = \frac{[1 - \exp(-x)][1 + a\exp(-x)]}{1 + \dfrac{a-1}{2}\exp(-x)} - x.$$

We have

$$\frac{du(x)}{dx} = \frac{1}{\left[1 + \dfrac{a-1}{2}\exp(-x)\right]^2}$$
$$\times \left\{\frac{a-1}{2}\exp(-x)[1 - \exp(-x)][1 + a\exp(-x)]\right.$$
$$+ \left(1 + \frac{a-1}{2}\exp(-x)\right)[\exp(-x) - a\exp(-x)$$
$$\left. + 2a\exp(-2x)] - \left[1 + \frac{a-1}{2}\exp(-x)\right]^2\right\}.$$

This derivative has the same sign as

$$B = \frac{a-1}{2}X(1 - X)(1 + aX)$$
$$+ \left(1 + \frac{a-1}{2}X\right)X[1 - a + 2aX) - \left[1 + \frac{a-1}{2}X\right]^2,$$

where $X = \exp(-x)$. After some simplifications we obtain

$$B = \frac{a(a-1)}{2}X^3 + \left[2a - \left(\frac{a-1}{2}\right)^2\right]X^2 - \tfrac{3}{2}(a-1)X - 1.$$

B is a polynomial of degree 3 whose derivative is

$$\frac{dB(X)}{dX} = \tfrac{3}{2}a(a-1)X^2 + \left[4a - \frac{(a-1)^2}{2}\right]X - \tfrac{3}{2}(a-1).$$

Its discriminant is

$$\Delta = \left[4a - \frac{(a-1)^2}{2}\right]^2 + 9a(a-1)^2 > 0,$$

and it follows that the derivative dB/dX has two real roots X_1 and X_2, with $X_2 > X_1$. Moreover, $dB(0)/dX$ and $\lim_{X \to \pm\infty} dB(X)/dX$ have opposite signs and $dB/dX(1) = (a+1)^2 > 0$.

We have now to examine two different cases:

Table 3.

X	0		X_2		X_0		1
$B(X)$	-1	$\searrow$		$\nearrow$	0	$\nearrow$	$\frac{(1+a)^2}{4}$

Table 4.

X	0		$-\log X_0$		α		∞
$u(X)$	0	$\nearrow$		$\searrow$	0	$\searrow$	$-\infty$

$a > 1$

The greatest root X_2 lies between 0 and 1, and the variations of the function B are as given in table 3. Therefore, there exists a unique value X_0 between X_2 and 1 such that $B(X) > 0$ for $X \in]X_0, 1]$.

$a \leqslant 1$

In the alternative case, the derivative $dB(X)/dX$ has a constant positive sign on [0, 1]. Then, there exists one value $X_0 \in]0, 1]$ such that $B(X) > 0$, for $X \in [X_0, 1]$.

(iii) The variations of the function u are summarized in table 4. It follows that there exists a unique value α such that

$$\begin{cases} u(X) > 0, & \text{if } X < \alpha \\ u(X) < 0, & \text{if } X > \alpha. \end{cases}$$

(iv) Then, the function f has a unique minimum obtained for this value α, given by

$$\alpha\left[1 + \frac{a-1}{2}\exp(-\alpha)\right] = [1 - \exp(-\alpha)][1 + a\exp(-\alpha)]$$

$$\Leftrightarrow \alpha\left[\exp\alpha + \frac{a-1}{2}\right] = [1 - \exp(-\alpha)](a + \exp\alpha).$$

Appendix 4: Maximum-Likelihood Estimators: Limiting Existence and Behavior about $t = 0$ and $t = +\infty$

(a) First, we briefly recall the notations: We consider n individuals at time $t = 0$: kn are unemployed and $(1-k)n$ are employed. $p_{0,t} =$

$c(1 - \exp(-\delta t))$ is the probability of unemployment at time t for an individual who was employed at $t = 0$; $p_{1,t} = (1 - c)(1 - \exp(-\delta t))$ is the probability of employment at time t for an individual who was unemployed at $t = 0$. $f_{0,t}$ and $f_{1,t}$ are the corresponding frequencies.

(b) We know that the variable $Z_{0,t} = (1 - k)n f_{0,t}$ is distributed as a binomial variable $\mathfrak{B}[(1 - k)n; p_{0,t}]$. It follows that the characteristic function of the frequency $f_{0,t}$ is

$$\varphi_{f_{0,t}}(u) = \left[1 + p_{0,t}\left(\exp\frac{iu}{n(1 - k)} - 1\right)\right]^{n(1-k)} \tag{1}$$

where $0 \leqslant p_{0,t} < c$ for every positive value of t. Since $p_{0,t}(\exp(iu/n(1 - k)) - 1)$ tends to zero uniformly in t as the sample size n tends to infinity, the Taylor's series expansion of the second characteristic function about $1/n = 0$ is

$$\log \varphi_{f_{0,t}}(u) = p_{0,t}\, iu - \frac{p_{0,t}(1 - p_{0,t})}{1 - k}\frac{u^2}{2n} + p_{0,t}^2\frac{u^2}{2n}\varepsilon_t\left(\frac{u}{n}\right) \tag{2}$$

where $\varepsilon_t(u/n)$ tends to zero as n tends to infinity, uniformly in t.

I. Asymptotic Behavior of the Frequencies $f_{0,t}$, $f_{1,t}$

(a) When t tends to infinity, we obtain the following result:

Lemma 1. When n and t tend to infinity, we have

(i) $\sqrt{n}(f_{0,t} - p_{0,t}) \xrightarrow{d} N\left(0, \dfrac{c(1 - c)}{1 - k}\right)$,

$\sqrt{n}(f_{1,t} - p_{1,t}) \xrightarrow{d} N\left(0, \dfrac{c(1 - c)}{k}\right)$.

(ii) If n is of greater order than $\exp(2\delta t)$

$\exp(\delta t)(f_{0,t} - c) \xrightarrow{p} -c$,

$\exp(\delta t)(f_{1,t} - (1 - c)) \xrightarrow{p} -(1 - c)$.

(iii) If $\lim \sqrt{n}\exp(-\delta t) = A$,

$\sqrt{n}(f_{0,t} - c) \xrightarrow{d} N\left[-cA; \dfrac{c(1 - c)}{(1 - k)}\right]$,

$\sqrt{n}(f_{1,t} - (1 - c)) \xrightarrow{d} N\left[-(1 - c)A; \dfrac{c(1 - c)}{k}\right]$.

(iv) If n is of smaller order than $\exp(2\delta t)$,

$$\sqrt{n}(f_{0,t} - c) \xrightarrow{d} N\left[0; \frac{c\,(1-c)}{1-k}\right],$$

$$\sqrt{n}(f_{1,t} - (1-c)) \xrightarrow{d} N\left[0; \frac{c(1-c)}{k}\right].$$

Proof. The expansion (2) of the characteristic function of $f_{0,t}$ leads to

$$\begin{aligned}\log \varphi_{\sqrt{n}(f_{0,t}-p_{0,t})}(u) &= -iu\sqrt{n}p_{0,t} + \log \varphi_{f_{0,t}}(\sqrt{n}u) \\ &= -\frac{p_{0,t}(1-p_{0,t})}{1-k}\frac{u^2}{2} + p_{0,t}^2\frac{u^2}{2}\varepsilon_t\left(\frac{u}{\sqrt{n}}\right).\end{aligned}$$

Whatever the relative behavior of n and t, we asymptotically obtain $\lim p_{0,t} = c$, $\lim u/\sqrt{n} = 0$. It follows that

$$\lim \log \varphi_{\sqrt{n}(f_{0,t}-p_{0,t})} = -\frac{c(1-c)}{1-k}\frac{u^2}{2}$$

That is,

$$\sqrt{n}(f_{0,t} - p_{0,t}) \xrightarrow{d} N\left[0; \frac{c(1-c)}{1-k}\right].$$

which leads to result i.

Moreover, the definition of the probability $p_{0,t}$ leads to the following equality:

$$\sqrt{n}(f_{0,t} - c) = \sqrt{n}(f_{0,t} - p_{0,t}) - c\sqrt{n}\exp(-\delta t).$$

The other results follow from the comparison of the two terms in the right member. □

(b) As t tends to zero, the convergences may be either to normal distributions or to Poisson distribution. More precisely, we have the following lemma:

Lemma 2. When n tends to infinity and t tends to zero we have

(i) If $\lim nt = 0$:

$$\frac{1}{t}f_{0,t} \xrightarrow{P} 0 \text{ and } \frac{1}{t}f_{1,t} \xrightarrow{P} 0.$$

(ii) If $\lim nt = M$:

$$(1-k)nf_{0,t} \xrightarrow{d} \mathscr{P}(m_0 = cdM(1-k)),$$

$$knf_{1,t} \xrightarrow{d} \mathscr{P}(m_1 = (1-c)dMk).$$

(iii) If $\lim nt = +\infty$:

$$\sqrt{nt}\left(\frac{f_{0,t}}{t} - c\delta + \frac{c\delta^2 t}{2}\right) \xrightarrow{d} N\left[0, \frac{c\delta}{1-k}\right],$$

$$\sqrt{nt}\left(\frac{f_{1,t}}{t} - (1-c)\delta + \frac{(1-c)\delta^2 t}{2}\right) \xrightarrow{d} N\left[0, \frac{(1-c)\delta}{k}\right].$$

Proof. We have

$$\log \varphi_{f_{0,t}}(u) = n(1-k)\log\left\{1 + p_{0,t}\left(\exp\frac{iu}{n(1-k)} - 1\right)\right\}$$
$$= n(1-k)\log\left\{1 + c(1-\exp(-\delta t))\left(\exp\frac{iu}{n(1-k)} - 1\right)\right\};$$

$$\log \varphi_{\frac{1}{t}f_{0,t}}(u) = n(1-k)\log\left[1 + c(1-\exp(-\delta t))\left(\exp\frac{iu}{nt(1-k)} - 1\right)\right].$$

(i) and (ii): As nt tends to a constant, eventually to zero, it is possible to write the following expansion:

$$\log \varphi_{\frac{1}{t}f_{0,t}}(u) \# nt(1-k)c\delta\left(\exp\frac{iu}{nt(1-k)} - 1\right)$$

When $\lim nt = 0$, we have $\lim \log \varphi_{\frac{1}{t}f_{0,t}}(u) = 0$, which implies that $\frac{1}{t}f_{0,t} \xrightarrow{P} 0$.

When $\lim nt = M \neq 0$, we have

$$\lim \log \varphi_{\frac{1}{t}f_{0,t}}(u) = M(1-k)c\delta\left(\exp\frac{iu}{M(1-k)} - 1\right)$$

and

$$\lim \log \varphi_{(1-k)nf_{0,t}}(u) = c\delta M(1-k)(\exp iu - 1).$$

This proves the convergence to a Poisson distribution with parameter $c\delta M(1-k)$.

(iii): As nt increases, we have

$$\log\varphi_{\sqrt{nt}[\frac{f_{0,t}}{t}-c\delta+\frac{c\delta^2 t}{2}]}(u)$$

$$= -iuc\delta\sqrt{nt} + iu\frac{c\delta^2}{2}t\sqrt{nt} + \log\varphi_{f_{0,t}}\left(\frac{\sqrt{n}}{\sqrt{t}}u\right)$$

$$= -iuc\delta\sqrt{nt} + iu\frac{c\delta^2}{2}t\sqrt{nt}$$

$$+ n(1-k)\log\left\{1 + c(1-\exp(-\delta t))\left(\exp\frac{iu}{\sqrt{nt}(1-k)} - 1\right)\right\}$$

$$\# -\frac{c\delta u^2}{2(1-k)}.$$

This leads to the result.

In particular, the last convergences show that the ratio $f_{0,t}/t$ tends to $c\delta = \lim P_{0,t}/t$ when nt tends to infinity.

II. Existence of the Maximum-Likelihood Estimators c_t^* and δ_t^*

We know that the M.L. estimator c_t^* exists if and only if $f_{0,t} \neq 0$ or $f_{1,t} \neq 0$. The other estimator δ_t^* exists if and only if $f_{0,t} + f_{1,t} < 1$. It is easy to deduce the limit existence's probabilities from the asymptotic distributions of the frequencies.

Proof of Property 6 (when t tends to zero).

(a) From the binomial distribution of the variable $Z_{0,t}$ it follows that

$$P[f_{0,t} = 0] = P[Z_{0,t} = 0] = [1 - p_{0,t}]^{n(1-k)}$$

$$= [1 - c[1 - \exp(-\delta t)]]^{n(1-k)}$$

$$\# \exp[-n(1-k)c\delta t].$$

(i) This term tends to 1 as nt tends to zero.

(ii) It tends to $\exp[-c\delta M(1-k)]$, as nt tends to $M \neq 0$.

(iii) It tends to zero as nt tends to infinity.

The limits of the existence's probability follow from the formula

$$\lim P_c(t, n) = 1 - \lim P[f_{0,t} = 0]\,\lim P[f_{1,t} = 0].$$

(b) Moreover, by Lemma 2 we have that $\text{plim} f_{0,t} = \text{plim} f_{1,t} = 0$ for all relative behavior of n and t. It follows that $(f_{0,t} + f_{1,t}) = 0$ and therefore

$$\lim P_\delta(t, n) = \lim P[f_{0,t} + f_{1,t} < 1] = 1.$$

Proof of Property 8 (as t tends to infinity).

(a) By Lemma 1 we have

$$f_{0,t} \xrightarrow{P} c \neq 0 \text{ and } f_{1,t} \xrightarrow{P} 1 - c \neq 0.$$

Therefore $P_c(t, n) = P[f_{0,t} \neq 0 \text{ or } f_{1,t} \neq 0]$ tends to zero.

(b) On the other hand, a more precise analysis is required to handle the other condition. We know that $\text{plim}(f_{0,t} + f_{1,t}) = 1$, but the problem is to establish that the convergence holds by values strictly smaller than 1.

By Lemma 1(i), we have

$$\sqrt{n}(f_{0,t} + f_{1,t} - p_{0,t} - p_{1,t}) \xrightarrow{d} N\left[0; \frac{c(1-c)}{k(1-k)}\right],$$

$$\sqrt{n}(f_{0,t} + f_{1,t} - (1 - \exp - \delta t)) \xrightarrow{d} N\left[0; \frac{c(1-c)}{k(1-k)}\right].$$

Denote U an $N(0, 1)$ random variable and Φ the associated cumulative distribution function. We obtain

$$P_\delta(t, n) \# P\left[U < \frac{1 - [1 - \exp(-\delta t)]}{\sqrt{\dfrac{c(1-c)}{nk(1-k)}}}\right]$$

$$\# \Phi\left[\sqrt{n}\exp(-\delta t)\sqrt{\frac{k(1-k)}{c(1-c)}}\right].$$

This leads to the three cases:

- If $\lim n \exp(-2\delta t) = +\infty$, then $\lim P_\delta(t, n) = 1$.
- If $\lim \sqrt{n}\exp(-\delta t) = A$, then $\lim P_\delta(t, n) = \Phi[A\sqrt{k(1-k)/c(1-c)}]$.
- If $\lim n \exp(-2\delta t) = 0$, then $\lim P_\delta(t, n) = \frac{1}{2}$.

III. Property 7: Asymptotic Distribution of the Maximum-Likelihood Estimators When t Tends to Zero

(a) (i) $c_t^* - c$ can be written as

$$c_t^* - c = \frac{f_{0,t}}{f_{0,t} + f_{1,t}} - c = \frac{(1-c)f_{0,t} - cf_{1,t}}{f_{0,t} + f_{1,t}}$$

$$= \frac{(1-c)\left(\frac{1}{t}f_{0,t} - c\delta + \frac{c\delta^2 t}{2}\right) - c\left(\frac{1}{t}f_{1,t} - (1-c)\delta + \frac{(1-c)\delta^2 t}{2}\right)}{\frac{1}{t}f_{0,t} + \frac{1}{t}f_{1,t}}.$$

By Lemma 2iii we obtain as nt tends to infinity:

$$\sqrt{nt}(c_t^* - c)$$

$$= \frac{(1-c)\sqrt{nt}\left(\frac{1}{t}f_{0,t} - c\delta + \frac{c\delta^2 t}{2}\right) - c\sqrt{nt}\left(\frac{1}{t}f_{1,t} - (1-c)\delta + (1-c)\frac{\delta^2}{c}\right)}{\delta}$$

$$+ o_p(1)$$

Therefore

$$\sqrt{nt}(c_t^* - c) \xrightarrow{d} N\left[0; \frac{c(1-c)}{\delta}\left(\frac{c}{k} + \frac{1-c}{1-k}\right)\right].$$

(ii) If nt tends to a limit M, the result follows immediately from the expression of $c_t^* - c$ in terms of $f_{0,t}$ and $f_{1,t}$, by application of Lemma 2ii.

(b) We know that the frequencies $f_{0,t}$ and $f_{1,t}$ always tend to zero with t. Therefore, the estimator δ_t^* can be approximated by

$$\delta_t^* = -\frac{1}{t}\log(1 - f_{0,t} - f_{1,t}) \# \frac{f_{0,t} + f_{1,t}}{t}.$$

By Lemma 2 it follows that:

(i) If $\lim nt = 0$, $\text{plim}\,\delta_t^* = 0$.

(ii) If $\lim nt = M$, we see that

$$\delta_t^* \# \frac{f_{0,t} + f_{1,t}}{t} \# \frac{nf_{0,t} + nf_{1,t}}{M} \xrightarrow{d} \frac{1}{M}\left(\frac{Z_0}{1-k} + \frac{Z_1}{k}\right).$$

(iii) Finally, if nt tends to infinity, we have

$$\delta_t^* \# \frac{f_{0,t} + f_{1,t}}{t} \xrightarrow{p} c\delta + (1-c)\delta = \delta.$$

(iv) When convergence of the estimator holds, we investigate its asymptotic distribution by deriving the expansions at the greater order. Let two independent normal random variables distributed as $N(0, c\delta/1-k)$ and $N(0,(1-c)\delta/k)$ be denoted respectively by y_0 and y_1. Lemma 2 leads to

$$f_{0,t} \# c\delta t - \frac{c\delta^2 t}{2} + y_0 \frac{t}{\sqrt{nt}},$$

$$f_{1,t} \# (1-c)\delta t - (1-c)\frac{\delta^2 t^2}{2} + y_1 \frac{t}{\sqrt{nt}}.$$

Therefore, with the notation $y = y_0 + y_1$,

$$f_{0,t} + f_{1,t} \# \delta t - \frac{\delta^2 t^2}{2} + y\frac{t}{\sqrt{nt}}.$$

It follows that

$$\begin{aligned}\delta_t^* &= -\frac{1}{t}\log(1 - f_{0,t} - f_{1,t})\\ &\# -\frac{1}{t}\log\left(1 - \delta t + \frac{\delta^2 t^2}{2} - y\frac{t}{\sqrt{nt}}\right)\\ &\# \delta + \frac{y}{\sqrt{nt}} - \frac{\delta^3 t^2}{2}.\end{aligned}$$

The comparison of the two last terms leads to the result.

IV. Property 9: Asymptotic Distribution of the Maximum-Likelihood Estimators When t Tends to Infinity

(a) From Lemma 1 it follows that

$$\sqrt{n}u_{0,t} = \sqrt{n}(f_{0,t} - p_{0,t}) \xrightarrow{d} N\left[0; \frac{c(1-c)}{1-k}\right],$$

$$\sqrt{n}u_{1,t} = \sqrt{n}(f_{1,t} - p_{1,t}) \xrightarrow{d} N\left[0; \frac{c(1-c)}{k}\right].$$

By the same argument as in Appendix 1i, we obtain

$$\begin{aligned}\sqrt{n}(c_t^* - c) &= (1-c)\sqrt{n}u_{0,t} - c\sqrt{n}u_{1,t} + o_p(1)\\ &\xrightarrow{d} N\left[0; c(1-c)\left[\frac{(1-c)^2}{(1-k)} + \frac{c^2}{k}\right]\right].\end{aligned}$$

(b) On the other hand, the expansion of $\delta_t^* - \delta$ derived in Appendix 1 is correct for a fixed t, but as t increases it can be used only if $u_{0,t}\exp(-\delta t)$ and $u_{1,t}\exp(-\delta t)$ tend in probability to zero. This evidently depends on the relative behavior of n and t.

(i) If $\lim[n\exp(-2\delta t)] = +\infty$, Lemma 1i leads to

$$\exp(\delta t)u_{0,t} = \frac{1}{\sqrt{n}\exp(-\delta t)}\sqrt{n}u_{0,t} \xrightarrow{P} 0.$$

Therefore

$$\delta_t^* - \delta = -\frac{1}{t}\log[1 - (u_{0,t} + u_{1,t})\exp(\delta t)]$$

$$= \frac{1}{t}(u_{0,t} + u_{1,t})\exp(\delta t)\,(1 + o_p(1));$$

and then

$$\sqrt{n}t(\exp(-\delta t))\,(\delta_t^* - \delta) = \sqrt{n}(u_{0,t} + u_{1,t}) + o_p(1) \xrightarrow{d} N\left[0; \frac{c(1-c)}{k(1-k)}\right].$$

(ii) and (iii) If $\lim[n\exp(-2\delta t)] = A^2$, where $A \geqslant 0$, we first write δ_t^* in terms of $v_{0,t} = f_{0,t} - c$ and of $v_{1,t} = f_{1,t} - (1-c)$. We obtain

$$\delta_t^* = -\frac{1}{t}\log[-v_{0,t} - v_{1,t}],$$

that is,

$$\exp(-\delta_t^* \cdot t) = -v_{0,t} - v_{1,t}, \qquad \text{for } v_{0,t} + v_{1,t} < 0.$$

It follows from Lemma 1 that we have, when δ_t^* exists,

$$\sqrt{n}\exp(-\delta_t^* t) \xrightarrow{d} N^+\left(A; \frac{c(1-c)}{k(1-k)}\right), \qquad \text{when } \lim\sqrt{n}\exp(-\delta t) = A.$$

Therefore, we have on the domain of existence of δ_t^*:

- If $\lim\sqrt{n}\exp(-\delta t) = A \neq 0$: $\exp[-t(\delta_t^* - \delta)] \xrightarrow{d} N^+\left(1; \frac{c(1-c)}{A^2 k(1-k)}\right)$.
- If $\lim\sqrt{n}\exp(-\delta t) = 0$: $\sqrt{n}\exp[-\delta_t^* \cdot t] \xrightarrow{d} N^+\left(0; \frac{c(1-c)}{k(1-k)}\right)$. □

References

Chamberlain, G. 1980, "Analysis of Covariance with Qualitative Date." *Review of Economics* 67: 225–238.

Cox, D., and D. Oakes. 1984. *Analysis of Survival Data.* Chapman and Hall.

Davidson, J., D. Hendry, F. Srba, and S. Yeo. 1978. "Econometric Modelling of the Aggregate Time Series Relationship between Consumers' Expenditure and Income in the U. K." *Economic Journal* 88(19): 661–692.

De Stavola, B. 1986. "Sampling Designs for Short Panel Data." *Econometrica* 54: 415–424.

Engle, R. 1987. "On the Theory of Cointegrated Economic Time Series." *Journal of Applied Econometrics*, submitted.

Engle, R., and C. Granger, 1987. "Co-integration and Error Correction: Representation, Estimation and Testing." *Econometrica* 55: 251–276.

Fourgeaud, C., C. Gouriéroux, and J. Pradel. 1987. Heterogeneity and Hazard Dominance in Duration Data Models. CEPREMAP D.P.

Gouriéroux, C., F. Maurel, and A. Monfort. 1987. Regression and Non Stationarity. INSEE D.P.

Kalbfleisch, J. D., and Prentice, R. L. 1980. *The Statistical Analysis of Failure Time Data.* Wiley.

Karlin, S., and R. Taylor. 1965. *A First Course on Stochastic Processes.* Academic.

Phillips, P. C. B., and S. Ouliaris. 1986. Testing for Cointegration. Cowles Foundation D.P. 809.

32 Bilinear Constraints: Estimation and Test

Christian Gouriéroux,
Alain Monfort, and
Eric Renault

The theory of asymptotic tests has been developed for null hypotheses in an implicit form,

$$H_0 = \{g(\theta) = 0\},$$

or in an explicit form,

$$H_0 = \{\theta = f(\alpha), \alpha \in \mathscr{a}\};$$

in the latter case the auxiliary parameter α provides a parameterization of the null hypothesis. However, there exists a third form, called the mixed form, which is

$$H_0 = \{\exists \alpha \in \mathscr{a}: g(\theta, \alpha) = 0\}.$$

In this form, there are implicit constraints in which an auxiliary parameter α appears, but, contrary to the explicit case, α cannot parameterize the null hypothesis. This kind of formulation is very general since implicit and explicit forms are special cases of mixed forms; moreover, a mixed form naturally appears in many problems.

In order to illustrate these various formulations of an hypothesis, let us consider a very simple example of "common roots" appearing in dynamic models (see Sargan 1980; Sargan and Mehta 1983; Gouriéroux, Monfort, and Renault 1988). We have two lag polynomials of degree one: $1 + \theta_1 B$ and $\theta_2 + \theta_3 B$, where B is the lag operator. The parameter of interest is $\theta = (\theta_1, \theta_2, \theta_3)'$ and the null hypothesis is the equality of the roots of the two polynomials. This hypothesis can be written

$$1 + \theta_1 B = 1 + \alpha_1 B, \quad \theta_2 + \theta_3 B = \alpha_2(1 + \alpha_1 B),$$

i.e., in an explicit form:

$$H_0 = \{\exists \alpha_1, \alpha_2: \theta_1 = \alpha_1, \theta_2 = \alpha_2, \theta_3 = \alpha_1 \alpha_2\}.$$

An equivalent implicit form is

$$H_0 = \left\{\det\begin{bmatrix} 1 & \theta_2 \\ \theta_1 & \theta_3 \end{bmatrix} \equiv \theta_3 - \theta_1\theta_2 = 0\right\}.$$

Finally, this hypothesis can also be written, using the colinearity of the column vectors of the determinant, as

$$H_0 = \{\exists\alpha, \theta_2 = \alpha, \theta_3 = \alpha\theta_1\}.$$

This form is a mixed form, which, moreover, is linear with respect to the parameter of interest θ and to the auxiliary parameter α, whereas the explicit and implicit forms exhibit nonlinear functions of θ or of an auxiliary parameter. This bilinearity, which is very frequent, allows us to propose very simple test procedures which will be studied in this article.

In section I, a generalized Wald test principle, proposed by Szroeter (1983), is applied to this kind of hypothesis in a mixed bilinear form. We show that, because of the linearity with respect to the auxiliary parameter, the test can easily be implemented with linear least squares procedures. Moreover, using the bilinearity, it is possible to obtain constrained estimators of the auxiliary parameter and of the parameter of interest, based on linear least squares. The asymptotic properties of these estimators are studied in section II. The other sections describe several cases where these methods can be applied: tests of rational distributed lags (section III), test of instrumental variables relevance (section IV), test of overidentification (section V), test of rational expectation (section VI), and test of separability and homothesis of translog functions (section VII).

I. Generalized Wald Tests

We have seen in the introduction that the hypothesis of common root can be presented as bilinear restrictions on the parameter of interest θ and the auxiliary parameter α. In this section, we consider such hypotheses in the general case and we develop Wald procedures for testing these hypotheses.

1. Definition of the Hypotheses

Let us denote by $\theta \in \Theta \subset \mathbb{R}^p$ and $\alpha \in \mathcal{A} \subset \mathbb{R}^q$ the two kinds of parameters and let us assume that the null hypothesis can be written under a mixed form, which is linear with respect to the auxiliary parameter α:

$$H_0 = \{\exists\alpha \in \mathcal{A}: h(\theta) - H(\theta)\alpha = 0\}, \tag{1.1}$$

where h and H are given functions defined on Θ and whose respective dimensions are $(r, 1)$ and (r, q).

We also impose the linearity of these constraints with respect to the other parameter θ. This means that the constraints system can be written in two ways, one linear with respect to α, and another one linear with respect to θ:

$$h(\theta) - H(\theta)\alpha \equiv a(\alpha) - A(\alpha)\theta, \tag{1.2}$$

where a and A are functions defined on $\mathcal{a}$ whose respective dimensions are $(r, 1)$ and (r, p).

Therefore, the jth constraint is made of a constant term, linear terms in α, linear terms in θ, and bilinear terms in α and θ. An extensive form of this constraint can be written

$$d_j + h_j'\theta + a_j'\alpha + \alpha' C_j \theta = 0, \qquad j = 1, \ldots, r$$

where $h_j\ \mathbb{R}^p$, $a_j \in \mathbb{R}^q$, and C_j is a matrix of size (q, p).

Using the notations

$$\underset{(r\times 1)}{d} = (d_1, \ldots, d_r)',$$

$$\underset{(p\times r)}{h} = (h_1, \ldots, h_r),$$

$$\underset{(q,r)}{a} = (a_1, \ldots, a_r),$$

$$C = \underset{(rp\times q)}{\begin{bmatrix} C_1' \\ \vdots \\ C_r' \end{bmatrix}},$$

$$\Gamma = \underset{(rq\times p)}{\begin{bmatrix} C_1 \\ \vdots \\ C_r \end{bmatrix}},$$

we get

$$h(\theta) = d + h'\theta,$$

$$a(\alpha) = d + a'\alpha,$$

$$H(\theta) = -a' - (Id \otimes \theta')C,$$

$$A(\alpha) = -h' - (Id \otimes \alpha')\Gamma.$$

The auxiliary parameter is only defined under the null hypothesis. Moreover, when this hypothesis is satisfied, we have to impose that this parameter is unambiguously defined. This identifiability condition on the auxiliary parameter can be written

$$\forall \theta_0 \in \Theta_0 = \{\theta: \exists \alpha \in \mathscr{A}: h(\theta) - H(\theta)\,\alpha = 0\}:$$

$$h(\theta_0) - H(\theta_0)\alpha_1 = h(\theta_0) - H(\theta_0)\alpha_2 \Rightarrow \alpha_1 = \alpha_2.$$

It can be summarized as follows:

Assumption A_1. Identifiability of the auxiliary parameter. $H(\theta_0)$ is of full column rank q for any $\theta_0 \in \Theta_0$.

We also impose another condition ensuring that the constraints are not redundant.

Assumption A_2. $A(\alpha)$, $\alpha \in \mathscr{A}$, is of full row rank r.

Let us note that the previous rank assumption implies the following order conditions:

$$q \leqslant r \leqslant p.$$

Finally, it is easily seen that the constraints system could also be written in an implicit form by eliminating the auxiliary parameter α. Such a form, with redundant equations, is, for instance,

$$h(\theta) - [H'(\theta)H(\theta)]^{-1}h(\theta) = 0.$$

Thus, once α is eliminated, the system is nonlinear with respect to θ.

2. The Test Principle

A Wald procedure (see Wald 1943; Andrews 1986; Gouriéroux and Monfort 1989a) consists of checking if the constraints on the parameter of interest are approximately satisfied by a consistent, asymptotically normal estimator of the parameter of interest.

Assumption A_3. $(\hat{\theta}_T, T \in \mathbb{N}^*)$ is a sequence of estimators such that, if $\theta_0 \in \mathring{\Theta}$ (the interior of Θ) is the true value of the parameter, $\sqrt{T}(\hat{\theta}_T - \theta_0)$ converges in distribution to $N[0, Q(\theta_0)]$, when $T \to \infty$. $Q(\theta_0)$ is assumed to be invertible.

Assumption A_1 implies that, under H_0, only one value α_0 of α is associated with θ_0. The constraint $h(\theta_0) - H(\theta_0)\alpha_0 = 0$ is exactly verified. Now, if we consider the "approximate constraints" $h(\hat{\theta}_T) - H(\hat{\theta}_T)\alpha_0$, there is no longer strict equality to zero. In fact, the asymptotic distribution of this function of $\hat{\theta}_T$ is easily found. Under the null hypothesis we have

$$\sqrt{T}[h(\hat{\theta}_T) - H(\hat{\theta}_T)\alpha_0] \xrightarrow{d} N[0, \Omega_0]$$

with

$$\Omega_0 = \left\{\frac{\partial}{\partial\theta'}[h(\theta) - H(\theta)\alpha_0]Q(\theta)\frac{\partial}{\partial\theta}[h(\theta) - H\theta)\alpha_0]'\right\}_{\theta=\theta_0}.$$

From the bilinearity of the constraints we get

$$\sqrt{T}[h(\hat{\theta}_T) - H(\hat{\theta}_T)\alpha_0] \xrightarrow{d} N[0, \Omega_0 = A(\alpha_0)Q(\theta_0)A(\alpha_0)']. \tag{1.3}$$

However, this result cannot be used directly, since $\sqrt{T}[h(\hat{\theta}_T) - H(\hat{\theta}_T)\alpha_0]$ depends on the unknown parameter α_0. We have to estimate first the auxiliary parameter under H_0.

From (1.3) we obtain the asymptotic linear model, under H_0:

$$h(\hat{\theta}_T) = H(\hat{\theta}_T)\alpha_0 + u_T$$

where $\sqrt{T}u_T$ is asymptotically distributed as $N[0, \Omega_0]$.

Now, it is natural to estimate the auxiliary parameter by a quasigeneralized least squares method (Q.G.L.S.).

Let $\hat{\Omega}_T$ be a consistent estimator of Ω_0. In order to apply the least squares method, we must be sure that the regressors are not colinear. This condition is summarized in the following assumption, which extends assumption A_1 to values of the parameter of interest belonging to the alternative.

Assumption A_4. $H(\theta)$ is of full column rank, except possibly on a Lebesgue negligible set.

The Q.G.L.S. estimator of α_0 is

$$\tilde{\alpha}_T^0 = [H'(\hat{\theta}_T)\hat{\Omega}_T^{-1}H(\hat{\theta}_T)^{-1}H'(\hat{\theta}_T)\hat{\Omega}_T^{-1}h(\hat{\theta}_T). \tag{1.4}$$

The "estimated constraints" are defined by

$$\begin{aligned} Z_T &= h(\hat{\theta}_T) - H(\hat{\theta}_T)\tilde{\alpha}_T^0 \\ &= (Id - M_T)h(\hat{\theta}_T), \end{aligned} \tag{1.5}$$

where M_T is the orthogonal projector on the space spanned by the columns of $H(\hat{\theta}_T)$, the orthogonality being the one associated with $\hat{\Omega}_T^{-1}$. The test consists in accepting H_0 if Z_T is sufficiently small and to reject H_0 otherwise. In order to find the critical value, we have to find the asymptotic distribution of these estimated constraints.

3. Asymptotic Behavior

Property 1. Under assumptions A_1 to A_4, the asymptotic distribution of $\sqrt{T}Z_T$ under H_0 is the same as that of $\sqrt{T}(Id - M_0)[h(\hat{\theta}_T) - H(\hat{\theta}_T)\alpha_0]$, where M_0 is the orthogonal projector on the space spanned by the columns of $H(\theta_0)$, the orthogonality being the one associated with Ω_0^{-1}; this implies

$$\sqrt{T}Z_T = \sqrt{T}[h(\hat{\theta}_T) - H(\hat{\theta}_T)\tilde{\alpha}_T^0] \xrightarrow{d} N[0, (Id - M_0)\Omega_0(Id - M_0)'].$$

Proof. See Appendix 1.

With this asymptotically normal vector, we can build a quadratic form whose asymptotic distribution is a χ^2.

Property 2. Under assumptions A_1–A_4, the statistic

$$\xi_T - T[h(\hat{\theta}_T) - H(\hat{\theta}_T)\tilde{\alpha}_T^0]'\hat{\Omega}_T^{-1}[h(\hat{\theta}_T) - H(\hat{\theta}_T)\tilde{\alpha}_T^0]$$

where $\tilde{\alpha}_T^0$ is given by (1.4), is asymptotically distributed under H_0 as χ^2 $(r - q)$.

Proof. See Appendix 2.

Thus, replacing α_0 by the estimator $\tilde{\alpha}_T^0$ in the random variable:

$$\xi_T^* = \boldsymbol{T}[h(\tilde{\theta}_T) - H(\tilde{\theta}_T)\alpha_0]'\tilde{\Omega}_T^{-1}[h(\tilde{\theta}_T) - H(\tilde{\theta}_T)\alpha_0]$$

whose asymptotic distribution is $\chi^2(r)$, provides a statistic ξ_T whose asymptotic distribution is still a χ^2, but with a number of degrees of freedom reduced by q.

4. The Test

From the previous results we immediately deduce a test procedure.

Definition 3. The generalized Wald test of the null hypothesis $H_0 = \{\exists\alpha: h(\theta) = H(\theta)\alpha\}]$ at the asymptotic level ε has a critical region given by $\{\xi_T > \chi^2_{1-\varepsilon}(r-q)\}$, where $\chi^2_{1-\varepsilon}(r-q)$ is the $(1-\varepsilon)$ quantile of the χ^2 distribution with $(r-q)$ degrees of freedom.

In fact, there are several test procedures corresponding to various possible choices for $\hat{\Omega}_T$. Among these choices, one leads to a particularly simple procedure since it involves only linear least-squares estimators. This procedure is as follows:

i. Regress by O.L.S. $h(\hat{\theta}_T)$ on the columns of $H(\hat{\theta}_T)$ and deduce the consistent estimator of α:

$\tilde{\alpha}_T = [H'(\hat{\theta}_T)]^{-1}H'(\hat{\theta}_T)^{-1}H'(\hat{\theta}_T)h(\hat{\theta}_T)$

ii. Compute $\hat{\Omega}_T = A(\tilde{\alpha}_T)Q(\hat{\theta}_T)A(\tilde{\alpha}_T)'$.

iii. Regress by G.L.S. $h(\hat{\theta}_T)$ on the columns of $H(\hat{\theta}_T)$, using the covariance matrix $\frac{\hat{\Omega}_T}{T}$. The generalized Wald statistic is simply what is usually called the "sum of squared residuals" in this regression, i.e., the squared norm of the vector of the residuals, this norm being computed with the metric corresponding to $T\hat{\Omega}_T^{-1}$

iv. Compare this statistic with $\chi^2_{1-\varepsilon}(r-q)$.

II. Constrained Estimation

1. The Classical Estimators

The information used in the previous test is basically contained in $\hat{\theta}_T$. Since this estimator asymptotically satisfies

$$\sqrt{T}(\hat{\theta}_T - \theta) \xrightarrow{d} N[0, Q(\theta)],$$

it is natural to determine the constrained estimators from the "likelihood" associated with this asymptotic distribution. Such estimators, denoted by $\hat{\theta}^0_T$, $\hat{\alpha}^0_T$, are obtained as solutions of

$$\begin{cases} \min\limits_{\theta,\alpha}(\hat{\theta}_T - \theta)'Q(\hat{\theta}_T)^{-1}(\hat{\theta}_T - \theta) \\ \text{under the constraints } h(\theta) - H(\theta)\alpha = 0. \end{cases} \tag{2.1}$$

We denote by $\hat{\mu}^0_T$ the values of the Lagrange multipliers associated with this problem.

We know, in particular, that, if the initial estimator $\hat{\theta}_T$ is asymptotically efficient under the maintained hypothesis $\hat{\theta}_T^0$ and $\hat{\alpha}_T^0$ are efficient under the null hypothesis (see Gouriéroux and Monfort 1989b, chapter X, section D).

If the Wald test leads us to accept the null hypothesis, it is useful to find simple constrained estimators whose asymptotic properties are satisfactory, for instance, asymptotically equivalent to that of the estimators $\hat{\theta}_T^0$ and $\hat{\alpha}_T^0$ introduced above. We shall see that such estimators can be obtained by linear regressions. Thus, not only the tests, but also the constrained estimation, can be implemented with standard linear least squares packages.

2. Estimators Based on the Q.G.L.S. Procedure

In order to compute the test statistic, we have used, in the second step, a Q.G.L.S. procedure. From this procedure we get another estimator of α:

$$\tilde{\alpha}_T^0 = [H'(\hat{\theta}_T)\hat{\Omega}_T^{-1}H(\hat{\theta}_T)]^{-1}H'(\hat{\theta}_T)\hat{\Omega}_T^{-1}h(\hat{\theta}_T). \tag{2.2}$$

The following result is a direct consequence of the algorithmic interpretation discussed in the following subsection.

Property 4. Under the null hypothesis $\tilde{\alpha}_T^0$ and $\hat{\alpha}_T^0$ are asymptotically equivalent:

$$\sqrt{T}(\tilde{\alpha}_T^0 - \alpha_0) = \sqrt{T}(\hat{\alpha}_T^0 - \alpha_0) + o_p(1).$$

Therefore we easily obtain a good estimator of the auxiliary parameter. This parameter is not sufficient to parameterize the null hypothesis and we may also need a good estimator of θ under H_0.

Let us consider the following program, where α is given:

$$\begin{cases} \operatorname*{Min}_{\theta}(\hat{\theta}_T - \theta)'Q(\hat{\theta}_T)^{-1}(\hat{\theta}_T - \theta) \\ h(\theta) - H(\theta)\alpha = 0 \end{cases} \Leftrightarrow \begin{cases} \operatorname*{Min}_{\theta}(\hat{\theta}_T - \theta)'Q(\hat{\theta}_T)^{-1}(\hat{\theta}_T - \theta) \\ a(\alpha) - A(\alpha)\theta = 0 \end{cases} \tag{2.3}$$

and let us denote by $\tilde{\theta}(\alpha) = \varphi(\hat{\theta}_T, \alpha)$ the solution of this program.

Comparing with (2.1), we immediately see that

$$\hat{\theta}_T^0 = \tilde{\theta}[\hat{\alpha}_T^0] = \varphi(\hat{\theta}_T, \hat{\alpha}_T^0).$$

Therefore, we have

$$\begin{aligned} \sqrt{T}(\hat{\theta}_T^0 - \theta_0) &= \sqrt{T}[\varphi(\hat{\theta}_T, \hat{\alpha}_T^0) - \theta_0] \\ &= \sqrt{T}[\varphi(\hat{\theta}_T, \tilde{\alpha}_T^0) - \theta_0] + o_p(1). \end{aligned}$$

Property 5. Let us consider the estimator $\tilde{\theta}_T^0$ solution of

$$\begin{cases} \underset{\theta}{\operatorname{Min}} (\hat{\theta}_T - \theta)' Q(\hat{\theta}_T)^{-1} (\hat{\theta}_T - \theta) \\ \text{under } a(\tilde{\alpha}_T^0) - A(\tilde{\alpha}_T^0)\theta = 0. \end{cases}$$

$\tilde{\theta}_T^0$ and $\hat{\theta}_T^0$ are asymptotically equivalent under H_0.

Note that the previous program reduces to a linear least-squares procedure under linear constraints.

3. Estimator Obtained by One Iteration of Newton's Method

How to explain the possibility of computing estimators with linear techniques, when the implicit constraints on θ are nonlinear? The results obtained are related to the method aiming at improving a consistent estimator with an iteration of Newton's method. Let us recall briefly the principle of this method.

Let us denote

$$\beta = \begin{bmatrix} \theta \\ \alpha \\ \mu \end{bmatrix}$$

and $\mathscr{L}(\beta)$ as the lagrangian associated with (2.1):

$$\mathscr{L}(\beta) = (\hat{\theta}_T - \theta)' Q(\hat{\theta}_T)^{-1} (\hat{\theta}_T - \theta) - \mu'[h(\theta) - H(\theta)\alpha]. \tag{2.4}$$

The constrained estimator $\hat{\beta}_T^0 = [\hat{\theta}_T^{0\prime}, \hat{\alpha}_T^{0\prime}, \hat{\mu}_T^{0\prime}]'$ converges, under H_0, to $\beta_0 = (\theta_0', \alpha_0', 0)'$ with the convergence rate $1/\sqrt{T}$; moreover it verifies the first-order condition

$$\frac{\partial \mathscr{L}}{\partial \beta}[\hat{\beta}_T^0] = 0. \tag{2.5}$$

Let $\hat{\beta}_T$ be an estimator converging to β_0 under H_0, with a convergence rate equal to $1/\sqrt{T}$; an iteration of Newton's method provides the new estimator:

$$\beta_T^* = \hat{\beta}_T - \left[\frac{\partial^2 \mathscr{L}}{\partial \beta\, \partial \beta'}(\hat{\beta}_T)\right]^{-1} \frac{\partial \mathscr{L}}{\partial \beta}(\hat{\beta}_T). \tag{2.6}$$

Using (2.5) it is easily seen that, under H_0,

$$\sqrt{T}(\beta_T^* - \beta_0) = \sqrt{T}(\hat{\beta}_T - \beta_0) - \left[\frac{\partial^2 \mathscr{L}}{\partial\beta\partial\beta'}(\hat{\beta}_T)\right]^{-1} \sqrt{T}\left[\frac{\partial \mathscr{L}}{\partial\beta}(\hat{\beta}_T) - \frac{\partial \mathscr{L}}{\partial\beta}(\hat{\beta}_T^0)\right]$$

$$= \sqrt{T}(\hat{\beta}_T - \beta_0) + \left[\frac{\partial^2 \mathscr{L}}{\partial\beta\partial\beta'}(\hat{\beta}_T)\right]^{-1} \frac{\partial^2 \mathscr{L}}{\partial\beta\partial\beta'}(\hat{\beta}_T)\sqrt{T}(\hat{\beta}_T^0 - \hat{\beta}_T)$$

$$+ o_p(1)$$

$$= \sqrt{T}(\hat{\beta}_T - \beta_0) + o_p(1).$$

The estimator given by (2.6) is asymptotically equivalent to $\hat{\beta}_T^0$ under H_0.

The simplifications appearing in the previous sections are mainly due to the easiness of computing (2.6) in our context.

(i) Let us first note that a consistent estimator of β_0, under H_0, is

$$\hat{\beta}_T = \begin{bmatrix} \hat{\theta}_T \\ \tilde{\alpha}_T \\ 0 \end{bmatrix}. \tag{2.7}$$

(ii) Let us now consider the first and second derivatives of the lagrangian. We have

$$\begin{cases} \dfrac{\partial \mathscr{L}}{\partial\theta}(\beta) = -2Q(\hat{\theta}_T)(\hat{\theta}_T - \theta) + A(\alpha)'\mu, \\[2ex] \dfrac{\partial \mathscr{L}}{\partial\alpha}(\beta) = +H(\theta)'\mu, \\[2ex] \dfrac{\partial \mathscr{L}}{\partial\mu}(\beta) = -[h(\theta) - H(\theta)\alpha], \end{cases}$$

$$\begin{cases} \dfrac{\partial^2 \mathscr{L}}{\partial\theta\partial\theta'}(\beta) = +2Q(\hat{\theta}_T), & \dfrac{\partial^2 \mathscr{L}}{\partial\theta\partial\alpha'}(\beta) = \dfrac{\partial}{\partial\alpha}[A(\alpha)'\mu]', \\[2ex] \dfrac{\partial^2 \mathscr{L}}{\partial\theta\partial\mu'}(\beta) = A(\alpha)', & \dfrac{\partial^2 \mathscr{L}}{\partial\alpha\partial\alpha'}(\beta) = 0, \\[2ex] \dfrac{\partial^2 \mathscr{L}}{\partial\alpha\partial\mu'}(\beta) = H(\theta)', & \dfrac{\partial^2 \mathscr{L}}{\partial\mu\partial\mu'}(\beta) = 0. \end{cases}$$

System (2.6) can be written as

$$\begin{bmatrix} 2Q(\hat{\theta}_T) & 0 & A(\tilde{\alpha}_T)' \\ 0 & 0 & H(\hat{\theta}_T)' \\ A(\tilde{\alpha}_T) & H(\hat{\theta}_T) & 0 \end{bmatrix} \begin{bmatrix} \theta_T^* - \hat{\theta}_T \\ \alpha_T^* - \tilde{\alpha}_T \\ \mu_T^* \end{bmatrix} = \begin{bmatrix} 0 \\ 0 \\ h(\hat{\theta}_T) - H(\hat{\theta}_T)\tilde{\alpha}_T \end{bmatrix},$$

or, in an extensive form, as

$$\begin{cases} 2Q(\hat{\theta}_T)(\theta_T^* - \hat{\theta}_T) + A(\tilde{\alpha}_T)'\mu_T^* = 0 \\ H(\hat{\theta}_T)'\mu_T^* = 0 \\ A(\tilde{\alpha}_T)(\theta_T^* - \hat{\theta}_T) + H(\hat{\theta}_T)(\alpha_T^* - \tilde{\alpha}_T) = h(\hat{\theta}_T) - H(\hat{\theta}_T)\tilde{\alpha}_T. \end{cases}$$

From the first equation, we get

$$\theta_T^* - \hat{\theta}_T = -Q(\hat{\theta}_T)^{-1}A(\tilde{\alpha}_T)'\frac{\mu_T^*}{2}, \tag{2.8}$$

and, using this expression in the third equation, we obtain

$$-\hat{\Omega}_T\frac{\mu_T^*}{2} + H(\hat{\theta}_T)(\alpha_T^* - \tilde{\alpha}_T) = h(\hat{\theta}_T) - H(\hat{\theta}_T)\tilde{\alpha}_T,$$

or

$$\frac{\mu_T^*}{2} = \hat{\Omega}_T^{-1}H(\hat{\theta}_T)(\alpha_T^* - \tilde{\alpha}_T) - \hat{\Omega}_T^{-1}[h(\hat{\theta}_T) - H(\hat{\theta}_T)\tilde{\alpha}_T]. \tag{2.9}$$

Multiplying both sides by $H(\hat{\theta}_T)'$ and using the second equation of the system, we get

$$\begin{aligned} \alpha_T^* &= \tilde{\alpha}_T + [H'(\hat{\theta}_T)\hat{\Omega}_T^{-1}H(\hat{\theta}_T)]^{-1}H'(\hat{\theta}_T)\hat{\Omega}_T^{-1}[h(\hat{\theta}_T) - H(\hat{\theta}_T)\tilde{\alpha}_T] \\ \alpha_T^* &= [H'(\hat{\theta}_T)\hat{\Omega}_T^{-1}H(\hat{\theta}_T)]^{-1}H'(\hat{\theta}_T)\Omega_T^{-1}h(\hat{\theta}_T). \end{aligned} \tag{2.10}$$

We immediately note that this estimator is simply the estimator $\tilde{\alpha}_T^0$ obtained by the Q.G.L.S. procedure in the second step. Therefore $\tilde{\alpha}_T^0$ is asymptotically equivalent to $\hat{\alpha}_T^0$, which provides a proof of Property 4.

III. Tests of Rational Distributed Lags

Let us consider the linear model

$$Y_t = \varphi' z_t + \theta_0 x_t + \theta_1 x_{t-1} + \cdots + \theta_k x_{t-k} + u_t, \ t = 1, \ldots, T,$$

where z_T, $(x_t, \ldots, x_{t-k})'$ are vectors of exogenous variables, φ, $\theta = (\theta_0, \ldots, \theta_k)'$ are vectors of unknown parameters, and u_t, $t = 1, \ldots, T$ are zero-mean, serially uncorrelated, homoscedastic disturbances.

We introduce the notation $\Theta(B) = \theta_0 + \theta_1 B + \cdots + \theta_k B^k$ where B is the lag operator and we want to test the null hypothesis under which $\Theta(B)$ is equal to the $k + 1$ first terms of the series expansion of

$$\frac{C(B)}{A(B)},$$

where

$$C(B) = c_0 + c_1 B + \cdots + c_s B^s$$

and

$$A(B) = 1 + \alpha_1 B + \cdots + \alpha_q B^q,$$

s and q being integers such that $s + q < k$.

This condition can be written

$$(1 + \alpha_1 B + \cdots + \alpha_q B^q)(\theta_0 + \theta_1 B + \cdots + \theta_k B^k + \theta^*_{k+1} B^{k+1} + \cdots)$$
$$= (c_0 + c_1 B + \cdots + c_s B^s).$$

The constraints imposed on the parameter θ are

$\exists c_0, \ldots, c_s, \alpha_1, \ldots, \alpha_q$ such that

$$c_0 = \theta_0$$

$$c_1 = \theta_1 + \alpha_1 \theta_0$$

$$c_s = \theta_s + \alpha_1 \theta_{s-1} + \cdots + \alpha_q \theta_{s-q}$$

$$0 = \theta_{s+1} + \alpha_1 \theta_s + \cdots + \alpha_q \theta_{s+1-q}$$

$$0 = \theta_k + \alpha_1 \theta_{k-1} + \cdots + \alpha_q \theta_{k-q}$$

with, by convention, $\theta_i = 0$ if $i < 0$.

Let us assume that, for any θ in H_0, the $k - s$ last equations uniquely determine $\alpha_1, \ldots, \alpha_q$; then the $s + 1$ first equations are automatically satisfied and can be omitted. Finally the constraints can be written

$$\begin{cases} \exists \alpha_1, \ldots, \alpha_q \text{ such that} \\ 0 = \theta_j + \alpha_1 \theta_{j-1} + \cdots + \alpha_q \theta_{j-q}, \qquad j = s+1, \ldots, k \\ \text{with } \theta_i = 0 \text{ if } i < 0. \end{cases}$$

This constraint has the form (1.2). The test procedure of section I can be applied by taking $\hat{\theta}_T$ equal to the O.L.S. estimator; the test statistic asymptotically follows under H_0 a χ^2 distribution with $k - s - q$ degrees of freedom. The methods of section II provide estimators of α and θ under H_0.

Let us consider some particular cases:

(i) $s = 0; q = 1$ *(Koyck lags).* The constraints are

$$\begin{cases} \exists\alpha\colon \theta_1 + \alpha\theta_0 = 0 \\ \text{-----------} \\ \theta_k + \alpha\theta_{k-1} = 0. \end{cases}$$

The asymptotic distribution of the test statistic under H_0 is $\chi^2(k-1)$.

(ii) $s = q = 1$. The constraints are

$$\begin{cases} \exists\alpha\colon \theta_2 + \alpha\theta_1 = 0 \\ \text{---------} \\ \theta_k + \alpha\theta_{k-1} = 0 \end{cases}$$

The asymptotic distribution of the test statistic under H_0 is $\chi^2(k-2)$.

(iii) $s = 0; q = 2$.

$$\begin{cases} \exists\alpha_1, \alpha_2\colon \theta_1 + \alpha_1\theta_0 = 0 \\ \qquad\theta_2 + \alpha_1\theta_1 + \alpha_2\theta_0 = 0 \\ \text{------------------} \\ \qquad\theta_k + \alpha_1\theta_{k-1} + \alpha_2\theta_{k-2} = 0 \end{cases}$$

The asymptotic distribution of the test statistic under H_0 is $\chi^2(k-2)$.

(iv) $s = 1; q = 2$.

$$\begin{cases} E\alpha_1;\alpha_2\colon \theta_2 + \alpha_1\theta_1 + \alpha_2\theta_0 = 0 \\ \text{------------------} \\ \qquad\theta_k + \alpha_1\theta_{k-1} + \alpha_2\theta_{k-2} = 0 \end{cases}$$

The asymptotic distribution of the test statistic under H_0 is $\chi^2(k-3)$.

Let us note that this kind of constraint associated with $\alpha_1 = -2$, $\alpha_1 = 1$ corresponds to Almon's formulation of degree 1. Therefore a test on α_1 and α_2 provides a test of this formulation.

IV. Test of Instrumental Variables Relevance

Let us consider a structural equation of a simultaneous equations system:

$$y_t = x_t'\alpha + u_t, \qquad t = 1, \ldots, T$$

where α is a vector of size q, x_t is a vector of exogenous or endogenous variables, and u_t, $t = 1, \ldots, T$ are zero-mean, serially uncorrelated disturbances whose variance is σ^2.

We want to test the null hypothesis requiring that a vector z_t, of size r, is a vector of instrumental variables, i.e., a vector satisfying

$$\operatorname*{plim}_T \frac{1}{T} \sum_{t=1}^{T} z_t u_t = 0$$

or

$$\exists\alpha\colon \operatorname*{plim}_T \frac{1}{T} \sum_{t=1}^{T} z_t y_t = \operatorname*{plim}_T \sum_{t=1}^{T} z_t x_t' \alpha.$$

With obvious notations, this can be written as

$$\exists\alpha\colon m_{zy} = M_{zx}\alpha. \tag{4.1}$$

This constraint has the form 1.2, the θ vector being the vector

$$\begin{pmatrix} \mathrm{vec} M_{zx}' \\ m_{zy} \end{pmatrix},$$

whose size is $r(q + 1)$. This parameter is estimated by

$$\hat{\theta}_T = \frac{1}{T} \begin{bmatrix} \mathrm{vec} \sum_{t=1}^{T} x_t z_t' \\ \sum_{t=1}^{T} z_t y_t \end{bmatrix}.$$

The matrix $H(\theta)$ appearing in (1.1) is here M_{zx}, which, from Assumption A_1, has a rank equal to q; this means that the orthogonal projections of the components of x_t on the subspace of L_2 spanned by the components of z_t are linearly independent.

Condition (4.1) can also be written

$$(I_r \otimes \alpha') \,\mathrm{vec} M_{zx}' - m_{zy} = 0 \tag{4.2}$$

Here $A(\alpha)$ is the matrix

$$(I_r \otimes \alpha', -I_r),$$

whose rank is always r; this implies that Assumption A_2 is satisfied.

Under classical conditions, the asymptotic covariance matrix of

$$\frac{1}{\sqrt{T}} \sum_{t=1}^{T} z_t u_t$$

is

$$\sigma^2 \operatorname*{plim}_T \frac{1}{T} \sum_{t=1}^{T} z_t z_t',$$

which does not depend on α. Therefore the generalized least squares procedure can be directly applied:

$$\min_\alpha \frac{1}{\sigma^2} \left[\frac{1}{T} \sum_{t=1}^{T} z_t y_t - \frac{1}{T} \sum_{t=1}^{T} z_t x_t \alpha \right] \left[\frac{1}{T} \sum_{t=1}^{T} z_t z_t' \right]^{-1} \times \left[\frac{1}{T} \sum_{t=1}^{T} z_t y_t - \frac{1}{T} \sum_{t=1}^{T} z_t x_t \alpha \right].$$

This approach can be used as soon as the number of observations is large enough to make the matrix $(1/T)\sum_{t=1}^{T} z_t z_t'$ invertible. We find the usual two-stage least-squares formula (see Malinvaud 1978, chapter 20, section 5):

$$\tilde{\alpha}_T^0 = [X'Z(Z'Z)^{-1}Z'X]^{-1}X'Z(Z'Z)^{-1}Z'y,$$

where X (resp. Z) is a matrix whose rows are x_t' (resp. z_t') and y is the vector whose components are y_t, $t = 1, \ldots, T$.

Using the notations $\hat{u} = y - X\tilde{\alpha}_T^0$ and $\hat{\sigma}^2 = (1/T)\|y - X\tilde{\alpha}_T^0\|^2$, the test statistic is

$$\xi_T = \frac{1}{\hat{\sigma}_T^2} \hat{u}'Z(Z'Z)^{-1}Z'\hat{u}$$

and the critical region of asymptotic size 5% is

$$\{\xi_T \geqslant \chi^2_{.95}(r - q)\}.$$

ξ_T is also equal to TR^2, where R^2 is the determination coefficient in the regression of $\hat{u}$ on the columns of Z.

Let us also note that the two-stage least-squares estimator can be seen as a particular case of the generalized moments method (Hansen 1982). The test described above is directly based on the optimal value of the criterion used in this method (Newey 1985).

V. Overidentification Test

This kind of application has been consider in Szroeter's (1983) article on the generalized Wald test. Let us recall the basic principle of this test.

We consider the reduced form of a simultaneous-equations model:

$$y_t = \Pi x_t + v_t,$$

where y_t is a g-vector of endogenous variables, x_t is a k-vector of exogenous variables, and the v_t's are zero-mean, non-serially correlated disturbance vectors, whose covariance matrices do not depend on t.

We want to test the null hypothesis H_0 assuming that this system is compatible with the structural form

$$A_1 y_t + A_2 x_t = u_t,$$

with $R\ \mathrm{vec}A = r$, $A = (A_1, A_2)$, where R is a known matrix whose size is $l \times g(g + k)$ of rank l and r is a known vector of size l.

This hypothesis can be written

$$\begin{cases} \exists A_1, A_2 & A_1 \Pi + A_2 = 0 \\ & R\ \mathrm{vec}A = r. \end{cases}$$

The equations $R\ \mathrm{vec}A = r$ are equivalent to

$$\mathrm{vec}A = a + S\alpha,$$

where a is a particular solution, S is a matrix whose size is $g(g \times k) \times [g(g + k) - l)$, which is of full column rank and whose columns are a basis of the kernel of R. Therefore the constraints can be written

$$\exists \alpha\colon A_1(\alpha)\Pi + A_2(\alpha) = 0,$$

or

$$[I_k \otimes A_1(\alpha)]\mathrm{vec}\Pi + \mathrm{vec}A_2(\alpha) = 0.$$

These constraints are of the form (1.2) with $\theta = \mathrm{vec}\Pi$.

$A(\alpha)$ is here $I_k \otimes A_1(\alpha)$, which is of full column rank (assumption A_2) if, and only if, $A_1(\alpha)$ is invertible: this is the usual coherency (or solvability) condition. Assumption A_1 imposes the uniqueness of the solution in α for any given θ; it is the identifiability condition

$$\begin{bmatrix} \Pi' \otimes I_9 & I_{9k} \\ & R \end{bmatrix} \text{ of full column rank,}$$

or

$$\mathrm{rank}\,[(I_9 \otimes A)R'] = g^2.$$

The general test and estimation methods of the previous sections apply directly. Since the same explanatory variables appear in all the equations of the reduced form, the overall G.L.S. estimator of Π is the same as the one obtained by the O.L.S. method applied to each equation. This estimator is the basic estimator for the test procedure and for the constrained estimation of Π and A. The test statistic is asymptotically distributed as a χ^2 whose number of degrees of freedom is

$$r - q = g \times k - [g(g + k) - l] = l - g^2.$$

The estimation of A (and Π) under H_0 requires only the O.L.S. or G.L.S. method under linear constraints; nevertheless it is asymptotically equivalent to the full-information maximum-likelihood estimator under the normality assumption.

This test procedure can be extended to a sequential testing procedure of predeterminedness, exogeneity, noncausality, and overidentification in dynamic models (see Monfort-Rabemananjara 1987).

VI. Test of the Rational Expectation Hypothesis

In macroeconomic models, the dynamics is often introduced through the expectations of some variables. Since these expectations are generally unobservable, it is necessary to define a model explaining their formation.

In this section, we consider a univariate dynamic linear model in which expectations appear. Following the same approach as in Wallis 1980 and Pesaran 1981, we derive the constraints on the reduced form, which are implied by the rational expectation hypothesis. These constraints can take a bilinear mixed form, to which we can apply the generalized Wald test.

1. Reduced Form Associated with the Rational Expectation Hypothesis

(i) The structural form. The structural model consists in a relationship giving the value y_t of the endogenous variable, in terms of the expectation ${}_{t-1}\hat{y}_t$ of this variable made at time $t - 1$, the values $x_t = (x_{1t}, \ldots, x_{kt})'$ of K exogenous variables and α disturbance u_t:

$$y_t = a\,{}_{t-1}\hat{y}_t + b'x_t + u_t. \tag{6.1}$$

We assume that the process of the disturbance is a sequenece of zero-mean, independent variables whose variances are σ^2 and which is independent from the process x_t.

Under the rational expectation hypothesis, the model is completed by imposing that ${}_{t-1}\hat{y}_t$ is equal to the best prediction of y_t based the information I_{t-1} available at the previous date. On the sequel, we assume that this information is

$$I_{t-1} = \{y_{t-1}, x_{t-1}, y_{t-2}, x_{t-2}, \ldots\}. \tag{6.2}$$

Thus, the rational expectation is

$$_{t-1}\hat{y}_t = E(y_t/I_{t-1}). \tag{6.3}$$

(ii) The reduced form. Replacing in (6.1) the expectation by its expression, we get

$$y_t = aE(y_t/I_{t-1}) + b'x_t + u_t.$$

Taking the conditional expectation of each side, we get

$$E(y_t/I_{t-1}) = aE(y_t/I_{t-1} + b'E(x_t/I_{t-1})$$

and we deduce

$$y_t = \frac{ab'}{1-a} E(x_t/I_{t-1}) + b'x_t + u_t. \tag{6.4}$$

Thus, we have transformed the problem of the formation of the expectations of the endogenous variable into that of the expectations of the exogenous variables. Let us assume that the expectations of the exogenous variables are linear functions of observable variables z, which may include lagged exogenous variables

$$E(x_t/I_{t-1}) = Cz_t, \tag{6.5}$$

where C is a $(K \times L)$ matrix.

Moreover, we assume that the prediction error,

$$v_t = x_t - E(x_t/I_{t-1}), \tag{6.6}$$

is a white noise whose covariance matrix is Σ. Since v is a function of the past values of y and the present and past values of x, we see that u_t and v_t are uncorrelated.

From (6.4), (6.5), and (6.6), we get

$$\begin{cases} y_t \dfrac{b'C}{1-a} z_t + u_t + b'v_t \\ x_t = Cz_t + v_t \end{cases} \tag{6.7}$$

with

$$V\begin{pmatrix} u_t \\ v_t \end{pmatrix} = \begin{pmatrix} \sigma^2 & 0 \\ 0 & \Sigma \end{pmatrix}.$$

2. Constraints on the Parameters

The form just obtained can be compared with the unrestricted reduced form

$$\begin{cases} y_t = \Pi_1 z_t + w_{1t} \\ x_t = \Pi_2 z_t + w_{2t} \end{cases} \tag{6.8}$$

where Π_1 and Π_2 are unconstrained as well as the covariance matrix

$$V\begin{pmatrix} w_{1t} \\ w_{2t} \end{pmatrix} = \begin{pmatrix} \Omega_{11} & \Omega_{12} \\ \Omega_{21} & \Omega_{22} \end{pmatrix}.$$

Under the assumption of rational expectation, the reduced form parameters are linked to the structural parameters by the equations

$$\begin{cases} \Pi_2 = C, \Pi_1 = \dfrac{b'C}{1-a} \\ \\ \Omega_{11} = \sigma^2 + b'\Sigma b, \Omega_{12} = b'\Sigma, \Omega_{22} = \Sigma. \end{cases} \tag{6.9}$$

The unrestricted reduced form depends on $L + LK + [K(K+1)/2] + 1 + K$ parameters, whereas the restricted form depends on $K + LK + 1 + [K(K+1)/2] + 1$ parameters. Therefore the rational expectation hypothesis can be characterized by $L-1$ independent constraints on the reduced-form parameters.

This hypothesis can be put under a mixed form which is bilinear with respect to $\theta = (\Pi_1, \Pi_2, \Omega_{11}, \Omega_{12}, \Omega_{22})$ and to $\alpha = (\alpha_0, \alpha_1, \ldots, \alpha_k)'$:

$$H_0 = \{\exists \alpha_1, \ldots, \alpha_k \in \mathbb{R}, \alpha_0 \in \mathbb{R}: \Omega_{12} = (\alpha_1, \ldots, \alpha_k)\Omega_{22}$$
$$\text{and } (\alpha_1, \ldots, \alpha_k)\Pi_2 - \alpha_0 \Pi_1 = 0\}. \tag{6.10}$$

When the null hypothesis is satisfied we have $(\alpha_1, \ldots, \alpha_k) = b'$ and $\alpha_0 = 1 - a$; therefore the auxiliary parameters have an interesting interpretation since they provide the structural form (6.1).

3. The Test Statistic

Let $\hat{\Pi}_1, \hat{\Pi}_2, \hat{\Omega}_{12}, \hat{\Omega}_{22}$ be the usual estimators of $\Pi_1, \Pi_2, \Omega_{12}, \Omega_{22}$ obtained by the O.L.S. method applied to the unrestricted model. We know that $(\hat{\Pi}_1, \hat{\Pi}_2)$ and $(\hat{\Omega}_{12}, \hat{\Omega}_{22})$ are asymptotically uncorrelated.

Denoting $(\alpha_1, \ldots, \alpha_k)$ by $\bar{\alpha}$, we deduce that the asymptotic covariance matrix of

$$\begin{pmatrix} \hat{\Pi}_2'\bar{\alpha}' - \Pi_1'\alpha_0 \\ \hat{\Omega}_{21} - \hat{\Omega}_{22}\bar{\alpha}' \end{pmatrix}$$

is block-diagonal. Let us denote by

$$\begin{pmatrix} \hat{S}_1 & 0 \\ 0 & \hat{S}_2 \end{pmatrix}$$

a consistent estimator of this matrix under H_0.

The test statistic is equal to T times the sum of squared residuals of the regression

$$\begin{pmatrix} 0 \\ \hat{\Omega}_{21} \end{pmatrix} = \begin{pmatrix} \hat{\Pi}_2' & -\hat{\Pi}_1' \\ \hat{\Omega}_{22} & 0 \end{pmatrix} \begin{pmatrix} \bar{\alpha}' \\ \alpha_0 \end{pmatrix} + \begin{pmatrix} \hat{v}_1 \\ \hat{v}_2 \end{pmatrix}$$

with

$$E\begin{pmatrix} \hat{v}_1 \\ \hat{v}_2 \end{pmatrix} = 0, \; V\begin{pmatrix} \hat{v}_1 \\ \hat{v}_2 \end{pmatrix} = \begin{pmatrix} \hat{S}_1 & 0 \\ 0 & \hat{S}_2 \end{pmatrix}.$$

Let us introduce the following notations:

$$\|\hat{\Pi}_2\|^2 = \hat{\Pi}_2\hat{S}_1^{-1}\hat{\Pi}_2', \; \|\hat{\Pi}_1\|^2 = \hat{\Pi}_1\hat{S}_1^{-1}\hat{\Pi}_1',$$
$$\langle\hat{\Pi}_1, \hat{\Pi}_2\rangle = \hat{\Pi}_1\hat{S}_1^{-1}\hat{\Pi}_2' = \langle\hat{\Pi}_2, \hat{\Pi}_1\rangle'$$

and, similarly,

$$\|\hat{\Omega}_{22}\|^2 = \hat{\Omega}_{22}\hat{S}_2^{-1}\hat{\Omega}_{22}, \; \|\hat{\Omega}_{21}\|^2 = \hat{\Omega}_{12}\hat{S}_2^{-1}\hat{\Omega}_{21},$$
$$\langle\hat{\Omega}_{22}, \hat{\Omega}_{21}\rangle = \hat{\Omega}_{22}\hat{S}_2^{-1}\hat{\Omega}_{21} = \langle\hat{\Omega}_{12}, \hat{\Omega}_{22}\rangle'.$$

We see that the test statistic is

$$\xi_T = T\{\|\hat{\Omega}_{21}\|^2 - \langle\hat{\Omega}_{12}, \hat{\Omega}_{22}\rangle\{\|\hat{\Pi}_2\|^2 - \langle\hat{\Pi}_2, \hat{\Pi}_1\rangle$$
$$(\|\hat{\Pi}_1\|^2)^{-1}\langle\hat{\Pi}_1, \hat{\Pi}_2\rangle + \|\hat{\Omega}_{22}\|^2\}\langle\hat{\Omega}_{22}, \hat{\Omega}_{21}\rangle\}. \tag{6.11}$$

VII. Separability and Homothesis of Translog Functions

Among the functional forms of production functions, one of the most popular is the translog one proposed by Christensen, Jorgenson, and Lau (1973). Let us consider the case of three inputs X_1, X_2, X_3, and one output Y, the idea is to approximate the true production function:

$$\log Y = F[\log X_1, \log X_2, \log X_3] \tag{7.1}$$

by its second-order expansion around $X_1 = X_2 = X_3 = 1$:

$$\log Y = \theta_0 + \sum_{i=1}^{3} \theta_i \log X_i + \tfrac{1}{2} \sum_{i=1}^{3} \sum_{j=1}^{3} \theta_{ij} \log X_i \log X_j \tag{7.2}$$

with $\theta_{ij} = \theta_{ji}$.

1. Separability

Let us first assume that the true production function has the translog form (7.2).

The groups of inputs (1, 2) and 3 are separable if the production function F can be written

$$F[\log X_1, \log X_2, \log X_3] = f[\log G(\log X_1, \log X_2), \log X_3], \tag{7.3}$$

where G is an aggregation function.

It is easily seen, using Leontief conditions, that this separability occurs in two cases.

(i) There is a linear separability if f is linear and if $\log G$ is quadratic in $\log X_1$, $\log X_2$. These constraints of linear separability are (see Berndt and Christensen 1973)

$$\theta_{12} = \theta_{13} = 0. \tag{7.4}$$

In this case, the production function appears as a Cobb-Douglas function of translog aggregates.

(ii) There is nonlinear separability if f is quadratic with respect to $\log G$, $\log X_3$ and if $\log G$ is linear with respect to $\log X_1$, $\log X_2$.

The nonlinear separability constraints are (see Berndt and Christensen 1973)

$$\frac{\theta^1}{\theta_2} = \frac{\theta_{13}}{\theta_{23}} = \frac{\theta_{11}}{\theta_{12}} = \frac{\theta_{12}}{\theta_{22}}. \tag{7.5}$$

In this case, the production function appears as a translog function of Cobb-Douglas aggregates.

It is clear that the hypothesis of nonlinear separability has a bilinear mixed form:

$$H_0 = \{\exists \alpha : \theta_2 = \theta_1 \alpha, \theta_{2i} = \theta_{1i} \alpha, \qquad i = 1, 2, 3\}. \tag{7.6}$$

2. Local Separability

The separability condition of a translog function implies, as seen above, very restrictive forms of the production function. In fact, if we retain the interpretation of this function as a second-order expansion, it seems preferable to examine under what conditions the representation (7.2) is the expansion of a separable function:

$$F[\log X_1, \log X_2, \log X_3] = f[\log G(\log X_1, \log X_2), \log X_3].$$

So it is sufficient to write the separability conditions around $X_1 = X_2 = X_3 = 1$. These conditions have been derived by Denny and Fuss (1977). They are

$$\frac{\theta_1}{\theta_2} = \frac{\theta_{13}}{\theta_{23}}. \tag{7.7}$$

The nonlinear local separability hypothesis is characterized by the bilinear mixed form

$$H_0 = \{\exists\alpha\colon \theta_2 = \theta_1\alpha, \theta_{23} = \theta_{13}\alpha\} \tag{7.8}$$

and is implied by (7.6).

3. Local Homothesis

The same approach can be followed for the homothesis property (see Hayes 1986). Function F is said to be homothetic if

$$F[\log X_1, \log X_2, \log X_3] = f[\log H(X_1, X_2, X_3)], \tag{7.9}$$

where H is homogeneous of degree one.

The first- and second-order conditions implied by (7.9) are

$$\begin{cases} \dfrac{\partial \log Y}{\partial \log X_i} = f' \dfrac{\partial \log H}{\partial \log X_i}, \qquad i = 1, 2, 3, \ldots \\[2ex] \dfrac{\partial^2 \log Y}{\partial \log X_i\, \partial \log X_j} = f' \dfrac{\partial^2 \log H}{\partial \log X_i\, \partial \log X_j} + f'' \dfrac{\partial \log H}{\partial \log X_i} \dfrac{\partial \log H}{\partial \log X_j}, \\[2ex] \quad i, j = 1, 2, 3. \end{cases}$$

From the homogeneity of H we obtain

$$\sum_{i=1}^{3} \frac{\partial \log H}{\partial \log X_i} = 1, \qquad \sum_{j=1}^{3} \frac{\partial^2 \log H}{\partial \log X_i\, \partial \log X_j} = 0$$

and, therefore,

$$\frac{\partial \log Y}{\partial \log X_i} \cdot \frac{f''}{f'} = \sum_{j=1}^{3} \frac{\partial^2 \log Y}{\partial \log X_i \, \partial \log X_j}, \qquad i = 1, 2, 3.$$

These conditions, evaluated at $X_1 = X_2 = X_3 = 1$, are the only ones implied by the homethesis condition. Denoting

$$\alpha = \frac{f''[\log H(1, 1, 1)]}{f'[\log H(1, 1, 1)]},$$

we see that the local homethesis hypothesis has the following bilinear mixed form:

$$H_0^* = \left\{ \exists \alpha \colon \sum_{j=1}^{3} \theta_{ij} = \alpha \theta_i, \qquad i = 1, 2, 3 \right\}. \tag{7.10}$$

VIII. Conclusion

The examples clearly show that a nonlinear constraint on a parameter θ often has a bilinear mixed form with respect to θ and an auxiliary parameter α. When it is the case, it is strongly recommended that this mixed form be used, since it provides particularly simple estimation and test procedures. These procedures require only linear least squares and, if the unconstrained estimator is asymptotically efficient, they lead to test and constrained estimation procedures that are asymptotically optimal.

Appendix 1: Asymptotic Equivalent of $\sqrt{T}[h(\theta_T) - H(\theta_T)\tilde{\alpha}_T^0] = \sqrt{T} Z_T$

We have

$$\sqrt{T}[h(\hat{\theta}_T) - H(\hat{\theta}_T)\tilde{\alpha}_T^0]$$
$$= \sqrt{T}[h(\hat{\theta}_T) - H(\hat{\theta}_T)[H(\hat{\theta}_T)' \hat{\Omega}_T^{-1} H(\hat{\theta}_T)]^{-1} H(\hat{\theta}_T)' \hat{\Omega}_T^{-1} h(\hat{\theta}_T)].$$

It is well known that $\hat{\Omega}^{-1}$ can be replaced by Ω_0^{-1}, therefore we have to find an equivalent to

$$\sqrt{T}[h(\hat{\theta}_T) - H(\hat{\theta}_T)[H(\hat{\theta}_T)'\Omega_0^{-1}H(\hat{\theta}_T)]^{-1}H(\hat{\theta}_T)'\Omega_0^{-1}h(\hat{\theta}_T)]$$
$$= \sqrt{T}[h(\hat{\theta}_T) - M(\hat{\theta}_T)h(\hat{\theta}_T)],$$

where $M(\hat{\theta}_T)$ is the orthogonal projector on the space spanned by the columns of $H(\hat{\theta}_T)$, the orthogonality being the one associated with Ω_0^{-1}.

A first-order expansion around θ_0 gives

$$\sqrt{T}[h(\hat{\theta}_T) - M(\hat{\theta}_T)h(\hat{\theta}_T)]$$

$$= \sqrt{T}[Id - M(\hat{\theta}_T)]h(\hat{\theta}_T)$$

$$= [Id - M(\theta_0)]\frac{\partial h}{\partial \theta'}(\theta_0)\sqrt{T}(\hat{\theta}_T - \theta_0)$$

$$- \sum_{j=1}^{P} \sqrt{T}(\hat{\theta}_{jT} - \theta_{j0})\frac{\partial M}{\partial \theta_j}(\theta_0)h(\theta_0) + o_P(1).$$

Since $M(\theta)$ is a projector, we have

$$M(\theta)H(\theta) = H(\theta).$$

Taking the derivative with respect to θ_j, we have

$$\frac{\partial M}{\partial \theta_j}(\theta_0)H(\theta_0) + M(\theta_0)\frac{\partial H}{\partial \theta_j}(\theta_0) = \frac{\partial H(\theta_0)}{\partial \theta_j}$$

and

$$\frac{\partial M}{\partial \theta_j}(\theta_0)H(\theta_0)\alpha_0 = [Id - M(\theta_0)\frac{\partial H}{\partial \theta_j}(\theta_0)\alpha_0.$$

Using this relation, the expansion becomes

$$\sqrt{T}[h(\hat{\theta}_T) - M(\hat{\theta}_T)h(\hat{\theta}_T)]$$

$$= [Id - M(\theta_0)]\left[\frac{\partial h}{\partial \theta'}(\theta_0) - \sum_{k=1}^{p}\frac{\partial H_k}{\partial \theta'}(\theta_0)\alpha_{k0}\right]\sqrt{T}[(\hat{\theta}_T - \theta_0) + o_p(1)$$

$$= [Id - M(\theta_0)]\sqrt{T}[h(\hat{\theta}_T) - H(\hat{\theta}_T)\alpha_0] + o_p(1).$$

Appendix 2: Associated Quadratic Form

We have

$$\xi_t = T[h(\hat{\theta}_T) - H(\hat{\theta}_T)\tilde{\alpha}_T^0]'\hat{\Omega}_T^{-1}[h(\hat{\theta}_T) - H(\hat{\theta}_T)\tilde{\alpha}_T^0]$$

$$= T[h(\hat{\theta}_T) - H(\hat{\theta}_T)\tilde{\alpha}_T^0]'\Omega_0^{-1}[(h(\hat{\theta}_T) - H(\hat{\theta}_T)\tilde{\alpha}_T^0] + o_p(1)$$

$$= T[h(\hat{\theta}_T) - H(\hat{\theta}_T)\alpha_0]'(Id - M_0)'\Omega_0^{-1}(Id - M_0)[h(\hat{\theta}_T) - H(\hat{\theta}_T)\alpha_0] + o_p(1).$$

Since

$M_0^2 = M_0$ and $(Id - M_0)'\Omega_0^{-1}M_0 = 0$,

we obtain

$$(Id - M_0)\Omega_0(Id - M_0)'(Id - M_0)'(Id - M_0)'\Omega_0^{-1}(Id - M_0)(Id - M_0)\Omega_0 \times (Id - M_0)'$$
$$= (Id - M_0)\Omega_0(Id - M_0)'\Omega_0^{-1}(Id - M_0)\Omega_0(Id - M_0)'$$
$$= (Id - M_0)\Omega_0(Id - M_0)'.$$

This means that $(Id - M_0)'\Omega_0^{-1}(Id - M_0)$ is a generalized inverse of $(Id - M_0)\Omega_0(Id - M_0)'$. Since $Z_t \xrightarrow{d} N[0, \Sigma]$, we have

$$Z_T'\Sigma^- Z_T \xrightarrow{d} \chi^2(\text{rank } \Sigma),$$

and property 2 follows since

$$\text{rank } [(Id - M_0)\Omega_0(Id - M_0)'] = \text{rank}(Id - M_0) = r - q.$$

References

Andrews, P. 1986. Asymptotic Results for Generalized Wald Tests. Cowles Foundation, 761R.

Berndt, E., and Christensen, L. 1973. "The Internal Structure of Functional Relationship: Separability, Substitution and Aggregation." *Review of Economic Studies* 40: 403–410.

Christensen, L., Jorgenson, D., and Lau, L. 1973. "Transcendental Logarithmic Production Frontiers." *Review of Economics and Statistics* 55: 28–42.

Denny, M., and Fuss, M. 1977. "The Use of Approximation Analysis to Test for Separability and the Existence of Consistent Aggregates." *American Economic Review* 67: 404–418.

Gouriéroux, C., and Monfort, A. 1989a. "A General Framework for Testing a Null Hypothesis in a Mixed Form." *Econometric Theory* 5: 63–82.

Gouriéroux, C., and Monfort, A. 1989b. *Statistique et modèles économétriques.* Economica.

Gouriéroux, C., Monfort, A., and Renault, E. 1988. "Testing for Common Roots." *Econometrica.*

Hansen, L. 1982. "Large Sample Properties of Generalized Method of Moments Estimators." *Econometrica* 50: 1029–1054.

Hayes, K. 1986. "Third Order Translog Utility Functions." *Journal of Business Economics and Statistics* 4: 339–346.

Malinvaud, E. 1978. *Méthodes statistiques de l'économétrie,* third edition. Dunod.

Monfort, A., and Rabemananjara, R. 1987. From a VAR Model to a Structural Model with an Application to the Wage Price Spiral. Document de travail ENSAE/INSEE No. 8707.

Newey, W. 1985. "Maximum Likelihood Specification Testing and Conditional Moment Tests." *Econometrica* 53: 1047–1070.

Pesaran, M. H. 1981. "Identification of Rational Expectations Models." *Journal of Econometrics* 16: 375–398.

Sargan, J. D. 1980. "Some Tests of Dynamic Specification for a Single Equation." *Econometrica* 48: 879–898.

Sargan, J. D., and Mehta, F. 1983. "A Generalisation of the Durbin Significance Test and its Application to Dynamic Specification." *Econometrica* 51: 1551–1568.

Szroeter, J. 1983. "Generalized Wald Methods for Testing Nonlinear Implicit and Overidentifying Restrictions." *Econometrica* 51: 335–353.

Wald, A. 1943. "Test of Statistical Hypotheses Concerning Several Parameter When the Number of Observations Is Large." *Transactions of the American Mathematical Society* 54: 426–482.

Wallis, K. 1980. "Econometric Implications of the Rational Expectations Hypothesis." *Econometrica* 48: 49–73.

33

Heterogeneity in Panel Data: Are There Stable Production Functions?

Jacques Mairesse and
Zvi Griliches

1. Introduction

Our paper is about heterogeneity in production relations at the micro level and a quest for an interpretation of it. We have been studying, for a number of years, the relationship between output and inputs, between labor productivity and the capital-labor ratio, and between technological change and investment in R&D. We have worked primarily with firm level data in France, the United States, and Japan and used the production function framework, and especially the Cobb-Douglas form, as an organizing device for our analysis.[1] In this work we were struck both by the surprising amount of variability in the basic economic ratios at the micro level and by a number of "anomalies" in the conventional estimates based on such data. Since the usual approaches impose a common specification with constant parameters across the different units, it is at least possible that some of the variability and apparent anomalies in our results could be due to the neglect of parameter heterogeneity.

We ask, in this paper, if the observed heterogeneity is "real" in some sense and if it makes a difference for our major conclusions. It will turn out, however, that it is much more difficult to provide a clear answer to the first question and we will, therefore, concentrate primarily on it. To illustrate the problem and to describe some of the major aspects of our data we shall focus on the analysis of the capital coefficient estimates and their heterogeneity across different firms. We shall make a number of simplifying assumptions to make the problem tractable and to help us communicate our major results. In particular, we shall abstract from various issues of simultaneity and other possible specification errors and conduct the analysis under the assumption of a constant-returns-to-scale Cobb-Douglas production function.[2]

In section 2 we shall outline briefly the various specifications of coefficient heterogeneity considered by us and the interrelations between them. In section 4 we shall take a first look at our major results: the observed variance of the individual parameters and of their estimated "true" variance. In sections 5 and 6, we shall estimate these variances directly within the framework of the random coefficients model, using maximum-likelihood methods and the more flexible two-stages approach of regressing the squares and the cross-products of residuals on comparable squares and cross-products of the independent variables. In the last section, we look for other ways of testing the "reality" and relevance of our findings, and try to provide interim conclusions.

2. Motivation

The story begins with our data: We have collected, constructed, cleaned, and analyzed annual data on the output and inputs of about 450 manufacturing firms each in France and the United States and 850 firms in Japan, for the thirteen years from 1967 through 1979. We imposed common production function coefficients across firms, and often also across industries within manufacturing, in order to provide us with a framework for an analysis of the sources of productivity growth in different countries and also to help us in exploring the contribution of R&D. We estimated simple production functions as a first step in such analyses. Continued experience with the data has convinced us that most of the encountered problems cannot be cured by fancier functional forms. We did not work with "complete systems" of production relations. These require the availability of relevant individual firm input and output prices at the micro level, something that is not within the feasible set at the moment.

Table 1 shows the results of fitting a standard constant-returns-to-scale Cobb-Douglas production function to various dimensions of the data. We present three types of estimates of the capital coefficient (elasticity) in two settings: levels (in logarithms of the variables) and first differences (of logarithms, or rates of change in these variables). The first column gives the "total" estimates in levels, the result of pooling all the data and imposing a common intercept and common slope in the regression using all the observations. The second and third columns give the corresponding "between" and "within" estimates, the first being equivalent to fitting the regression to the averages, over 13 years, for each firm, while the second allows each firm to have its own intercept and gets its estimate from the "within-firm" time series variations. It allows thereby for the presence of

Table 1.
Alternative Estimates of Capital Elasticity.

	Dependent variable: log Q/L					
	Levels			First differences		
Regressions	Total	Between	Within	Total	Between	Within
France						
(1967–1979)						
($N = 441$)						
($T = 13$)						
$\hat{\beta}$	0.303	0.313	0.196	0.260	0.163	0.266
	(0.009)	(0.031)	(0.011)	(0.014)	(0.039)	(0.014)
$\hat{\sigma}$	0.362	0.338	0.133	0.122	0.024	0.119
R^2	0.174	0.192	0.052	0.064	0.038	0.066
Japan						
(1967–1979)						
($N = 845$)						
($T = 13$)						
$\hat{\beta}$	0.452	0.469	0.278	0.183	0.359	0.170
	(0.007)	(0.023)	(0.009)	(0.010)	(0.029)	(0.010)
$\hat{\sigma}$	0.375	0.343	0.148	0.118	0.026	0.115
R^2	0.292	0.326	0.082	0.031	0.151	0.026
United States						
(1967–1979)						
($N = 462$)						
($T = 13$)						
$\hat{\beta}$	0.221	0.222	0.213	0.289	0.178	0.294
	(0.007)	(0.024)	(0.008)	(0.009)	(0.030)	(0.009)
$\hat{\sigma}$	0.286	0.266	0.106	0.099	0.019	0.097
R^2	0.154	0.163	0.096	0.149	0.073	0.153

Note: $\hat{\beta}$ are the capital elasticity estimates, the slope coefficients in the regressions of log Q/L (logarithm of deflated output per employee) on log C/L (logarithm of capital per employee) in levels, or in the regressions of DQ/L on DC/L (corresponding log rates of changes) in first differences. All regressions also contain industry year constants, for fourteen industries (i.e. $(14 \times 13) = 182$ for the regression in levels and $(14 \times 12) = 118$ for those in first differences). $\hat{\sigma}$ is the standard deviation of estimated residuals.

correlated individual firm effects in the sense of Mundlak (1978) and Chamberlain (1984). It should be noted also that all the equations contain a set of fourteen industry-specific year dummy variables, allowing also for flexible and industry-specific time trends (or for different industry output deflators than the ones we have used). The total estimates in first differences (column 4) are in a sense close to the "within" ones in levels since they also allow for the presence of individual firm constants by differencing them out of the data. The corresponding "between" estimates (column 5) are based on the "longest" difference (i.e., the average growth rates of the variables over the whole 13-year period), while the "within" estimates allow also for individual firm differences in trends.

The overall results are not particularly surprising. Total and between estimates in levels are close together [the bulk of the variance in the data is between firms and accounts for about 88 percent of the total variance in the logarithm of labor productivity in all three countries] and are higher, especially for France and Japan, than the within estimates. Only in the U.S. data are the "between" and "within" differences minor. These differences are even more striking, also in the U.S. data, if one does not impose the constant-returns-to-scale assumption.[3] These are the kind of "anomalies" that have preoccupied us for some time.

Now the fact that "within" estimates of economic coefficients tend to be lower than "between" estimates is not new and has been much commented on in the past. The very simple model that underlies these estimates may be subject to many misspecifications which could account for such discrepancies. An incomplete list would include the assumption of constant returns to scale, the use of gross rather than net output measures, and the omission of measures of material use, R&D capital, and other aspects of quality of labor and capital; the lack of measures of input utilization and the associated simultaneity problems and short-run versus long-run productivity movements issues, and the possibility of serious measurement error in most of our variables. Some of these issues have already been explored in other contexts and on other occasions. Several of the others, especially issues of capacity utilization and measurement error, we plan to pursue further in the near future. Here we want to explore the underlying heterogeneity in firm responses as another possible source of the observed anomalies in our results.

The reason why we thought of this as a promising line of attack is that if firms really differ in their response coefficients, estimates based on different cuts of the data would represent a different weighting of the underlying distribution of parameters. For example, "between" estimates of production coefficients would weight the individual coefficients in proportion to the square distance between their input ratios and the economy- or industry-wide averages, while "within" estimates of the same coefficients would weight the same individual parameters by the relative variance of their input ratios over time. The two weight structures are very different and if there were some correlation between such weights and the underlying true parameters, the resulting average parameters could differ quite a bit from each other even if the underlying parameter distribution was stable in some sense. A negative correlation of the individual parameters with the "within" weights could account for the finding that the "within" estimates are, in general, smaller than the "between" estimates. Such a correlation could arise if firms whose environments are changing more rapidly and whose capital-labor ratios fluctuate more have managed to acquire technologies with less responsive, smaller capital coefficients.[4]

To see whether this could indeed provide at least a partial explanation for our observed results we embarked on the task of estimating a separate production function for each of our firms in all three countries and summarizing the massive results in some comprehensible fashion. It was clear from the beginning that with only 13 observations for each firm we could estimate only a few rather simple parameter relationships, and that the individual results were unlikely to be very precise. We were hoping to make up what we were losing in precision at the individual level by a clearer picture of the distribution of the parameters across firms. We were not prepared, however, for the amount of heterogeneity that we encountered in our data.

Besides allowing for the possible heterogeneity across firms one could also relax the assumption of the constancy of the slope parameters in the time dimension. Then we would be discussing the issue of "stability" rather than "heterogeneity." It turns out that "instability" may be the main problem with our data rather than heterogeneity and we shall explore this a bit toward the end of this paper. The original emphasis of most of our work in this paper is, however, on the appropriate characterization of the "individuality" of our firms.

3. General Framework

Within the general model of the constant-returns-to-scale Cobb-Douglas production function, we consider a number of different specifications of coefficient heterogeneity using both level and first differenced data. Our general model can be written as the following simple equation:

$$y_{it} = \alpha_i + \beta_i x_{it} + \varepsilon_{it}, \qquad i = 1, \ldots, n, \quad t = 1, \ldots, T$$

where y_{it} is logarithm of output per employee of firm i in year t, x_{it} is the logarithm of capital per employee, and ε_{it} is a disturbance distributed independently of the x_{it}'s. In this formulation the intercept parameters α_i and the slope parameters β_i are allowed to differ across firms and different versions of the model correspond to different assumptions as to how they differ. There is also a parallel first differences formulation:

$$y_{it} - y_{it-1} = \beta_i(x_{it} - x_{it-1}) + \varepsilon_{it} - \varepsilon_{it-1}, \quad i = 1, \ldots, n, \quad t = 2, \ldots, T.$$

The different specifications we look at can be summarized as follows, with $\sigma_\alpha^2 = E(\alpha_i - \alpha)^2$, $\sigma_\beta^2 = E(\beta_i - \beta)^2$, and $\sigma_{\alpha\beta} = E(\alpha_i - \alpha)(\beta_i - \beta)$:

Levels	First differences
A. $\alpha_i = \alpha$, $\beta_i = \beta$	a. $\beta_i = \beta$
B. $E\alpha_i = \alpha$, σ_α^2, $\beta_i = \beta$	b. $E\beta_i = \beta$, σ_β^2
C. $E\alpha_i = \alpha$, $E\beta_i = \beta$; σ_α^2, σ_β^2, $\sigma_{\alpha\beta}$	c. β_i distinct and fixed
D. α_i distinct and fixed, $\beta_i = \beta$	
E. α_i and β_i distinct and fixed	

These different combinations go from more-constraining to less-constraining sets: (A) both coefficients constant across firms (the usual linear regression assumption on pooled data); (B) random intercepts and constant slopes (the simple error components or random effects model); (C) both intercepts and slopes random across firms (the random coefficients model); (D) firm-specific intercepts and a common slope parameter (the fixed effects or covariance model); (E) firm-specific, fixed and different, intercepts and slopes (the fixed coefficients model).

Since differencing eliminates the individual intercepts, we are left with only three comparable first differences versions, all with no intercepts: (a) a single common slope, (b) randomly differing slopes, and (c) firm specific slopes.

The content of the distinction between "random" and "fixed" or firm-"specific" effects is partly in the assumption that the former are independent of the other variables in the equation, the x's (i.e., the firm effects are "uncorrelated," $E(\alpha_i|x) = \alpha$). This assumption is not imposed on the data in fitting the fixed effects versions (E and c) of the model. These versions, which allow for complete heterogeneity across firms, are the most general ones and all the other versions are nested within them and can be tested for as different restrictions on them. Note that the uncorrelation assumption applies to the absence of a relationship between the individual parameters and the individual x's and not to the absence of a relationship between the parameters themselves.[5] We will indeed be estimating a covariance between the intercept and slope parameters also in the "random" effects model, but our main emphasis will be on the slope parameter β and its variance.

Since differencing eliminates the individual intercepts, we are left with only three comparable first difference versions, all with no intercepts: (a) a single common slope, (b) randomly differing slopes, and (c) firm specific slopes.

We have not been particularly explicit about the structure of the variance-covariance matrix of the disturbances (Σ). In most of what follows we shall assume that there is no serial correlation (or heteroskedasticity) beyond that which arises from the presence of the individual firm effects which are to be modeled explicitly, or that the serial correlation has been adequately eliminated or reduced by the first difference transformation. The issue of the correct specification of Σ is considered in the appendix, where we try to deduce the correct sampling errors for our individual firm estimates. Note also that we have not allowed for time variation in these parameters. The variability over time in the α_i would be absorbed in the ε_{it}. Allowing β_i also to vary over time would strain our already overextended computational framework.[6] But we shall come back to this possibility in discussing some of our results below.

3. A First Look at the Major Results

Table 2 presents the results of estimating the simple production function separately for each firm. It lists the averages and observed dispersions of the estimated capital coefficients across firms both for the levels version, which is now a "within" equation with a separate constant and slope for each firm (specification E), and the first difference version (specification C). For comparison purposes we also list similar statistics for five other variables (which are not regression coefficients): the annual levels (in logarithms) and the annual growth rates of labor productivity and of capital intensity, and the "share of capital" in value added, which could be thought of as another independent estimate of the capital coefficient. (The share of capital can be computed only for the French and Japanese samples.) The first row of the table thus gives the averages for the individual firm capital coefficients and for the firm means of the various variables; the second row gives their observed dispersion in the data. The average values for the estimated coefficients are remarkably close to their least squares counterparts in table 1, the "within" levels and the "total" first differences ones, but their dispersion is immense. The estimated standard deviations do not provide, however, an adequate impression of this dispersion. At this point a picture is worth more than several paragraphs of description.

Figure 1 plots the distribution of the capital coefficients for France (the pictures are very similar for Japan and the United States) against their estimated precision (the inverse of their standard errors). The estimated range is enormous: for a coefficient with a prior mean of about 0.3 and a reasonable range between 0.1 and 0.5 we get an actual range from -1.7 to ± 2.3, with more than a third of the estimates being actually negative!

We did expect to see some heterogeneity at the individual level and did assume that it would be magnified by the large sampling errors arising from the rather short time series available for their estimation, but we were not really prepared for this amount of dispersion. We turned then to an attempt to determine more precisely the amount of "pure" sampling variance in the results and the complementary effort to determine the "real" amount of dispersion in these estimates and an exploration of the sense in which this dispersion is indeed "real," if any.

The next two lines in table 2 attempt to provide a first round answer to this question. Line 3 lists the estimated "true" dispersion or heterogeneity of the β_i coefficients based on the methodology described in Swamy (1970, 1971). Among the different estimates of coefficient heterogeneity, the Swamy estimates are the most straightforward to obtain. They are computed as the difference between the observed variance of the individually estimated firm coefficients and an average of the corresponding sampling variances. Being based on the individual regression estimates, they are robust to the possibility of correlated effects (between the α_i and β_i and the x's) contrary to the maximum likelihood estimates and those based on the regression of the squares and cross-products of the residuals. But since these estimates are computed as a difference, they may yield negative values (in this case, the "true" variance is set to zero), and may be seriously affected by even small biases in the estimates of the observed and sampling variances. This would be the case, in particular, if the errors are heteroskedictic and/or serially correlated. A positive serial correlation in both the errors and the x's can account for part of the discrepancy that we see between our Swamy estimates of σ_β in levels and in first differences. (See the Appendix for a discussion of the sensitivity of the Swamy estimates to the misspecification of the variance-covariance matrix of the errors.)

Table 2.
Heterogeneity: Different Indicators

	Variables						
	Log output per employee		Log capital per employee			β coefficients	
Country and indicator	Levels	Growth rates	Levels	Growth rates	Capital share	Levels	First differences
France							
($N = 441$)							
Average[a]	16.9	.045	10.5	.046	.256	.194	.232
s_b observed dispersion[b]	.375	.025	.526	.030	.096	.542	.414
"True" dispersion σ_β^c	.373	0*	.524	0*	.094	.440	.213
F test[d]	90.7	.4	132.1	.7	21.2	2.9	1.4
Japan							
($N = 845$)							
Average	29.5	.087	14.7	.107	.316	.273	.161
s_b observed dispersion	.418	.028	.508	.031	.103	.625	.434
"True" dispersion σ_β	.415	0*	.506	0*	.098	.539	.258
F test	87.6	.6	122.3	.8	11.1	3.9	1.5
United States							
($N = 462$)							
Average	29.8	.021	16.2	.051	—	.219	.283
s_b observed dispersion	.291	.020	.528	.030	—	.403	.321
"True" dispersion σ_β	.289	0*	.526	0*	—	.323	
F test	81.5	.4	126.5	.5	—	2.8	1.9

[a] The averages are the simple arithmetic means, except for the levels of the output per employee and of the capital per employee where they are the geometric means in thousand dollars per employee in 1970 prices. Thus, the averages of the individual estimates of the capital coefficients $\hat{\beta}_i$ are simply $\bar{\beta} = (1/N)\sum_i \hat{\beta}_i$, and that of the variables x_{it}:

$$x_{..} = \frac{1}{NT}\sum_i \sum_t x_{it} = \frac{1}{N}\sum_i x_i$$

[b] The observed dispersions s_b are the standard deviations between firms, i.e.,

$$s_B^2 = \frac{1}{(N-1)}\sum_i (\hat{\beta}_i - \bar{\beta})^2$$

or

$$s_B^2 = \frac{1}{N-1}\sum_i (x_{i.} - x_{..})^2$$

[c] The true dispersions are computed by adjusting the observed dispersions for sampling variability. For the capital coefficients, they are the Swamy estimates:

$$\sigma_\beta^2 = s_B^2 - \frac{1}{N}\sum_i v_i^2$$

where the sampling variance $v_i^2 = s_{e_i}^2/\sum_t (x_{it} - x_{i.})^2$, $s_{e_i}^2$ being the estimated variance of the errors in the individual regressions. For the variables, we have similarly

$$``\sigma_\beta^{2}" = s_b^2 - \frac{1}{T}s_w^2$$

where

$$s_w^2 = \frac{1}{N(T-1)}\sum_i \sum_t (x_{it} - x_{i.})^2$$

When its computed value would be negative, the estimated σ_β^2 is set to zero (marked by an * in the table).

[d] With this notation, it can be shown that the F tests can be computed simply as $F = s_b^2/(s_b^2 - \sigma_\beta^2)$. See Mairesse 1988 for more detail.

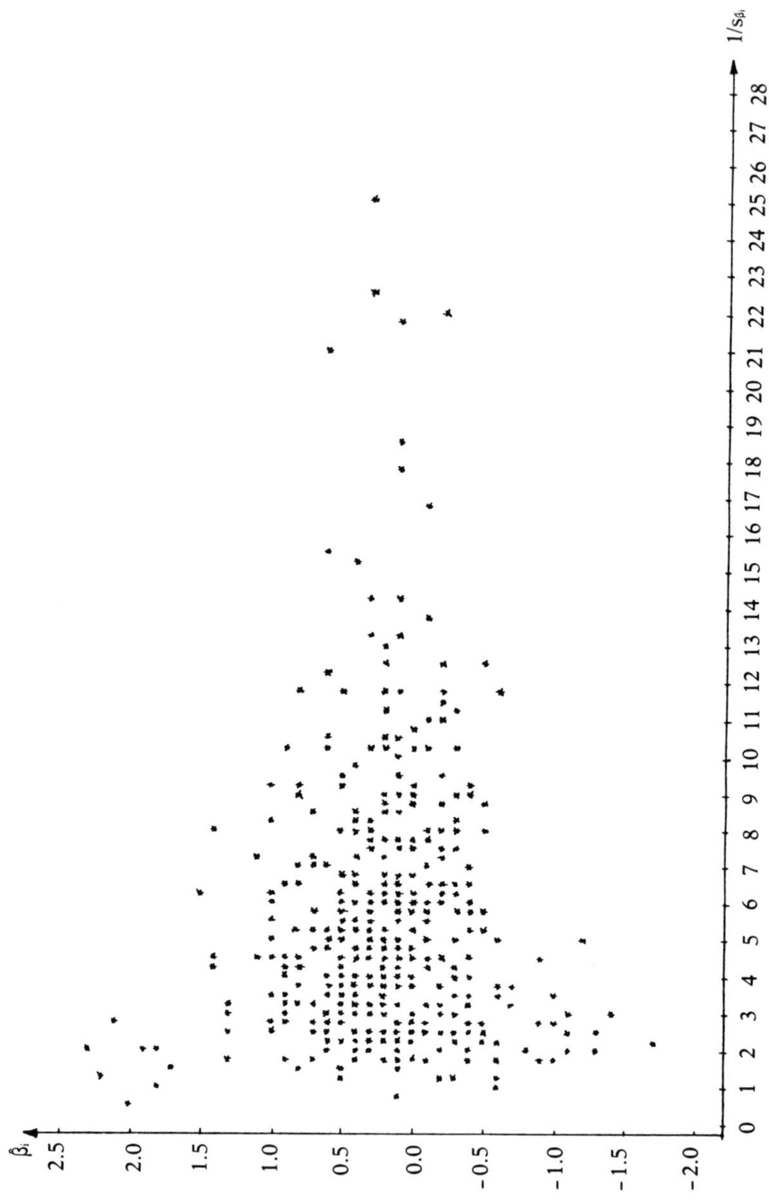

Figure 1.
Estimates of individual capital elasticities ($\hat{\beta}_i$) versus their estimated precision ($s_{\hat{\beta}_i}^{-1}$). France, 1967–1979 levels, $N = 441$.

However, what is most striking in our Swamy estimates is their order of magnitude: σ_β of about 0.20 to 0.25 in first differences ($\sigma_\beta^2 = 0.05$) and between 0.30 to 0.55 in levels (σ_β^2 from 0.10 to 0.30). These estimates are still much too large to be indicators of a credible amount of heterogeneity given our prior information about the possible magnitude of the capital elasticities which would correspond to a "true" dispersion σ_β of about 0.10 to (σ_β^2 of 0.01) for an average β of 0.3. It is interesting to stress, in contrast, that the estimated "true" dispersion in the capital share is much smaller and more credible: σ_β being exactly 0.10. It is interesting also to note the zero estimate for the "true" dispersion in the growth rates of labor productivity and capital intensity. As far as these two last variables are concerned, Gibrat's Law applies and we find no trace of persistent individual firm differences in them: all the observed variability is either common to all firms within an industry or is transitory.

Another approach is testing for coefficient heterogeneity. The fourth line in table 2 lists the F statistics for the hypothesis of equality of the production coefficients (or variables) across firms. Given the large number of degrees of freedom in our data, all the computed F statistics are very "significant" at conventional significance levels of 5 percent or even 1 percent (the critical F ratios barely exceed one for our sample sizes). One can question, however, whether they should be used in this fashion in such large samples, reducing the probability of type II error (of accepting homogeneity, if there is heterogeneity) as our sample sizes increase but keeping the type I error (of rejecting homogeneity, if there is homogeneity). A more symmetric treatment of the inference problem, advocated by Leamer (1978), would lead to the use of much higher values for the "critical" F (about 10 for our data) and much less certainty in rejecting the hypothesis of homogeneity.

Another way of getting an impression of the "significance" of such numbers is to compare them to the F's computed for the between firms dispersion in labor productivity, capital intensity, and capital share. These are on the order of 100 for the first two variables in levels and 11 (Japan) to 21 (France) for the capital shares, as against 3 to 4 for the capital elasticities estimates in levels, and 1.5 to 2 for the estimates in first differences. Now that is heterogeneity![7]

A related view of the testing problem is indicated by figure 2, which plots the frequency distribution of the estimated t-ratios for the individual capital coefficients and superimposes on it the theoretically expected t-distribution for this sample size (11 degrees of freedom). It is clear from this picture that the rejection of the homogeneity assumption comes from the

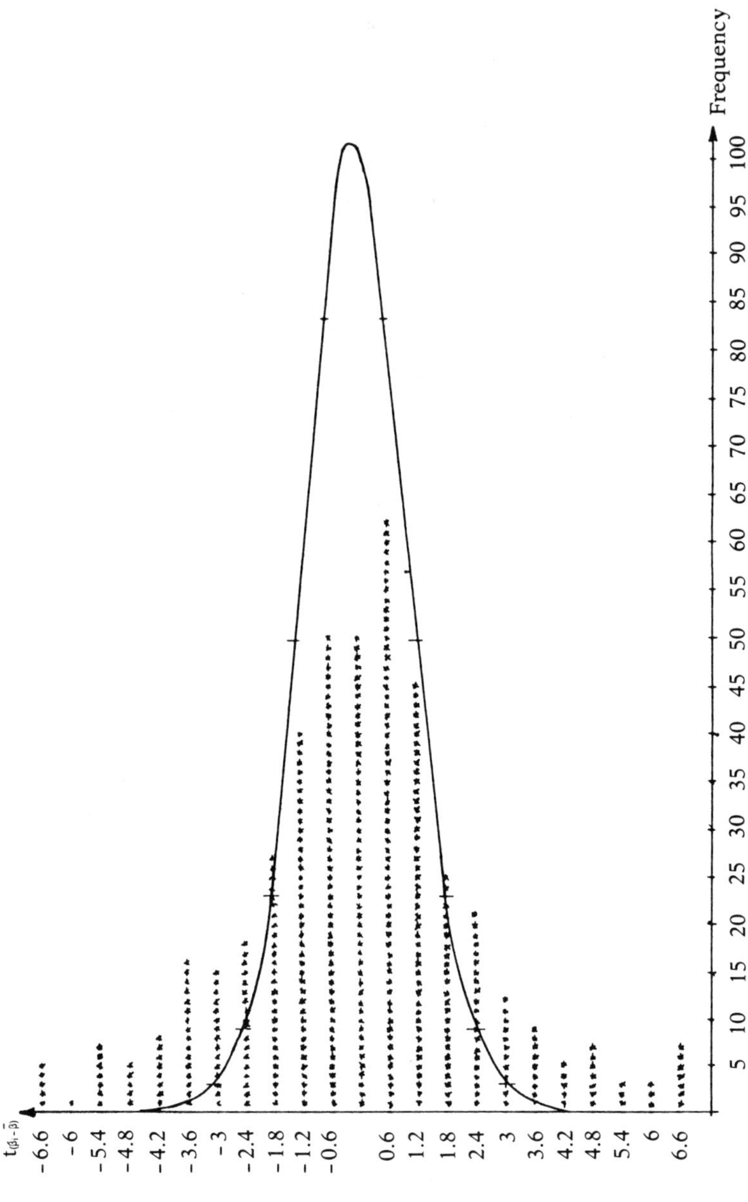

Figure 2.
Frequency distribution of the t-ratios for the individual capital elasticities β_i. France, 1967–1979 levels, $N = 441$.

presence of too many extreme values and is not the result of just a few outliers. We can use it also to ask the heterogeneity question in a slightly different multiple-comparisons approach.[8] Since we are looking at a large number of independent test statistics, what is the right critical value for a single statistic given that we want to keep a combined 5 percent significance level for the testing process as a whole? For (approximately) 500 comparisons, as in the French sample, the individual significance level should be set at about 0.0001 or a critical t-value of about 6.3 instead of the conventional 2.2 level. A single observation of a t-ratio in excess of 6.3 (or less than -6.3) would be enough to reject the hypothesis that all the observations arise from the population with the same mean and differ only from each other because of sampling variability. But in the French data we have 12 such observations![9]

This first round look at the dispersion in our data leaves us with rather ambiguous conclusions. The observed dispersion in the estimates of individual firm capital coefficients is very large and not really credible as an indicator of "reasonable" heterogeneity. The idea that the results could be due just to sampling variability is not supported by standard statistical tests, but the level at which the observed statistics fail the homogeneity hypothesis is not particularly impressive. The latter point of view is reinforced by the fact that the estimates of sampling error and the associated F-statistics, as we already noted, are very sensitive to the underlying distributional assumptions and especially to the assumption of homoskedasticity and serial independence (see appendix).

5. Maximum-Likelihood Estimates

In tables 3 and 4 we present several maximum-likelihood estimates for our three samples and our different specifications. We estimated the specifications B, C, and b, using the maximum likelihood framework. In each case the log likelihood function is the sum of individual firm likelihood values expressed in terms of the summary statistics for each firm and the parameters to be estimated: α, β, σ_α^2, σ_β^2, $\sigma_{\alpha\beta}$, and σ_ε^2.[10] For the constant parameters and the fixed effects cases, the maximum likelihood estimates are equivalent to different OLS versions and we have used the latter. For specifications A and a, they are the "total" estimates in levels and in first differences; for D they are the "within" estimate in levels and for E and c they are the previously described individual firm estimates.

The maximum-likelihood estimates, contrary to those presented in table 2, assume either the independence of the β_i's or the independence of both

Table 3.
Maximum-Likelihood Estimates on Levels

Specifications[a]	L(ML)	β	σ_ε^2	σ_α^2	$\sigma_{\alpha\beta}$	σ_β^2
France						
(A) α = Ct, β = Ct	2949.2	0.303	0.1315			
		(0.009)[b]	(0.0025)	—	—	—
		(0.032)[c]	(0.0097)			
(B) α = Rd, β = Ct	7511.2	0.210	0.0192	0.114		
		(0.011)	(0.0004)	(0.008)	—	—
		(0.028)	(0.0011)	(0.010)		
(C) α = Rd, β = Rd	7890.2	0.212	0.0148	0.123	−0.018	0.145
		(0.022)	(0.0003)	(0.009)	(0.008)	(0.014)
		(0.022)	(0.0007)	(0.013)	(0.009)	(0.019)
(D) α = Fs, β = Ct	8702.3	0.196	0.0192	[0.118]	—	—
(E) α = Fs, β = Fs	9732.1	[0.194]	[0.0146]	[0.194]	[−0.054]	[0.294]
Japan						
(A) α = Ct, β = Ct	5290.9	0.452	0.1404			
		(0.007)	(0.0019)	—	—	—
		(0.023)	(0.0065)			
(B) α = Rd, β = Ct	13255.8	0.303	0.0239	0.121		
		(0.009)	(0.0003)	(0.006)	—	—
		(0.021)	(0.0008)	(0.007)		
(C) α = Rd, β = Rd	14112.7	0.291	0.0176	0.135	−0.010	0.213
		(0.019)	(0.0003)	(0.007)	(0.007)	(0.014)
		(0.019)	(0.0006)	(0.008)	(0.008)	(0.016)
(D) α = Fs, β = Ct	15476.4	0.278	0.0238	[0.118]	—	—
(E) α = Fs, β = Fs	17700.3	[0.273]	[0.0173]	[0.207]	[0.020]	[0.391]
United States						
(A) α = Ct, β = Ct	4507.1	0.221	0.0820			
		(0.007)	(0.0015)	—	—	—
		(0.034)	(0.0084)			
(B) α = Rd, β = Ct	9232.2	0.214	0.0122	0.069		
		(0.008)	(0.0002)	(0.005)	—	—
		(0.019)	(0.0007)	(0.008)		
(C) α = Rd, β = Rd	9530.3	0.225	0.0100	0.068	−0.001	0.069
		(0.016)	(0.0002)	(0.005)	(0.004)	(0.007)
		(0.016)	(0.0006)	(0.008)	(0.005)	(0.008)
(D) α = Fs, β = Ct	10468.0	0.213	0.0122	[0.071]	—	—
(E) α = Fs, β = Fs	11374.1	[0.219]	0.0099	[0.122]	[−0.023]	[0.163]

[a] Ct, constant; Rd, random; Fs, firm specific (fixed effects).
[b] First line: usual standard errors obtained from the maximum likelihood method.
[c] Second line: "robust" standard errors obtained from the pseudo-maximum likelihood method (White 1980, 1982; Gourieroux et al. 1984). Average estimate computed from the individual estimates (means for β and σ_ε^2; variance and covariance for σ_α^2, σ_β^2 and $\sigma_{\alpha\beta}$).

Table 4.
Maximum-Likelihood Estimates in First Differences

Specifications[a]	L(ML)	β	σ_ε^2	σ_β^2
France				
(a) β = Ct	8506.7	0.260	0.0148	
		(0.014)[b]	(0.0003)	—
		(0.022)[c]	(0.0007)	
(b) β = Rd	8577.6	0.246	0.0137	0.064
		(0.019)	(0.0003)	(0.010)
		(0.019)	(0.0007)	(0.010)
(c) β = Fs	8904.5	[0.232]	[0.0139]	[0.172]
Japan				
(a) β = Ct	16588.9	0.183	0.0140	
		(0.010)	(0.0002)	—
		(0.015)	(0.0005)	
(b) β = Rd	16684.2	0.168	0.0131	0.061
		(0.014)	(0.0002)	(0.007)
		(0.014)	(0.0004)	(0.007)
(c) β = Fs	17308.4	[0.161]	[0.0132]	[0.188]
United States				
(a) β = Ct	10071.5	0.289	0.0097	
		(0.009)	(0.0002)	—
		(0.018)	(0.0004)	
(b) β = Rd	10186.1	0.300	0.0088	0.040
		(0.014)	(0.0002)	(0.005)
		(0.014)	(0.0004)	(0.005)
(c) β = Fs	10554.0	[0.283]	[0.0089]	[0.103]

[a] See footnote *a* to table 3.
[b] See footnote *b* to table 3.
[c] See footnote *c* to table 3.

α_i and β_i from the x's, i.e., the absence of "correlated effects." They also assume that ε and the coefficients α and β are distributed normally, or more generally that their distribution belongs to the linear exponential family.[11] The standard errors of the estimates under the normality assumption (computed from the inverse of the information matrix) are given in the first line of parentheses; the more general standard errors robust under heteroskedasticity and nonnormality are given in the second line of parentheses.

The first column in tables 3 and 4 gives the estimated values of the log likelihood, allowing one to compute directly the various likelihood ratio (LR) tests for the randomness of the parameters (i.e., the nullity of the variances σ_β^2 and/or σ_α^2) or for their equality across firms (i.e., the equality of β_i and/or α_i for all i). We shall turn first to the tests of heterogeneity, before looking at the orders of magnitude themselves. Table 5 recapitulates the 2LR values per degrees of freedom p of the tests (where p is the number of additional parameters under the alternative hypothesis or the number of restrictions under the null hypothesis) and the corresponding critical values of the χ^2 or F statistics at the 1 percent level of significance: $\chi^2_{0.01}(p)/p = F_{0.01}(p,\infty)$.

The pattern of the results is quite similar for all three samples. All of the rejections appear to be very significant statistically. There are, however, large differences between them, if one takes an eclectic view of comparing gains in likelihood per additional parameters. In this sense, the largest benefit comes from relaxing the constancy of the intercept parameter α. With only one additional parameter σ_α^2, the random effects specification is extremely parsimonious, this one parameter being "equivalent" to about 80 percent of the $(N-1)$ additional parameters of the fixed effects specification. The additional improvement arising out of the relaxation of the constancy of the slope parameter, although less dramatic, is still quite sizeable. Again the random coefficient specification performs relatively well. The additional variance parameter σ_β^2 is "equivalent" to about 30 to 40 percent of the residual variance reduction achieved by the $N-1$ firm-specific coefficients β_i in levels, and about 15 to 25 percent of it in first differences.[12]

The LR tests of equality of the slope parameters β (D if E and a if c) are equivalent to the usual F tests that have been discussed in the introduction.[13] As we have noted already, although those tests are very "significant" at conventional significance levels, they are not all that "high" if one takes into consideration our large sample sizes and follows Leamer's view of using a critical value which increases with the number of degrees of freedom.

Table 5.
Likelihood Ratio Tests of Homogeneity versus Random or Fixed Coefficients Heterogeneity[a]

	France		Japan		United States		
Tests	p	$2LR/p$	p	$2LR/p$	p	$2LR/p$	$\chi^2_{0.01}(p)/p = F_{0.01}(p, \infty)$
(A) if (B): $\sigma_\alpha^2 = 0$	1	9124.0	1	15929.8	1	9450.2	6.6
(B) if (E): $\sigma_\alpha^2 = \sigma_\beta^2 = 0$	2	4941.0	2	8821.8	2	5023.2	4.6
(B) if (E): $\sigma_\beta^2 = 0$, $\sigma_\alpha^2 \neq 0$	1	758.0	1	1713.8	1	596.2	6.6
(A) if (D): $\alpha_i = \alpha$	440	26.2	844	24.1	461	25.9	~ 1
(A) if (E): $\alpha_i = \alpha$, $\beta_i = \beta$	880	15.4	1688	14.7	922	14.8	~ 1
(D) if (E): $\beta_i = \beta$, $\alpha_i \neq \alpha$	440	4.7	844	5.3	461	3.9	~ 1
(a) if (b): $\sigma_\beta^2 = 0$	1	141.8	1	190.6	1	229.2	6.6
(a) if (c): $\beta_i = \beta$	440	1.8	844	1.7	461	2.1	~ 1

[a] LR, likelihood ratio; p, degrees of freedom.

We are, however, primarily interested in the order of magnitude of our heterogeneity estimates. The more relevant numbers are the estimated variances (σ_β^2) for the two random coefficient specifications C and b given in tables 3 and 4. The corresponding figures in brackets for the fixed coefficient specifications are the empirical variances of the firm-specific estimated β_i. As expected they are much greater than the estimated "true" σ_β^2, most of the differences corresponding to the sampling variances (i.e., the variances due to the errors in the model) and our limited study period. Although unaffected by the imprecision of the individual estimation of the β_i, the estimated σ_β^2 remains large, and far too large for numbers which a priori we would expect to be of the order 0.01 ($\sigma_\beta = 0.10$) and not to exceed 0.04 ($\sigma_\beta = 0.20$). In this respect, they are quite comparable (unfortunately) to our previously reported Swamy estimates. The σ_β^2's estimated in first differences are much smaller than those estimated in levels, but they still seem too large, being about 0.06 in France and Japan and 0.04 in the U.S. (the corresponding estimates in levels are about 0.15, 0.21, and 0.07, respectively).[14]

The reasons why the variances are so different when estimated in levels and in first differences (and nearer to what we would deem acceptable for the latter) are unclear. A plausible explanation is, of course, the possibility of correlated effects, since maximum likelihood estimation in levels assumes that the random intercept effects α_i are uncorrelated with the capital-labor ratio. Going to first differences disposes of that problem. The fact that our estimates of the (mean) capital elasticity β tend to be higher (clearly for Japan, more or less so also for France, but rather the opposite for the United States) in specifications which are affected by the presence of correlated effects (A, B, and C) is another indication of the same phenomenon. There may also be some coherence in the observed discrepancies in the estimated β and σ_β^2 in levels and first difference: they are both quite wide for Japan and both modest for the United States, France being in a somewhat intermediate position. This first explanation, however, does not apply to the Swamy estimates, which show the same discrepancies between the estimated σ_β^2 in levels and first differences.

Another explanation for the discrepancies in the σ_β^2 (not the β) is the positive correlation of the errors ε in the regression, and hence their negative autocorrelation in first differences. This would cause a positive bias in the level estimates of σ_β^2, since the x themselves are strongly positively correlated, but only a negligible one in the first difference estimates, the differenced Δx's being only weakly serially correlated. This explanation has the advantage of also working for the Swamy estimates (see appendix).

6. Estimates from Regressions on Squares and Cross-Products of Residuals

There is another way of estimating the variance components of heterogeneity suggested by the random coefficients model literature.[15] This method relies on the fact that the variances and covariances of the dependent variable y, conditional on the explanatory variable x, are linear functions of the relevant squares and cross-products of the x's. Thus, if the mean parameters of the model have been estimated consistently in a first stage (for N large and T fixed) and the corresponding residuals u_{it} computed in this stage, it can be shown that regressing their squares and cross-products on the corresponding squares and cross-products of the x's yields consistent estimates of the variance parameters (for N large and T fixed). Since these different regressions constitute a system of related equations (with appropriate cross-equations restrictions on the parameters), they can be estimated more efficiently (given the mean parameters) by quasi-generalized least squares (QGLS). We have estimated them both by OLS and QGLS, but shall report here only on the latter.

Letting u_{it} and Δu_{it} be the residuals from the simple OLS estimates of our model in levels and in first differences (A and a), we have two systems of equations across firms (the observations being over i). The first one in levels consists of T equations on squares, of $(T-1)$ on cross-products lagged by 1 year, of $(T-2)$ on cross-products lagged by 2 years, ... or a total of $T(T+1)/2 = 91$ of them. Similarly, in first differences there are such $(T-1)$ equations on squares, $(T-2)$ on cross-products lagged by one year, ..., for a total of $T(T-1)/2 = 78$. Assuming that ε's are uncorrelated over time, they can be written respectively as

$$u_{it}^2 = \sigma_\beta^2 x_{it}^2 + 2\sigma_{\alpha\beta} x_{it} + (\sigma_\alpha^2 + \sigma_\varepsilon^2) + v_{it'} \qquad (t = 1, \dots T)$$

$$u_{it}u_{it'} = \sigma_\beta^2 x_{it}x_{it'} + \sigma_{\alpha\beta}(x_{it} + x_{it'}) + \sigma_\alpha^2 + v_{itt'}$$

$$(t \neq t';\, t = 1, \dots T;\, t' = 1, \dots T)$$

$$\Delta u_{it}^2 = \sigma_\beta^2 \Delta x_{it}^2 + \sigma_{\Delta\varepsilon}^2 + w_{it}, \qquad (t = 1, \dots (T-1))$$

$$\Delta u_{it}\Delta u_{it'} = \sigma_\beta^2 \Delta x_{it}\Delta x_{it'} + w_{itt'},$$

$$(t \neq t';\, t = 1, \dots (T-1);\, t' = 1, \dots (T-1)).$$

Although somewhat cumbersome (because of the number of equations), this approach is more flexible than the maximum-likelihood method. It is easier to investigate various assumptions about the error terms or the

Table 6.
Estimates from Systems of Regressions on Squares and Cross-Products of Residuals, Fully Constrained (MCQG estimates)

	$\sigma_{\varepsilon}^{2a}$	σ_{β}^{2}	$\sigma_{\alpha\beta}$	σ_{α}^{2}
France levels	0.003	0.042	0.001	0.078
		(0.003)	(0.003)	(0.007)
Japan levels	0.002	0.062	−0.009	0.084
		(0.002)	(0.003)	(0.006)
U.S. levels	0.002	0.052	−0.001	0.030
		(0.002)	(0.002)	(0.004)
France Chamberlain's II	0.003	0.035	0.003	0.085
		(0.003)	(0.003)	(0.007)
Japan Chamberlain's II	0.002	0.037	−0.007	0.086
		(0.002)	(0.002)	(0.005)
U.S. Chamberlain's II	0.001	0.039	−0.002	0.030
		(0.001)	(0.002)	(0.004)
France first difference	0.007	0.051	—	—
	(0.000)	(0.003)		
Japan first difference	0.008	0.041	—	—
	(0.000)	(0.003)		
U.S. first difference	0.004	0.032	—	—
	(0.000)	(0.002)		

[a] σ_{ε}^{2}, for levels computed as the difference between the intercepts of the square and cross-product coefficients. For first differences, it is an estimate of $\sigma_{\Delta\varepsilon}^{2}$.

random parameters themselves within this framework. In particular, we can accommodate serial correlation of the errors by not imposing the assumption that the intercepts of the different cross-product equations of the system in levels are equal and allow also for nonstationarity of the errors by not assuming them to be equal within various groups of equations. Similarly, we can allow for unsynchronized random shocks on our response parameter β by relaxing the equality constraints on the coefficients of the squares and cross-products of the x's in different ways.

It is also possible to use first-stage residuals corresponding to alternative variants of the (first-order) specification of our model. In particular, we have allowed for the possibility of systematic (synchronized) changes over time in the capital elasticity β, and for correlated (with the x's) firm effects by including all the available x_{it} in the first-stage regressions, using what is known as Chamberlain's Π matrix approach (1984).

We have taken advantage of the flexibility of the approach by estimating more or less constrained versions of the system of equations, for the

Table 7.
Estimates from System of Regressions on Squares and Cross-Products of Residuals, Unconstrained across Groups of Equations[a] (MCQG estimates)

	σ_β^2 estimated from equations on								
	Levels			Chamberlain's			First differences		
	France	Japan	U.S.	France	Japan	U.S.	France	Japan	U.S.
SQ	0.037	0.055	0.056	0.030	0.030	0.043	0.117	0.106	0.082
CP1	0.036	0.055	0.056	0.029	0.031	0.042	0.083	0.027	0.047
CP2	0.036	0.055	0.055	0.029	0.031	0.042	0.022	0.006	0.048
CP3	0.035	0.056	0.055	0.028	0.030	0.041	0.031	0.024	−0.011
CP4	0.035	0.056	0.054	0.028	0.030	0.040	0.042	−0.005	−0.006
CP5	0.034	0.056	0.052	0.028	0.030	0.039	0.031	0.035	0.003
CP6	0.035	0.055	0.050	0.029	0.030	0.037	−0.041	0.046	0.006
CP7	0.034	0.055	0.048	0.028	0.030	0.035	−0.015	−0.004	0.020
CP8	0.033	0.055	0.045	0.028	0.030	0.033	−0.003	0.050	−0.008
CP9	0.033	0.055	0.042	0.028	0.029	0.031	0.070	0.008	0.048
CP10	0.034	0.054	0.039	0.029	0.029	0.028	0.101	−0.010	−0.014
CP11	0.032	0.052	0.035	0.028	0.028	0.028	0.095	0.099	0.017
CP12	0.030	0.050	0.033	0.025	0.027	0.023	—	—	—

[a] Dependent variables: SQ, squared residuals; CPh, cross-products of residuals h periods apart.

three types of residuals computed in the first stage from the specifications in terms of levels, first differences and Chamberlain's π matrix.

The results of our main computations are summarized in tables 6, 7, and 8, respectively, for the fully constrained estimates, and for those constrained only within groups of equations (in this case we have as many estimates as the number of groups), and for those obtained without imposing any cross-equations restrictions (in this case we have as many estimates as the number of equations, and we give in table 8 only the estimates pertaining to the equation on squares and the cross-products lagged by four years).

In comparison with our previous ML estimates, there is a pleasant surprise: the fully constrained estimates of σ_β^2 in levels are much smaller, and now they are also quite close to the first difference estimates, and also quite close to the ones resulting from Chamberlain's approach (table 6). But these estimates are still on the high side of what would seem a priori reasonable: the estimated σ_β^2 range from 0.03 ($\sigma_\beta = 0.18$) for the United States in first difference, to 0.06 ($\sigma_\beta^2 = 0.25$) for Japan in levels.

Table 8.
Estimates from Regressions on Squares and Four Year Apart Cross-Products of Residuals, Unconstrained across Equations (OLS Estimates)

	Levels			Chamberlain's II			First differences		
Year	France	Japan	U.S.	France	Japan	U.S.	France	Japan	U.S.
SQ[a]									
1979	.035	.034	.127	.030	.028	.106	.107	.124	.104
1978	.042	.033	.149	.036	.022	.128	.076	.363	.070
1977	.035	.036	.184	.030	.030	.151	.149	.094	.185
1976	.053	.024	.154	.044	.033	.138	.182	.103	.202
1975	.033	.032	.191	.029	.034	.149	.183	.099	.170
1974	.055	.063	.157	.039	.053	.124	.490	.080	.155
1973	.019	.045	.170	.012	.035	.130	.231	.136	.114
1972	.021	.046	.163	.017	.033	.115	.186	.128	.089
1971	.034	.048	.150	.031	.033	.110	.129	.091	.146
1970	.017	.043	.136	.012	.031	.096	.154	.135	.105
1969	.006	.026	.078	.002	.020	.052	.125	.085	.087
1968	.009	.042	.059	.004	.038	.044	.095	.136	.078
1967	.015	.035	.027	.005	.033	.014	—	—	—
CP4[b]									
1979–75	.040	.034	.165	.035	.024	.132	−.178	.019	−0.89
1978–74	.045	.045	.160	.036	.035	.131	.163	−.050	.005
1977–73	.027	.043	.185	.022	.032	.145	.098	.056	−.071
1976–72	.036	.043	.172	.029	.036	.135	.056	−0.12	.180
1975–71	.038	.046	.171	.034	.037	.127	−.033	−.107	−.023
1974–70	.031	.059	.145	.024	.045	.110	−.001	.044	−.103
1973–69	.011	.042	.122	.008	.030	.087	.067	.062	.040
1972–68	.020	.055	.099	.016	.042	.070	.072	−.074	.019
1971–67	.021	.053	.073	.016	.041	.048	—	—	—

[a] squared residuals
[b] cross-products of residuals 4 years apart

While these results do not change our main conclusions significantly they do raise some new puzzles. It is not clear why they should be so different from our earlier maximum-likelihood estimates of σ_β^2 in levels. In particular, correlated intercept effects and serial correlation of the errors should affect them both similarly (at least if we impose the full set of equality constraints on the intercepts in the system of square and cross-product regressions). It is also puzzling why our new estimates of σ_α^2 (in levels) and of σ_ε^2 (in levels and first differences) are smaller than their maximum-likelihood counterparts. These anomalies point to some, still unclear, misspecifications in our model.

The incompletely constrained estimates (in tables 7 and 8) may shed some light on this mystery. They show that there is much instability in our results, especially in first differences. The example of the French sample is most striking. We find a first difference estimate of σ_β^2 of about 0.12 for the squares equations, with corresponding estimates for individual year equations varying from 0.08 (for 1978) up to 0.42 (in 1974/73). This estimate goes down to 0.04 in the 4 year apart cross-products equations with corresponding separate estimates ranging again from −0.18 (!) (for 1979–75) to 0.16 (for 1978–74). It drops down again to −0.04 (!) in 6 year apart cross-product equations, and up again to 0.10 in the 11 year apart cross-product equations. For the American and Japanese samples, the pattern is roughly similar, though less extreme. The estimates of σ_β^2 in levels are much more stable; they do indicate, however, a clear downward trend when we go from those estimated on squares to the estimates based on the 12 year lagged cross-products. This could be due to some form of random shocks on the β's, unsynchronized but strongly correlated over time, in addition to the fixed heterogeneity component β_i. Such shocks unfortunately do not seem to account for what we see in first differences.

7. An Analysis by Periods and Other Extensions

It is not easy to summarize our various results. There are two numbers worth keeping in mind: our prior expectation about a reasonable heterogeneity in the true β's is a standard deviation of 0.1. The observed standard deviation of the individual estimates is about 0.5 in levels and about 0.4 in first differences. A direct subtraction of an estimate of the sampling variance (the Swamy method) results in a "residual" estimate of the true dispersion σ_β between 0.4 in levels and 0.2 in first differences, the latter still being about twice as high as our prior expectations. More "direct" estimates of σ_β which associate it with the coefficient of the squared x's (or their cross-products) in the squares and cross-products of residuals regressions or their maximum likelihood analogues, hover also, at their lower range, around 0.2. Thus, allowing for sampling variability or estimating the dispersion directly, still yields estimates that are "too high."

At this point there are two possibilities. We could accept the 0.2 estimate as real and revise our expectations. If we allow for the fact that our simple production function equation may be seriously misspecified (there may be decreasing or increasing returns to scale, capacity utilization fluctuations may matter, capital may be mismeasured, etc.), then it may be reasonable to expect the β in a misspecified equation to have a different prior distribution. For example, a more agnostic view would still keep it between zero and one but would not be surprised by a standard deviation of 0.2. An alternative, though not mutually exclusive possibility, would lead us to inquire into the "reality" of this heterogeneity and its stability over time. Unless the misspecification is in some sense permanent, there will be some instability in the estimates.

We have actually explored a number of first-order extensions of our model and found that they do not reduce the estimated σ_β significantly. Neither letting go of the constant returns assumption or using value added output measures or including materials as another input (in the French and Japanese samples) changes our results significantly. The "improvement" in the specification is counterbalanced by the decline in the "net" variance of the capital-labor ratio from which the β's have to be estimated.[16] The impact of capacity utilization fluctuations remains still to be explored because we do not have a good handle on it in our data. However, its effect is unlikely to be "stable," and we would expect that it differs from period to period.

We also worried about the possibility that the observed heterogeneity is just an artifact of a few outliers and that using some alternative more "robust" approach may make it go away. A look at figure 1 should be enough to convince one that this is not the case. Nevertheless, we pursued two approaches toward robustness. In one approach, we eliminate all firms whose (within) variance in x was either very small or extremely large. This had essentially zero effect on our estimated "true" σ_β^2, since it reduced the observed variance and the estimated sampling variance about equally. The other approach computes a robust estimate of the observed variance of the β's from their interquartile range and subtracts from it the *median* of the estimated sampling variances (rather than their mean). This resulted also in only minor changes in the final estimates of the "true" σ_β^2.[17] It is clear that the "overdispersion" that we observe is not the result of a few errant firms, but is actually a pervasive aspect of our data and our approach to them.

Why do we care about heterogeneity? If people differ in their response coefficients and if we contemplate some experiment that will impinge differentially on them, then it would be valuable to know how they differ and how this is related to any policy change we may wish to pursue. It they do differ but these differences are not permanent, then knowing their heterogeneity today may not help us any tomorrow. This leads us to question also the time stability of the β's and not just their cross-sectional heterogeneity. One way of asking this question is to divide our period into two, redo the analysis, and investigate the question of whether the estimated heterogeneity is more or less the "same" in both periods and whether the estimated within period β's are correlated with each other.

The results of reestimating our model for each firm in each of the countries, separately for the two subperiods (before and after the first oil shock): 1967–1973 and 1974–1979, are given in table 9.

The correlation between the estimated $\hat{\beta}_i$'s in the two subperiods for our three samples and both in levels and first differences (the last two columns of row 4), are remarkably low, on the order .05 to .10. Even if we take into account the attenuation resulting from sampling errors, they imply a rather substantial time instability in these estimates and throw serious doubt on the "reality" of our previous estimates of heterogeneity. The associated estimates of σ_β (row 3), which are consistent with these correlations (σ_β^2 being estimated by the between subperiod covariance), are in fact much lower than the total period based estimates (and much lower also than the estimates based on each subperiod separately).[18] They are now much closer to what we might think is a priori reasonable. Moreover, the levels and first differences based estimates are now very close to each other.

For comparison purposes we also list similar numbers for the intercept coefficients α (in the equation in levels) and capital shares. The intercepts (or constant terms) are not as "constant" as one might have thought, since the correlations between their periods estimates are of the order of 0.50; they are, however, much more stable than the slope parameter β and the heterogeneity in them is much more "permanent."[19] The same remarks apply, even more markedly, to the capital shares. It seems, however, that the capital elasticity β, at least the way we estimated it, is a much less stable aspect of average firm behavior.[20]

The most common way of allowing for heterogeneity in such studies as ours using individual firm data is to estimate separate equations for different industries. We have already done something along these lines by

Table 9.
Heterogeneity Estimates, from the analysis in the two periods: 1967–1973 and 1974–1979[a]

	Capital share	Intercept coefficients (α)	Capital coefficients (β) Levels	Capital coefficients (β) First differences
France				
s_b observed	.096	.442	.542	.414
σ_β "true" (tp)	.094	.414	.440	.213
σ_β "true" (bp)	.089	.348	.110	.113
Corr bp	.76	.45	.05	.05
Corr (sc, $\hat{\beta}$)			.04	−.01
Japan				
s_b observed	.103	.455	.625	.434
σ_β "true" (tp)	.098	.427	.539	.258
σ_β "true" (bp)	.094	.345	.186	.180
Corr bp	.68	.41	.06	.09
Corr (sc, $\hat{\beta}$)			−.01	.02
United States				
s_b observed		.349	.403	.321
σ_β "true" (tp)		.306	.323	.218
σ_β "true" (bp)		.308	.152	.154
Corr bp		.55	.09	.12

[a] s_b observed, computed from the dispersion of the separately estimated coefficients (or the firm variable means). From table 2. σ_β "true" (tp), estimated "true" dispersion, based on the total period 1967–1979 (tp). From table 2. σ_β "true" (bp), estimated from the covariance between the separately estimated capital coefficients in the two periods (or the means of the variables). Corr bp, observed correlation between the separately estimated capital coefficients in the two periods. Corr (sc, $\hat{\beta}$), correlation between the average capital share and the estimated (total period) capital coefficients. Unavailable for U.S.

allowing fourteen separate industry-year constants. But we can ask the additional question: Does the estimated heterogeneity have any "industrial" content? A priori, we would think that it should have some. Otherwise, the "reality" of the estimated dispersion in the β_i's may be doubtful and also the usefulness of knowing it, even if it were present. To check on this, we can run an analysis of variance of the estimated individual slope coefficients using fourteen industry dummy variables. They account, however, for about 2 to 7 percent of the observed variance in the $\hat{\beta}_i$'s. In both levels and first differences, and in all three countries, only two or three industries (moreover different in each of the three countries) display average coefficients which are statistically significantly different and that barely from the overall manufacturing average. Hence there does not seem to be any consistent industry differences in the firm heterogeneity as estimated by us. (See table 12 in appendix 2 for separate estimates at the individual industry level, which convey the same message.)

Still another way of investigating the "reality" of the observed dispersion in the β's is to ask how they are correlated with other independent estimates of the same parameter. Under the assumption of competition and constant returns to scale the capital share should equal β. Even if one relaxes these assumptions and allows for deviation from purely competitive conditions or constant returns to scale, one would still expect a significant positive correlation between the regression estimates and the capital shares. These correlations can be computed for the French and Japanese samples (line 5 of table 9); they are negligible. Even if one takes the maximal number of 0.04 for France and adjusts it upward for the attenuation due to sampling error, one would still get only 0.05 (!), which is much too small to allow us to think of either of the two estimates as being a reflection of the other. Once again, it appears that the estimated dispersion in the β's has little to do with what we may think a priori reasonable.

8. Interim Conclusions

What can we conclude about the average of our estimated β's, the capital elasticity of output, rather than its dispersion? The major conclusion is that we have not solved the between-within puzzle. Heterogeneity is not the answer to it. This can be seen by comparing the different overall estimates (or means of individual estimates) that are reproduced, for convenience sake, in table 10.

Except for the United States, the within and between estimates (lines 1 and 2) differ significantly, but the within estimates and the unweighted

Table 10.
Alternative Estimates of the Capital-Output Elasticity β

	France	Japan	United States
Levels			
1. Between[a]	.313	.469	.222
	(.031)	(.023)	(.024)
2. Within[a]	.196	.278	.213
	(.011)	(.009)	(.008)
3. Average of individual β's[b,e]	.194	.273	.219
	(.026)	(.022)	(.019)
4. ML random effects $\bar{\beta}$[e]	.212	.291	.225
	(.022)	(.019)	(.016)
First differences			
5. Average of individual β's[b,e]	.232	.161	.283
	(.020)	(.015)	(.015)
6. ML random effects $\bar{\beta}$[d]	.246	.168	.300
	(.019)	(.014)	(.014)

[a] From table 1.
[b] From table 3.
[c] Standard errors computed from the observed variance across firms divided by $N - 1$.
[a] From tables 1 and 5
[b] From table 2
[c] From table 3
[d] From table 4
[e] Standard errors for average estimates are computed from observed variance across firms divided by $N - 1$.

(arithmetic) means of the individually estimated β's do not. Thus there is no (negative) correlation between the weighting scheme of the within estimator and the individual β's, and hence this correlation is not the culprit for its "lowness." On the other hand, there do appear to be real correlated effects, a least for the French and Japanese samples (i.e., a positive correlation between the individual intercepts α and the x's) which might be taken as substantiating a positive bias in the between estimator.

There is not evidence, however, of a significant correlation of the β's (and the x's). The maximum-likelihood estimates (lines 4 and 6) which impose the no correlation assumption turn out to be essentially the same as the means of the individual estimates (lines 3 and 5). In a sense, this evidence of no real relation between the individually estimated β's and the capital-labor ratios is another indication of the "unreality" or irrelevance of their estimated heterogeneity. What is comforting in table 10 is, however, the relative closeness of the various estimates of the average β is compared to our different estimates of the true dispersion σ_β, even though there remain quite significant discrepancies between them.

What is then the answer to the rhetorical (and somewhat ambiguous) question in the title of this paper? It is negative given the current status of our data and the variables available to us. Without information on factor prices at the micro level and on actual capacity utilization, we are unlikely to find stable production relationships at the individual firm level. Moreover, the simple production function model, even when augmented by additional variables and further nonlinear terms, it at best just an approximation to a much more complex and changing reality at the firm, product, and factory floor level. While one can hope to get reasonable estimates of the average response coefficients that are consistent across different data sets and different estimation methods, there does not appear to be much promising content in the estimated dispersion. In this sense, if we are interested in the average behavior of productivity, then "aggregation," or more correctly pooling (i.e., estimating a common coefficient across a large number of firms), may not be "necessarily bad."[22]

Much more could be said about the various estimates than we have been able to do here. One could explore more the differences that arise from the assumption of correlated individual effects, from different treatments of serial correlation in the disturbances, and from the results of alternative estimation methods. But the main problem facing us remains the inadequacy of the underlying simple production function model. We need to figure out ways of allowing for the discrepancy between recorded inputs and actually used levels, for lags and anticipations, and the simultaneity in the various behavior relations associated with production decisions. As always, much work remains to be done, but then one needs also to start somewhere.

Appendix: Swamy-Type Estimates and Their Sensitivity to Heteroskedasticity and Serial Correlation

Since the Swamy-type estimates can be very sensitive to second-order misspecification of our model, we have computed them under alternative assumptions about the variance-covariance matrix of the errors. A worthwhile extension of this work would be to base them on more robust estimates of the variances, using nonparameteric methods such as the jackknife or the bootstrap.

We use the following matrix notation, in addition to that given in section 3 of the text: Δ is the (2,2) variance-covariance matrix of the coefficients (i.e., $\delta_{11} = \sigma_\beta^2$, $\delta_{22} = \sigma_\alpha^2$, $\delta_{12} = \delta_{21} = \sigma_{\alpha\beta}$), Σ_i is the (T, T) variance-covariance matrix of the errors ε_{it} for firm i ($\Sigma_i = E(\varepsilon_i \varepsilon_i')$), x_i is the $(T, 2)$ matrix of observations on x for firm i and the constant (i.e., $X_i = (x_i, 1_T)$), and $\boldsymbol{\beta}$ stands for the (2,2) vector of mean coefficients (i.e., $\boldsymbol{\beta} = (\beta, \alpha)'$).

The individual firm OLS estimates and their corresponding sampling variances are as follows:

$$\hat{\boldsymbol{\beta}}_i = (X_i'X_i)^{-1}X_i'y_i,$$

$$V(\hat{\beta}_i|X_i, \beta_i) = (X_i'X_i)^{-1}X_i'\Sigma_i X_i(X_i'X_i)^{-1}.$$

The observed variance-covariance matrix of the individual firm OLS estimates is

$$\hat{V}(\beta_i) = \frac{1}{N-1}\sum_{i=1}^{N} (\hat{\beta}_i - \bar{\beta})(\hat{\beta}_i - \bar{\beta})' \quad \text{with } \bar{\beta} = \frac{1}{N}\sum_{i=1}^{N} \hat{\beta}_i.$$

We can show that

$$V(\bar{\beta}_i) = VE(\hat{\beta}_i|X_i, \beta_i) + EV(\hat{\beta}_i|X_i, \beta_i)$$

$$= \Delta + EV(\hat{\beta}_i|X_i, \beta_i).$$

The matrix $E(V(\hat{\beta}_i|X_v, \beta_i)$ can be estimated by the average of the individual sampling variance-covariance matrices:

$$\bar{V}(\hat{\beta}_i|X_i, \beta_i) = \frac{1}{N}\sum_{i=1}^{N} V(\hat{\beta}_i|X_i, \beta_i)$$

assuming that ε_{it} are uncorrelated across firms. Hence the variance-covariance matrix of the "true" coefficients Δ can be estimated by

$$\hat{\Delta} = V(\beta_i) - \bar{V}(\hat{\beta}_i|X_i, \beta_i).$$

This formula generalizes that given by Swamy, where heteroskedasticity is allowed only across firms, i.e., $\Sigma_i = \sigma_{\varepsilon_i}^2 I$ (I being the (T, T) identity matrix).[23]

Thus, different assumptions about Σ_i yield alternative estimates of Δ. This is conditional, however, on obtaining consistent estimates of Σ in the panel data context, with N going to "infinity" for a fixed T.[24] The most simple case is that of homoskedasticity and independence of the errors:

$$\Sigma_i = \sigma_\varepsilon^2 I$$

and

$$V(\hat{\beta}_i) = \frac{1}{N}\sigma_\varepsilon^2 \sum_{i=1}^{N} (X_i'X_i)^{-1}.$$

It is also possible to allow for heteroskedasticity across firms (as Swamy originally did): $\Sigma_i = \sigma_{\varepsilon_i}^2 I$, the sampling variance being computed then as the arithmetic average of the individually estimated sampling variances:

$$\frac{1}{N}\sum_{i=1}^{N} \sigma_{\varepsilon_i}^2 (X_i'X_i)^{-1}$$

Another case is that of heteroskedasticity within firms only, where Σ_i is a constant diagonal matrix.[25]

In order to deal with serial correlation, we assume a (T, T) autocorrelation matrix of the errors TCOR corresponding to an autoregression of the first order with autocorrelation parameter $\rho = 0.5$ in levels (and the corresponding autocorrelation matrix in first differences). Following Solon (1984), a close examination of the first three serial autocorrelation coefficients of the residuals computed both from the fixed effects specifications in levels and in first differences, indeed suggests that a first-order autoregression with a ρ of about 0.5 would be an adequate description of the error process. To take into account the serial correlation of the errors, we have also used the Cochran-Orcutt transformation to compute the Swamy estimates in quasi-difference form (i.e., $(y_{it} - 0.5y_{it-1})$, and $(x_{it} - 0.5x_{it-1})$).

The various estimates of the "true" variance in the coefficients, that we can compute under these different assumptions, are given in table 11. We also present in this table the corresponding QGLS estimates of the mean β. These results are given only for the French sample, since they are very similar for our other two samples.

The direction of the potential biases that we see in the estimated σ_β^2 is what one might have expected, but their magnitude is more of a surprise. Allowing for heteroskedasticity across firms or within firms increases the estimated σ_β^2 by about 0.01 to 0.03. This increase is relatively minor for the level estimates, but is more serious for the first difference estimates, since they are much smaller than the former and of about the same order of magnitude. Such bias, however, corresponds to a negative correlation (across or within firms) between the variance of the residuals and the corresponding squares of the x's (or Δx's), which may be in part spurious (due to sampling errors or outliers: very small or very large squares of the x's or Δx's).

Taking into account the serial autocorrelation of the errors affects our level estimates more, changing the estimated σ_β^2 from about 0.18 to 0.13.

Table 11.
Alternative Swamy's Estimates for the French Sample

Various types of estimates	Estimates in levels β	σ_α^2	$\sigma_{\alpha\beta}^2$	σ_β^2	Estimates in first differences β	σ_β^2	Estimates in quasi-differences[a] β	σ_β^2
1. Observed	0.194	0.194	−0.054	0.293	0.232	0.171	0.227	0.187
2. "True" if $\sum_i = \hat{\sigma}_\varepsilon^2 I$[b]	0.212	0.167	−0.050	0.181	0.254	0.011	0.227	0.072
	(0.024)				(0.015)		(0.018)	
3. "True" if $\sum_i = \hat{\sigma}_{\varepsilon i}^2 I$	0.196	0.171	−0.048	0.193	0.233	0.045	0.220	0.089
	(0.024)				(0.016)		(0.018)	
4. "True" if $\sum_i = \text{diag}(\hat{\sum})$	0.211	0.171	−0.050	0.195	0.251	0.023	0.229	0.078
	(0.024)				(0.015)		(0.018)	
5. "True" if $\sum_i = \hat{\sigma}_\varepsilon^2 TCOR$[c]	0.219	0.152	−0.050	0.132	0.248	0.011	—	—
	(0.023)				(0.014)			

[a] Quasi-differences: $y_t - .5y_{t-1}$, $x_t - .5x_{t-1}$.
[b] $\sum_i$, variance-covariance matrix of the residuals for firm i.
[c] TCOR is the autocorrelation matrix that corresponds to $\rho_\tau = \rho^\tau$, with $\rho = 0.5$ in levels, and the derived autocorrelation matrix in first differences.

Table 12.
Heterogeneity Estimates by Industry[a]

Sectors		France				Japan				United States			
		N	β_i	s_β	σ_β	N	β_i	s_β	σ_β	N	β_i	s_β	σ_β
All	Total manufacturing	441	.232	.414	.213	845	.161	.434	.258	462	.283	.321	.218
1	Food industries	31	.321	.357	.135	70	.236	.376	.228	38	.492	.329	.164
2	Paper and allied products	14	.240	.342	0*	28	.419	.345	0*	22	.248	.344	.229
3	Chemicals (e.g., drugs)	14	.327	.683	.534	87	.140	.392	.199	20	.353	.264	.197
4	Rubber, misc. plastic products	25	.028	.357	0*	36	.221	.391	.233	18	.490	.315	.234
5	Stone, clay, and class products	62	.295	.364	.085	44	.092	.439	.229	18	.185	.242	.131
6	Primary metal industries	22	.279	.454	.234	49	.156	.426	.248	30	.229	.372	.174
7	Fabricated metal products	39	.182	.414	.165	66	.226	.633	.493	32	.260	.339	.253
8	Machinery and instruments	84	.104	.435	.233	156	.050	.492	.225	72	.257	.242	.100
9	Electrical equipment	55	.277	.464	.331	135	.154	.364	.172	60	.337	.277	.190
10	Autos and ground transp. equip.	23	.245	.336	0*	42	.228	.399	.300	21	.124	.464	.403
11	Aircraft, boats, and space vehicles	11	.144	.271	0*	23	.057	.288	0*	15	.287	.331	.141
12	Textiles and appareils	32	.318	.379	.063	50	.320	.373	.218	34	.218	.296	.169
13	Drugs	17	.361	.350	.242	33	.033	.302	.181	43	.244	.315	.239
14	Miscellaneous industries	12	.392	.307	.193	26	.178	.397	.301	39	.223	.328	.240

[a] See notes to table 2 for definitions.

This is confirmed by the quasi-differenced estimates, which are even smaller, with estimated σ_{β}^2 of about 0.08. The first differences based estimates of the sampling variance are not, however, biased by the (negative) serial correlation in the differenced errors, because the differenced Δx's are practically uncorrelated over time (contrary to the x's in levels which are strongly positively correlated).

It is interesting to note that there is little difference in the various QGLS estimates of β corresponding to the various weighting schemes. Contrary to the variance estimators, they are all consistent under the alternative (second-order) misspecification of the variance-covariance matrix of the errors.

Acknowledgments

We are indebted to the National Science Foundation (SES-82-0806), CNRS, the Sloan Foundation, and the NBER Productivity Program for financial support. We are grateful to Thomas Abbott, Jean Marie Chanut, and Ghazala Mansuri for research assistance and to Bronwyn Hall for many useful discussions. We have also benefited from comments by Gary Chamberlain, Christian Gourieroux, Bill Mason, Alain Monfort, Bill Randolph and Alain Trognon.

Notes

1. For examples of this work see Griliches and Mairesse 1983, 1984, and 1985 and Mairesse 1988.

2. What is visible in this paper is only the tip of an iceberg of a great deal of work with these data. There are many interesting but tangential issues, both substantive and econometric, which could be taken up as we traverse this range of topics.

3. The first differences results exhibit similar discrepancies, between the total and within estimates on the one hand and the between estimates on the other. For more details on such results, see Mairesse, 1988 and 1990.

4. Using the notations and framework given in the next section, the between estimates can be written as

$$\hat{b}_{\mathrm{b}} = \sum_i b_i d_i^2,$$

where

$$\hat{b}_i = (\bar{y}_{i\cdot} - \bar{y}_{\cdot\cdot})/(\bar{x}_{i\cdot} - \bar{x}_{\cdot\cdot})$$

and

$$d_i^2 = (\bar{x}_{i\cdot} - \bar{x}_{\cdot\cdot})^2 \Big/ \sum_i (\bar{x}_{i\cdot} - \bar{x}_{\cdot\cdot})^2.$$

While the within estimates are equivalent to

$$b_w = \sum_i \hat{\beta}_i w_i^2,$$

where

$$\hat{\beta}_i = \sum_t (x_{it} - \bar{x}_{i\cdot})(y_{it} - \bar{y}_{i\cdot}) \Big/ \sum_t (x_{it} - \bar{x}_{i\cdot})^2$$

and

$$w_i^2 = \sum_t (x_{it} - \bar{x}_{i\cdot})^2 \Big/ \sum_j \sum_t (x_{it} - x_{j\cdot})^2.$$

The argument in the text assumes that $E\hat{b}_i = E\hat{\beta}_i = \beta_i$, which implies the absence of "correlated effects" ($\hat{\alpha}_i$'s related to the x's). $E(b_w)$ will be less than $E(\hat{b}_b)$, if there is a negative correlation between the β_i's and the w's.

5. Since the x's are also economic choice variables, this assumption may not be reasonable for either the α's or the β's. In a nonconstant returns case, with x (the capital-labor ratio) fully variable, it would be proportional to $\beta_i/(1 - \beta_i)$. This could introduce a correlated effects problem in the cross-sectional estimates, but would not be a problem in the time-series dimension, where most of the variability in x would come from changes in the relevant factor prices.

6. See Hsiao 1986 for more elaborate versions, which allow for variability in both dimensions. However, the simple specification of the form $\beta_{it} = \beta_i + \lambda_t$, which allows only for synchronized changes across firms, does not fit the data any better. More elaborate specifications—such as $\beta_{it} = (1 - \psi)\beta_i + \psi_{it-1} + \mu_{it}$, proposed by Rosenberg (1973), or $\beta_{it} = \beta_i + \mu_i\lambda_t$, proposed by Cragg (1987)—might be more satisfactory. For a more general approach to the problem of specifying and testing parameter heterogeneity and stability see Dutta and Leon 1986.

7. In the opposite direction, the F statistics computed for the growth rates of labor productivity and capital intensity are smaller than 1 and do not reject the hypothesis of homogeneity—which is consistent with our previous remark on growth rates differentials across firms.

8. See Scheffe 1959 for the relation between this approach and the overall standard F test.

9. Both figures 1 and 2 plot the levels based β_i. The corresponding graphs for the first differences based β_i are similar in shape but the dispersion is smaller. In the French sample, there are only three β_i's whose t-ratios fall outside the 6.3 range.

10. See Swamy 1971, and also Anderson 1973 and Magnus 1978.

11. See White 1981, 1982, and also Gouriéroux, Monfort, and Trognon 1984.

12. Note that the estimated $\sigma_{\alpha\beta}$ in table 3 are not significantly different from zero. Our ML estimates are almost unchanged if we assume $\sigma_{\alpha\beta} = 0$.

13. With our large number of observations, $2LR/p$ values are in fact equal or almost so to F values; they differ here only because the F given in table 2 are based on a different weighting.

14. Given our large number of observations, the standard errors of the estimated coefficients are very small. As could be expected, the robust standard errors are larger than the usual ones for specifications A, B, and c. It is interesting to note that the two types of standard errors are almost the same for specifications C and b. Except for numerical errors of approximation, they should be in fact strictly equal, since the heteroskedasticity of the type generated by random coefficients is the only one to enter into their computations.

15. See among others Hildreth and Houck 1968, Goldfeld and Quandt 1972, Amemiya 1977, MaCurdy 1981, 1985, or Randolph 1986.

16. This can be illustrated by considering parallel results that do not include separate time-industry constants, putting all of the trend effects into the capital-labor ratio. Such estimates yield, obviously, a much higher $\bar{\beta}$ (e.g., 0.41 versus 0.16 in first differences for Japan), but also a much *smaller* dispersion (an observed σ_β of 0.31 versus 0.43) and the implication of no true heterogeneity, all of the observed dispersion being attributable to sampling variability. Thus, adding statistically important variables, the industry year dummies, and reducing thereby the potential misspecification of the model, increases the estimated heterogeneity of β's instead of reducing it.

17. The observed variance estimated from the interquartile range is smaller than the one "normally" computed: 0.20 instead of 0.29 in levels and 0.14 instead of 0.17 in first differences, in the case of the French sample. However, the median of the sampling variances is also smaller than the mean: 0.05 instead of 0.10 in levels, and 0.08 instead of 0.12 in first differences. In total, these two reductions largely offset each other: σ_β^2 goes down only from 0.19 to 0.15 in levels (σ_β from 0.44 to 0.39) and remains about 0.05 in first differences (σ_β of 0.22).

18. Assuming that the sampling errors affecting our individual estimates in each of the subperiods, are independent, we can write: $\hat{\beta}_i^1 = \beta_i^1 + e_i^1$ and $\hat{\beta}_i^2 = \beta_i^2 + e_i^2$ with $\text{cov}(e_i^1, e_i^2) = 0$. The observed correlation (between $\hat{\beta}_i^1$ and $\hat{\beta}_i^2$) will underestimate the true correlation (between β_i^1 and β_i^2), in a proportion that can be computed from the estimated sampling variances. Assuming also the stability of the individual coefficients over time ($\beta_i = \beta_i^1 = \beta_i^2$), the covariance between the subperiods estimates provides also a direct estimate of the true variance $\sigma_\beta^2 = \text{var}(\beta) = \text{cov}(\hat{\beta}_i^1, \hat{\beta}_i^2)$.

19. If we adjust it for the sampling error bias, the correlation between the periods estimates is raised, in the case of the French sample, from .05 to .18 for β, as against from .45 to .88 for α. Or else: the true variance based on the between periods covariance is about 6 percent of that based on the total period observed variance for β in levels (28 percent in first differences), while it is about 70% for α.

20. However, it does not seem that the time instability in β could be simply characterized by pure random (and independent) shocks. It will correspond better to shocks which would be strongly correlated and most likely non stationary (with some kind of "drift" from year to year and possible "accidents" in specific years). That is what is suggested, as we already noted, by our estimates based on the system of (non-constrained) regressions on the squares and cross-products of residuals obtained in levels or with Chamberlain's approach. This is also what is suggested by an analysis in which we break our data into even and odd years, rather than the early and latter periods. The correlation between the β's are in this case much higher: .50 instead of .05 for the French sample.

21. Such comparisons can be interprated as specification tests a la Hausman (Hausman 1978; Hausman and Taylor 1981). The estimates being either very close, or very different, it is superfluous, given our large number of observations, to perform the tests explicitly and compute their levels of significance.

22. See Grunfeld and Griliches 1961.

23. The Swamy estimate given in table 2 are computed in this way.

24. This condition raises certain difficulties; see for example Carter and Yang 1986 and Kiefer 1980.

25. There is an identification problem in discussing heteroskedasticity in the context of random coefficient models. It is not always possible to distinguish the heteroskedasticity coming from the random coefficients and that pertaining to the overall disturbance in the model. The only heteroskedasticity that matters here is one that is a function of the x's but that, in principle, should be in the definition of β_{it}. Since our main focus is on the variability of β_{it} in the i (individual) dimension, it is sufficient for us to define $\beta_{it} = \beta_i + e_{it}$, where β and μ_{it} are independently distributed, and to throw the $(\mu_{it}x_{it})$ terms into the definition of the overall disturbance ε_{it}.

References

Amemiya, T. 1977. "A Note on a Heteroskedastic Model." *Journal of Econometrics* 5: 295–299.

Anderson, T. W. 1973. "Asymptotically Efficient Estimation of Covariance Matrices with Linear Structure." *Annals of Statistics* 1: 135–141.

Carter, R. L., and M. C. K. Yang. 1986. "Large Sample Inference in Random Coefficient Regression Models." *Communications in Statistics, Part A, Theory and Methods* 15(8): 2507–2525.

Chamberlain, G. 1984. "Panel Data." In *Handbook of Econometrics,* volume 2, ed. Z. Griliches and M. Intriligator (North-Holland).

Cragg, J. G. 1987. A Bilinear Model for Heteroskedastic Panel Data. University of British Columbia Department of Economics Discussion Paper No. 87–23.

Dutta, J., and H. L. Leon. 1986. Testing for Heterogeneous Parameters in a Least Squares Framework. First Boston Working Paper Series 86–32, Columbia University Graduate School of Business.

Goldfeld, S. R., and R. M. Quandt. 1972. *Non-Linear Methods in Econometrics.* North-Holland.

Gouriéroux, C., A. Monfort, and A. Trognon. 1984. "Pseudo Maximum Likelihood Methods." *Econometrica* 52: 681–720.

Griliches, Z., and J. Mairesse. 1983. "Comparing Productivity Growth: An Exploration of French and U.S. Industrial and Firm Data." *European Economic Review* 21: 89–119.

Griliches, Z., and J. Mairesse. 1984. "Productivity and R&D at the Firm Level." In *R-D Patents and Productivity*, ed. Z. Griliches (University of Chicago Press).

Griliches, Z., and J. Mairesse. 1985. R&D and Productivity Growth: Comparing Japanese and U.S. Manufacturing Firms. National Bureau of Economic Research Working Paper No. 1778.

Grunfeld, Y., and Z. Griliches. 1960. "Is Aggregation Necessarily Bad?" *Review of Economics and Statistics*: 1–13.

Hausman, J. A. 1978. "Specification Tests in Econometrics." *Econometrica* 46: 1251–1273.

Hausman, J. A., and Taylor, W. E. 1981. "Panel Data and Unobservable Individual Effects." *Econometrica* 49: 1377–1398.

Hildreth, C., and J. P. Houck. 1968. "Some Estimates for a Linear Model with Random Coefficients." *Journal of the American Association* 63: 584–595.

Hsiao, C. 1986. *Analysis of Panel Data.* Cambridge University Press.

Kiefer, N. M. 1980. "Estimation of Fixed Effect Models for Time Series of Cross-Sections with Arbitrary Intertemporal Covariance." *Journal of Econometrics* 14: 195–202.

Leamer, E. E. 1978. *Specification Searches: Ad hoc Inference with Nonexperimental Data.* Wiley.

MaCurdy, T. 1981. Multiple Time-Series Models Applied to Panel Data. National Bureau of Economic Research Working Paper No. 646.

MaCurdy, T. 1985. A Guide to Applying Time Series Models to Panel Data. Unpublished paper, Stanford University.

Magnus, J. R. 1978."Maximum Likelihood Estimation of the GLS Model with Unknown Parameters in the Disturbance Covariance Matrix." *Journal of Econometrics* 7: 281–312.

Mairesse, J. 1988. "Les lois de la production ne sont plus ce qu'elle etaient: une introduction a l'econometrice des panels." *Revue Economique* (1): 225–271.

Mairesse, J. 1990. "Time-series and Cross-sectional Estimates on Panel Data: Why Are They Different and Why Should They Be Equal?" In *Panel Data and Labor Market Studies*, ed. J. Hartog, G. Ridder, and J. Theeuwes (North-Holland).

Mundlak, Y. 1978. "On the Pooling of Time Series and Cross-Section Data." *Econometrica* 46: 69–85.

Randolph, W. C. 1986. Consistent Least Squares Estimation of Error Covariance Parameters for Regression Models with Linear Covariance Structure. United States Bureau of Labor Statistics, unpublished paper.

Rosenberg, B. 1973. "The Analysis of a Cross-section of Time Series by Stochastically Convergent Parameter Regression." *Annals of Economic and Social Measurement* 2: 399–428.

Scheffe, H. 1959. *The Analysis of Variance*. Wiley.

Solon, G. 1984. Estimating Autocorrelation in Fixed Effects Models. National Bureau of Economic Research Technical Working Paper No. 32.

Swamy, P. A. V. B. 1970. "Efficient Inference in a Random Coefficient Model." *Econometrica* 38: 311–323.

Swamy, P. A. V. B. 1971. *Statistical Inference in Random Coefficient Regression Models*. Springer-Verlag.

White, H. 1980. "A Heteroskedasticity-Consistent Covariance Matrix Estimation and a Direct Test for Heteroskedasticity." *Econometrica* 48: 817–838.

White, H. 1982. "Maximum Likelihood Estimators of Misspecified Models." *Econometrica* 50(1): 1–25.

34

A Note on the Efficiency of Two-Step Estimation Methods

Alain Trognon and
Christian Gouriéroux

The progress of theoretical economics has yielded econometric modeling of very high complexity. In such a context the maximum-likelihood principle has been at first the single inference method capable of giving an answer to the statistical questions of the practitioners. Those economic researchers are facing the calculus constraint of the computers and the very high costs for the construction of their models by maximizing likelihood functions. Thus, the econometric theory has developed some general principles which yield to some estimation methods whose implementation are less costly than the maximum-likelihood technique. Furthermore those methods do not involve all the parameters of the true model. They can be applied to smoother specifications where the parameters of interest play the more important roles. Such a class of estimation methods contains pseudo-maximum-likelihood estimation, *M*-estimation, generalized methods of moments, and asymptotic least squares. All these methods are computed by maximizing a data-dependent objective function with respect to the parameters of interest.

Even for those attractive methods, the numerical part of parameter estimation can be cumbersome. It can often be simplified a lot by using a two-step estimation method. Two-step methods are very common in the case of generalized linear models since the quasi-generalized least-squares estimator is one of them. It is well known that QGLS is asymptotically as efficient as GLS. Such a property is unfortunately very rare. In effect, the asymptotic variance of the first round estimator has in general an influence on the asymptotic variance of the second round estimator.

In the present paper, our question is: Is it possible by modifying the initial objective function to produce a two-step estimation method without any efficiency loss? If it is possible, there will be numerical gains in the estimation of the parameters of interest without more dispersion.

The modifications of the objective function are based on some ancient ideas developed by Hartley (1961) and for instance applied in the context of autocorrelated autoregressive models by Hatanaka (1974).

In section I the general framework is described. Section II gives some general indications on the two-step methods and produces an approximated objective function which has the required properties. The following sections are devoted to several applications of the approximated objective function: nonlinear least-squares and Hatanaka's estimation, efficient two-step estimation of TOBIT models, and two-step techniques for marginal and conditional maximum-likelihood estimators.

I. The General Framework

Applied econometricians are using more and more frequently estimation methods based upon the maximization of a data-dependent objective function. Those methods cover a large class of estimation procedures: maximum-likelihood method, least-squares method, *M*-estimator, generalized method of moment (GMM), or asymptotic least squares (ALS). Whatever the method used is, the estimator of the parameter of interest is defined by

$$\hat{\theta}_T = \underset{\theta}{\operatorname{argmax}}\ \Psi_T(\theta), \tag{1}$$

where $\Psi_T(\cdot)$ is a real random function which depends upon the observed sample of size T. When the econometrician has at his disposal T observations on an endogenous variable y and K exogenous variables $x' = (x_1, \dots, x_K)$ the *M*-estimator of θ is associated with

$$\Psi_T(\theta) = \sum_{t=1}^{T} \psi(y_t, x_t, \theta),$$

where ψ is a real function. When

$$\psi(y_t, x_t, \theta) = -(y_t - x_t'\theta)^2,$$

$\hat{\theta}_T$ is the OLS estimator. In the case of GMM, $\Psi_T(\theta)$ is a distance between an estimator and an associated function of the parameters; for ALS the objective function is some quadratic form of the identifiable conditions of the parameters.

In the sequel, Ψ_T will be two times differentiable with respect to θ. In that case, if the set of variation for θ is open, $\hat{\theta}_T$ is given by the first-order conditions

$$\frac{\partial \Psi_T}{\partial \theta}(\hat{\theta}_T) = 0.$$

If θ_0 is the true value of the parameter of interest, it can be shown (see White 1985, for example) that under the following assumptions:

$$\frac{1}{T}\Psi_T(\theta) \xrightarrow{\text{p.s.}} \Psi_\infty(\theta), \tag{A1}$$

$$\theta_0 = \underset{\theta}{\operatorname{argmax}}\, \Psi_\infty(\theta), \tag{A2}$$

$$\frac{1}{\sqrt{T}}\frac{\partial \Psi_T}{\partial \theta}(\theta_0) \xrightarrow{L} N(0, I_0), \tag{A3}$$

$$-\frac{1}{T}\frac{\partial^2 \Psi_T}{\partial \theta \partial \theta'}(\theta_0) \xrightarrow{\text{p.s.}} J_0^{-1} I_0 J_0^{-1}. \tag{A4}$$

Then

$$\frac{1}{\sqrt{T}}\frac{\partial \Psi_T}{\partial \theta}(\theta_0) - J_0\sqrt{T}(\hat{\theta}_T - \theta_0) \xrightarrow{P} 0$$

and

$$\sqrt{T}(\hat{\theta}_T - \theta_0) \xrightarrow{L} N(0, J_0^{-1} I_0 J_0^{-1}).$$

II. Case When There Exists a Previous Consistent Estimation of a Part of the Parameter of Interest

Very often the optimization program (1) is very complicated but it is very simple for a subvector of the parameter when the complement subvector is known. In such a situation it is very attractive to proceed in two steps if there exists a consistent estimator of the second part of the parameter. More clearly, if $\theta = (\alpha, \beta)$ and if $\tilde{\beta}_T$ is a consistent estimation of β, the initial program (1) can be replaced by

$$\tilde{\alpha}_T = \underset{\alpha}{\operatorname{argmax}}\, \Psi_T(\alpha, \tilde{\beta}_T). \tag{2}$$

Program (2) is simpler than (1) since the dimension of the problem is smaller. But, sometimes the gain in proceeding in two steps as for (2) is much more important. For example, consider the case of the autocorrelated model $y_t = x_t'\alpha + u_t$, $u_t = \beta u_{t-1} + v_t$, $v_t \sim \text{iid}(\alpha, \sigma^2)$. The Cochrane-Orcutt or the Hildreth-Lu method yields an estimator of $\theta' = (\alpha', \beta')$ which minimizes

$$\Psi_T(\alpha, \beta) = \sum_{t=1}^{T} (y_t - \beta y_{t-1} - (x_t' - \beta x_{t-1}')\alpha)^2.$$

When β is estimated by $\tilde{\beta}_T$, (2) yields to the feasible generalized least squares for α, which can be computed by OLS on the quasi-first-differentiated model. The first-order conditions are nonlinear for (1) but linear for (2).

Unfortunately, this numerical simplification is not always neutral with respect to the asymptotic properties of α. This is particularly true if there exists some lagged endogenous variables among x_t. In that context, the asymptotic distribution of $\tilde{\alpha}_T$ depends heavily on the asymptotic distribution of $\tilde{\beta}_T$. The question is: Is it possible to modify $\Psi_T(\alpha, \tilde{\beta}_T)$ into $\Pi_T(\alpha, \tilde{\beta}_T)$ such that the optimization program based on Π_T yields to an estimator of α as efficient as the one based on Ψ_T and whose asymptotic distribution is independant of $\tilde{\beta}_T$?

To solve such a problem, it is convenient to consider the second-order expansion of $\Psi_T(\alpha, \beta)$ around $(\alpha, \tilde{\beta}_T)$,

$$\Psi_T(\alpha, \beta) \simeq \Psi_T(\alpha, \tilde{\beta}_T) + \frac{\partial \Psi_T}{\partial \beta'}(\alpha, \tilde{\beta}_T)(\beta - \tilde{\beta}_T)$$
$$+ \tfrac{1}{2}(\beta - \tilde{\beta}_T)' \frac{\partial^2 \Psi_T}{\partial \beta \partial \beta'}(\alpha, \tilde{\beta}_T)(\beta - \tilde{\beta}_T),$$

and let

$$\Phi_T(\alpha, \beta/\tilde{\beta}_T) = \Psi_T(\alpha, \tilde{\beta}_T) + \frac{\partial \Psi_T}{\partial \beta'}(\alpha, \tilde{\beta}_T)(\beta - \tilde{\beta}_T)$$
$$- \tfrac{1}{2}(\beta - \tilde{\beta}_T)' T J_T(\alpha)(\beta - \tilde{\beta}_T), \tag{3}$$

where $J_T(\alpha)$ is a random matrix such that

$$\operatorname*{Plim}_{T \to \infty} \left[J_T(\alpha_0) + \frac{1}{T} \frac{\partial^2 \Psi_T}{\partial \beta \partial \beta'}(\alpha_0, \beta_0) \right] = 0.$$

In the following, Φ_T will be called "approximated objective function."

Property 1. If Assumptions A1–A4 are fulfilled by Ψ_T, if $\sqrt{T}(\tilde{\beta}_T - \beta_0)$ converges in distribution and if Φ_T is defined by (3), then

$$(\tilde{\alpha}_T, \tilde{\beta}_T) = \underset{\alpha, \beta}{\text{argmax}}\ \Psi_T(\alpha, \beta)$$

and

$$(\alpha_T^*, \beta_T^*) = \underset{\alpha, \beta}{\text{argmax}}\ \Phi_T(\alpha, \beta/\tilde{\beta}_T)$$

are asymptotically equivalent, that is to say,

$$\operatorname*{Plim}_{T\to\infty} \sqrt{T}(\tilde{\alpha}_T - \alpha_T^*) = 0 \text{ and } \operatorname*{Plim}_{T\to\infty} \sqrt{T}(\hat{\beta}_T - \beta_T^*) = 0. \quad ■$$

Proof. See Appendix 1.

This property brings an answer to the question asked before. In effect, β_T^* can be directly expressed as a function of α_T^* and $\hat{\beta}_T$:

$$\beta_T^* = \hat{\beta}_T + [J_T(\alpha_T^*)]^{-1} \frac{1}{T} \frac{\partial \Psi_T}{\partial \beta} (\alpha_T^*, \hat{\beta}_T) \tag{4}$$

and α_T^* is the solution of the program $\operatorname*{Max}_{\alpha} \Pi_T(\alpha, \hat{\beta}_T)$ where

$$\Pi_T(\alpha, \hat{\beta}_T) = \Psi_T(\alpha, \hat{\beta}_T) + \frac{1}{2} \frac{\partial \Psi_T(\alpha, \hat{\beta}_T)}{\partial \beta'} [TJ_T(\alpha)]^{-1} \frac{\partial \Psi_T(\alpha, \hat{\beta}_T)}{\partial \beta}. \tag{5}$$

Comments

i. Starting with an objective function (Ψ_T), which produces some consistent estimators of α and β, it is possible to build a new objective function (Π_T) such that the estimator $\alpha_T^* = \text{argmax}\ \Pi_T(\alpha, \tilde{\beta}_T)$ has an asymptotic distribution that does not depend upon the asymptotic distribution of $\tilde{\beta}_T$. In such a case if β_0 is the true value of β the replacement of $\tilde{\beta}_T$ by β_0 brings no efficiency loss for the estimation of α.

ii. On the contrary, the initial objective function Ψ_T does not bear this property. In effect $\hat{\alpha}_T^0 = \text{argmax}\ \Psi_T(\alpha, \beta_0)$ and $\hat{\alpha}_T = \text{argmax}\ \Psi_T(\alpha, \hat{\beta}_T)$ do not have the same asymptotic distribution except if:

$$\operatorname*{Plim}_{T\to\infty} \frac{1}{T} \frac{\partial^2 \Psi_T}{\partial \alpha \partial \beta'} (\alpha_0, \beta_0) = 0.$$

In general $\hat{\alpha}_T^0$ is more efficient than $\hat{\alpha}_T$ (see Gouriéroux and Monfort 1989). The two-step method implies an efficiency loss. Simple calculus shows that Π_T verifies

$$\underset{T\to\infty}{\text{Plim}}\ \frac{1}{T}\frac{\partial^2\Pi_T}{\partial\alpha\partial\beta'}(\alpha_0, \beta_0) = 0.$$

Consequently, with Π_T there is no efficiency loss but the two-step estimator of α is not better than the estimator deduced from $\hat{\theta} = \text{argmax}_\theta$ $\Psi_T(\alpha, \beta)$.

iii. If Ψ_T is the log-likelihood function, $\Pi_T(\alpha, \tilde{\beta}_T)$ produces an efficient estimator.

iv. Assume $\beta = \theta$ and Ψ_T is a log-likelihood: $\log L_T(\theta)$. Then (4) is the so-called first-order improved estimator:

$$\theta_T^* = \hat{\theta}_T + \left[-\frac{\partial^2 \log L_T(\hat{\theta}_T)}{\partial\theta\partial\theta'}\right]^{-1}\frac{\partial \log L_T(\hat{\theta}_T)}{\partial\theta}$$

(see Gouriéroux and Monfort 1989).

v. If $\hat{J}_T$ is a consistent estimator of

$$\text{Plim} - \frac{1}{T}\frac{\partial^2\Psi_T}{\partial\beta\partial\beta'}(\alpha_0, \beta_0),$$

$J_T(\alpha)$ can be replaced by $\hat{J}_T$ (see Appendix 1) in all the previous equations.

III. Applications to Some Models and Some Estimation Methods

1. A Simple Interpretation in the Case of the Linear Model[1]

Let the matrix form of the linear model be

$$y = X\alpha + Z\beta + u,\ X(T \times p),\ Z(T \times q). \tag{6}$$

$\theta = (\alpha, \beta)$ can be estimated by least squares method. In this case $\hat{\theta}_T = \text{argmax}\ \Psi_T(\alpha, \beta)$ where $\Psi_T(\alpha, \beta) = -\|y - X\alpha - Z\beta\|^2$.

The approximated objective function relies on the following derivatives:

$$\frac{\partial\Psi_T}{\partial\alpha} = 2X'(y - X\alpha - Z\beta), \frac{\partial\Psi_T}{\partial\beta} = 2Z'(y - X\alpha - Z\beta), \frac{\partial^2\psi_T}{\partial\beta\partial\beta'} = -2Z'Z.$$

It appears that Π_T does not depend on $\tilde{\beta}_T$, since, after some computations,

$$\Pi_T(\alpha, \tilde{\beta}_T) = -(y - X\alpha), M_Z(y - X\alpha) \text{ where } M_Z = I_T - Z(Z'Z)^{-1}Z'.$$

In such a case, α_T^* is the result of the linear regression of $M_Z y$ on $M_Z X \ldots$; this is the Frish-Waugh theorem!

2. The Case of M-Estimation

(a) *Some definitions*: The objective function has the form

$$\Psi_T(\theta) = \sum_{t=1}^{T} \psi(y_t, x_t, \theta).$$

The endogenous and exogenous variables (x_t, y_t) are assumed iid for simplicity sake. The results presented in the sequel could be extended to more general processes such as strongly mixing processes (see White 1985). For our purpose the expectation of the marginal distribution will be denoted E_x and the expectation of the conditional distribution of y_t upon x_t is denoted E_o. With these notations we know that

$$I_o = \underset{x}{E}\,\underset{o}{E}\,\frac{\partial\psi}{\partial\theta}(y, x, \theta_o)\frac{\partial\psi}{\partial\theta'}(y, x, \theta_o)$$

and

$$J_o = -\underset{x}{E}\,\underset{o}{E}\,\frac{\partial^2\psi}{\partial\theta\partial\theta'}(y, x, \theta_o).$$

Those two matrices are consistently estimable by

$$\hat{I}_o = \frac{1}{T}\sum_{t=1}^{T}\frac{\partial\psi}{\partial\theta}(y_t, x_t, \hat{\theta}_T)\frac{\partial\psi}{\partial\theta'}(y_t, x_t, \hat{\theta}_T)$$

and

$$\hat{J}_o = -\frac{1}{T}\sum_{t=1}^{T}\frac{\partial^2\psi}{\partial\theta\partial\theta'}(y_t, x_t, \hat{\theta}_T).$$

Since the asymptotic variance of $\hat{\theta}_T$ is $J_o^{-1}I_oJ_o^{-1}$, $\hat{J}_o^{-1}\hat{I}_o\hat{J}_o^{-1}$ is a consistent estimator of this one.

(b) *Consistent estimators of the asymptotic variance of two-step estimators*: For M-estimators the initial objective function and the approximated one can be written as a sum of elementary functions:

$$\Phi_T(\theta, \tilde{\beta}_T) = \sum_{t=1}^{T} \varphi(y_t, x_t, \theta, \tilde{\beta}_T)$$

where

$$\varphi(y_t, x_t, \theta, \tilde{\beta}_T) = \psi(y_t, x_t, \alpha, \tilde{\beta}_T) + \frac{\partial \psi}{\partial \beta'}(y_t, x_t, \alpha, \tilde{\beta}_T)(\beta - \tilde{\beta}_T)$$
$$+ \tfrac{1}{2}(\beta - \tilde{\beta}_T)' J_T(\alpha)(\beta - \tilde{\beta}_T).$$

In such a case, one has the following result:

Property 2. The matrices I_T^* and J_T^* defined by

$$I_T^* = \frac{1}{T}\sum_{t=1}^{T} \frac{\partial \varphi}{\partial \theta}(\varphi_t, x_t, \theta_T^*, \tilde{\beta}_T)\frac{\partial \varphi}{\partial \theta'}(y_t, x_t, \theta_T^*, \tilde{\beta}_T)$$

and

$$J_T^* = -\frac{1}{T}\sum_{t=1}^{T} \frac{\partial^2 \varphi}{\partial \theta \partial \theta'}(y_t, x_t, \theta_T^*, \tilde{\beta}_T)$$

converge toward I_o and J_o, respectively.

Proof. See Appendix 2.

This property shows that the standard formulas for the computation of the covariance matrices can be used as if $\tilde{\beta}_T$ was fixed in the approximated objective function $\Phi_T(\alpha, \beta/\tilde{\beta}_T)$.

(c) *Application to nonlinear least squares*: Assume that $E(y_t/x_t) = f(x_t, \theta)$ and $V(y_t/x_t) = \sigma^2 \forall t$. θ can be estimated by the mean of nonlinear least squares through an initial objective function based on $\psi(y_t, x_t, \theta) = -(y_t - f(x_t, \theta))^2$ (Malinvaud 1978).

Since for that model

$$\text{Plim} -\frac{1}{T}\frac{\partial^2 \Psi_T}{\partial \beta \partial \beta'} = J_{o\beta\beta} = 2\, E_x \frac{\partial f}{\partial \beta}(x, \theta_o)\frac{\partial f}{\partial \beta'}(x, \theta_o),$$

$J_T(\alpha)$ can be

$$J_T(\alpha) = \frac{2}{T}\sum_{t=1}^{T} \frac{\partial f}{\partial \beta}(y_t, \alpha, \tilde{\beta}_T)\frac{\partial f}{\partial \beta'}(x_t, \alpha, \tilde{\beta}_T).$$

With this particular definition of J_T, the approximated objective function has a very appealing interpretation since

$$\varphi_T(\alpha, \beta/\tilde{\beta}_T) = -\sum_{t=1}^{T}\left\{y_t - f(x_t, \alpha, \tilde{\beta}) - \frac{\partial f}{\partial \beta'}(x_t, \alpha, \tilde{\beta}_T)(\beta - \tilde{\beta}_T)\right\}^2, \tag{7}$$

in which $\tilde{\beta}_T$ is assumed to be fixed. Furthermore Property 2 shows that the standard formulas for the computation of the asymptotic variances are valid for α_T^*. In the econometric literature the technique that yields to 7 is known to be the Gauss-Newton method. For more details see Fuller (1976) or Hartley 1961.

Remark. If one has a consistent estimation $\tilde{\alpha}_T$ of α, the approximated linear model defined in 8 produces nonlinear least squares estimators of α and β, asymptotically equivalent to α_T^*, β_T^* and $\hat{\alpha}_T$, $\hat{\beta}_T$:

$$y_t = f(x_t, \alpha, \hat{\beta}_T) + \frac{\partial f}{\partial f'}(x_t, \tilde{\alpha}_T, \tilde{\beta}_T)(\beta - \tilde{\beta}_T) + v_t^*. \tag{8}$$

An example is Hatanaka's estimation for autoregressive autocorrelated models. Consider the model

$$\begin{cases} y_t = \alpha_1 y_{t-1} + \alpha_2 x_t + u_t, & t = 1, \dots, T \\ u_t = \beta u_{t-1} + v_t \\ v_t \sim \text{iid}(0, \sigma^2). \end{cases}$$

The Wallis estimation, which is based on a consistent estimator of β in a first step and a QGLS estimation for α_1 and α_2 in a second step, produces estimators whose asymptotic distributions depend heavily on the distribution of the first step estimator of β. To solve this problem Hatanaka has proposed estimating α_1, α_2, and β by ordinary least squares on the auxiliary model defined by

$$y_t - \tilde{\beta}_T y_{t-1} = \alpha_1(y_{t-1} - \tilde{\beta}_T y_{t-2}) + \alpha_2(x_t - \tilde{\beta}_T x_{t-1}) + \tilde{u}_{t-1}(\beta - \tilde{\beta}_T) + \tilde{v}_t$$

where $\tilde{u}_t$ is the residual of some previous instrumental variable estimation of the model. If the disturbances are normally distributed Hatanaka's procedure is asymptotically efficient.

The procedure has a simple interpretation in this article if we consider the quasidifference sum of squares:

$$\Psi_T(\alpha, \beta) = -\sum_{t=1}^{T} (y_t - f_t(\alpha_1, \alpha_2, \beta))^2$$

with

$$f_t(\alpha_1, \alpha_2, \beta) = (\alpha_1 + \beta) y_{t-1} - \alpha_1 \beta y_{t-2} + \alpha_2 x_t - \alpha_2 \beta x_{t-1}.$$

Hatanaka's auxiliary model is simply

$$y_t = f_t(\alpha_1, \alpha_2, \tilde{\beta}_T) + \frac{\partial f}{\partial \beta}(\tilde{\alpha}_1, \tilde{\alpha}_2, \tilde{\beta}_T)(\beta - \tilde{\beta}_T) + \tilde{v}_t.$$

3. Application to Some Maximum Likelihood Estimations

(a) *An efficient two-step estimation method for the TOBIT model*: Consider the TOBIT model:

$$\begin{cases} y_t = x_t'b + u_t, & \text{if } x_t'b + u_t > 0 \\ y_t = 0 & \text{otherwise} \end{cases}$$

where $u_t \sim \text{Niid}(0, \sigma^2)$.

For this model the log-likelihood function is

$$L_T(b, \sigma^2) = \sum_{t=1}^{T} \left\{ -\frac{1}{2}\log 2\pi - \frac{1}{2}\log\sigma^2 - \frac{1}{2\sigma^2}(y_t - x_t'b)^2 \right\} \mathbb{1}[y_t > 0]$$
$$+ \sum_{t=1}^{T} \log\Phi\left[\frac{x_t'b}{\sigma}\right] \mathbb{1}[y_t > 0]$$

where

$$\Phi(x) = \int_{-\infty}^{x} \frac{1}{\sqrt{2\pi}} e^{-t^2/2}\, dt.$$

This likelihood function can be expressed as a function of $\alpha = 1/\sigma$ and $\beta = b/\sigma$. In the following, we set $\Psi_T(\alpha, \beta)$ for $L_T(\beta/\alpha, 1/\alpha^2)$.

To avoid the maximization of Ψ_T, Heckman has proposed the following two-step estimation method:

(i) Estimate β through the associated Probit model: $\tilde{\beta}_T$;

(ii) Estimate b and σ by regressing the positive values of y_t on x_t and $h(x_t'\tilde{\beta}_T)$ where

$$h(x) = \frac{\varphi(x)}{\Phi(x)}, \quad \varphi(x) = \frac{1}{\sqrt{2\pi}} \exp\left[-\frac{x^2}{2}\right], \quad \Phi(x) = \int_{-\infty}^{x} \varphi(t)\, dt.$$

The Heckman estimations of b and σ bear some drawbacks. First, they are not asymptotically efficient; second, the computation of the estimated asymptotic variance-covariance matrix is very cumbersome.

The general method developed earlier can be applied in the context of the TOBIT model. The obtained two-step method is in that case efficient.

The computation of $\Pi_T(\alpha, \tilde{\beta}_T)$ associated with the log-likelihood function $\Psi_T(\alpha, \beta)$ rest upon

$$\frac{\partial \Psi_T}{\partial \beta} = \sum_{t=1}^{T} \{(\alpha y_t - x_t'\beta)\mathbb{1}[y_t > 0] + h(x_t'\beta)\mathbb{1}[y_t = 0]\}\, x_t$$

and upon

$$\frac{\partial^2 \Psi_T}{\partial \beta \partial \beta'} = -\sum_{t=1}^{T} \{\mathbb{1}[y_t > 0] - \dot{h}(x_t'\beta)\mathbb{1}[y_t = 0]\}x_t x_t'.$$

Since the last second derivatives do not depend upon α, $J_T(\alpha)$ is independent of α and we can set

$$TJ_T(\alpha) = \tilde{J}_T = \sum_{t=1}^{T} \{\mathbb{1}[y_t > 0] - \dot{h}(x_t'\tilde{\beta}_T)\mathbb{1}[y_t = 0]\}x_t x_t'.$$

To obtain α_T^*, we have to maximize the following objective function in which n denotes the number of strictly positive y_t:

$$\begin{aligned}\Pi_T(\alpha, \tilde{\beta}_T) = {} & -\frac{n}{2}\log 2\pi + n\log\alpha - \frac{1}{2}\sum_{t=1}^{T} (\alpha y_t - x_t'\tilde{\beta}_T)^2 \mathbb{1}[y_t > 0] \\ & + \sum_{t=1}^{T} \log\Phi(x_t'\tilde{\beta}_T)\mathbb{1}[y_t = 0] \\ & + \frac{\partial \Psi_T}{\partial \beta'}(\alpha, \tilde{\beta}_T)\tilde{J}_T^{-1}\frac{\partial \Psi_T}{\partial \beta}(\alpha, \tilde{\beta}_T).\end{aligned}$$

α_T^* verifies the first-order condition

$$\begin{aligned}& \frac{n}{\alpha} - \sum_{t=1}^{T} (\alpha y_t - x_t'\tilde{\beta}_T)y_t\mathbb{1}[y_t > 0] - \left(\sum_{t=1}^{T} y_t\mathbb{1}[y_t > 0]x_t'\right)\tilde{J}_T^{-1}\cdots \\ & \cdots\sum_{t=1}^{T} \{(\alpha y_t - x_t'\tilde{\beta}_T)\mathbb{1}[y_t > 0] + h(x_t'\tilde{\beta}_T)\mathbb{1}[y_t = 0]\}x_t = 0,\end{aligned} \tag{9}$$

which yields to

$$A_T\alpha^2 + B_T\alpha + C_T = 0,$$

where

$$A_T = -\sum_{t=1}^{T} \mathbb{1}[y_t > 0]y_t^2 + \left(\sum_{t=1}^{T} \mathbb{1}[y_t > 0]y_t x_t'\right)\tilde{J}_T^{-1}\left(\sum_{t=1}^{T} \mathbb{1}[y_t > 0]y_t x_t\right),$$

$$\begin{aligned}B_T = {} & \sum_{t=1}^{T} \mathbb{1}[y_t > 0]y_t x_t'\tilde{\beta}_T - \left[\sum_{t=1}^{T} \mathbb{1}[y_t > 0]y_t x_t'\right]\tilde{J}_T^{-1}\cdots \\ & \cdots\sum_{t=1}^{T} \{(x_t'\tilde{\beta}_T\mathbb{1}[y_t > 0] - h(x_t'\tilde{\beta}_T)\mathbb{1}[y_t = 0])\}x_t,\end{aligned}$$

and

$C_T = n.$

As A_T is negative (cf. Appendix 3), there exists only one positive root for this equation. We retain this positive value for α_T^*. And β_T^* is given by

$$\beta_T^* = \tilde{\beta}_T + \tilde{J}_T^{-1} \sum_{t=1}^{T} \{(\alpha_T^* y_t - x_t'\tilde{\beta}_T)\mathbb{1}[y_t > 0] + h(x_t'\tilde{\beta}_T) + h(x_t'\tilde{\beta}_T)\mathbb{1}[y_t = 0]\}x_t.$$

Whatever $\tilde{\beta}_T$ is, the two-step estimator α_T^*, β_T^* are asymptotically efficient. Furthermore, the estimation of σ, $\sigma_T^* = 1/\alpha_T^*$ is positive; this was not necessary the case for the Heckman estimator.

(b) *Conditional and marginal maximum-likelihood estimators*: For a lot of socioeconomic phenomenon, econometricians have observations on couples of iid vector-valued random variables (y_t, x_t), $t = 1, 2, \ldots, T$ whose density function can be written as

$$l(y_t, x_t, \alpha, \beta) = l^c(y_t/x_t, \alpha, \beta)l^m(x_t, \beta).$$

In this case, α and β are in the conditional distribution whereas β is the only parameter of the marginal distribution of x_t. Such a situation is common for choice models: nested logit model, bivariate logit model, Nerlove-Press model, etc. (see Amemiya 1978, 1985; Gouriéroux 1984; Hausman McFadden 1984, etc.).

The log-likelihood function is the sum of the marginal and conditional log-likelihood functions:

$$L_T(\alpha, \beta) = L_T^C(\alpha, \beta) + L_T^m(B)$$

with

$$L_T^C(\alpha, \beta) = \sum_{t=1}^{T} \log l^C(y_t/x_t, \alpha, \beta)$$

and

$$L_T^m(\beta) = \sum_{t=1}^{T} \log l^m(x_t, \beta).$$

Amemiya proposed for this model the use of a simplified two-step method:

(i) Maximize the marginal likelihood function to obtain a first round estimator $\tilde{\beta}_T$ of β.

(ii) Compute then $\tilde{\alpha}_T$ as the result of the maximization of $L_T^C(\alpha, \tilde{\beta}_T)$.

Such an estimation procedure is not asymptotically efficient. Some experiments tend to show that the variance of the two-step estimators are much greater than the variance of the ML estimator. Furthermore, if Amemiya's procedure is numerically less costly than the ML estimation this gain is lost if we compute the asymptotic estimated variance of $\tilde{\alpha}_T$ (Small and Brownstone 1982).

The technique of the approximated log-likelihood function can be worked out in this context:

$$\Phi_T(\alpha, \beta/\tilde{\beta}_T) = L_T^{\mathrm{C}}(\alpha, \tilde{\beta}_T) + L_T^{\mathrm{m}}(\tilde{\beta}_T) + \left[\frac{\partial L_T^{\mathrm{C}}}{\partial \beta'}(\alpha, \tilde{\beta}_T) + \frac{\partial L_T^{\mathrm{m}}}{\partial \beta'}(\tilde{\beta}_T)\right](\beta - \tilde{\beta}_T) + \frac{1}{2}(\beta - \tilde{\beta}_T)'\left[\frac{\partial^2 L_T^{\mathrm{C}}}{\partial \beta \partial \beta'}(\alpha, \tilde{\beta}_T) + \frac{\partial^2 L_T^{\mathrm{m}}}{\partial \beta \partial \beta'}(\tilde{\beta}_T)\right](\beta - \tilde{\beta}_T).$$

Since $\partial L_T^{\mathrm{m}}/\partial \beta(\tilde{\beta}_T) = 0$, and as $\tilde{V}^{-1} = -(\partial^2 L_T^{\mathrm{m}}/\partial \beta \partial \beta')((\beta - \tilde{\beta}_T))$ is the inverse of the estimated asymptotic covariance matrix of $\tilde{\beta}_T$, α_T^* is given by

$$\Pi_T(\alpha, \tilde{\beta}_T) = L_T^{\mathrm{c}}(\alpha, \tilde{\beta}_T) - \frac{1}{2}\frac{\partial L_T^{\mathrm{c}}}{\partial \beta'}(\alpha, \tilde{\beta}_T)\left[\frac{\partial^2 L_T^{\mathrm{c}}}{\partial \beta \partial \beta'}(\alpha, \tilde{\beta}_T) - \tilde{V}^{-1}\right]^{-1}\frac{\partial L_T^{\mathrm{c}}}{\partial \beta}(\alpha, \tilde{\beta}_T)$$

and β_T^* by

$$\beta_T^* = \tilde{\beta}_T - \left[\frac{\partial^2 L_T^{\mathrm{c}}}{\partial \beta \partial \beta'}(\alpha_T^*, \tilde{\beta}_T) - \tilde{V}^{-1}\right]^{-1}\frac{\partial L_T^{\mathrm{c}}}{\partial \beta}(\alpha_T^*, \tilde{\beta}_T).$$

In this framework, α_T^* and β_T^* are asymptotically efficient.

V. Conclusion

The applicability of the approximated objective function seems to be very large. Very few examples have been presented here. Those examples have been chosen to help the reader in the understanding of the procedures and in a case to produce a new simple and efficient method. Some systematic researches have to be conducted for the promotion of the notion of approximated objective function. It is also necessary to produce genuine and Monte Carlo experiments to judge the real interest of the two-step methods produced by our general framework.

Appendix 1: Asymptotic Equivalence between $\theta_T^* = (\alpha_T^*, \beta_T^*)$ and $\hat{\theta}_T = (\hat{\alpha}_T, \hat{\beta}_T)$

The first-order conditions of the approximated program define θ_T^*:

$$\frac{\partial \Phi_T}{\partial \theta}(\theta_T^* / \tilde{\beta}_T) = 0.$$

Those conditions are

$$\frac{\partial \Psi_T}{\partial \alpha_j}(\alpha_T^*, \tilde{\beta}_T) + \frac{\partial^2 \Psi_T}{\partial \alpha_j \partial \beta'}(\alpha_T^*, \tilde{\beta}_T)(\beta_T^* - \tilde{\beta}_T)$$

$$-\tfrac{1}{2}(\beta_T^* - \tilde{\beta}_T)' \, T \frac{\partial J_T}{\partial \alpha_j}(\alpha_T^*)(\beta_T^* - \tilde{\beta}_T) = 0,$$

where $j = 1, \ldots, p$ if $\alpha \in \mathbb{R}^p$, and

$$\frac{\partial \Psi_T}{\partial \beta}(\alpha_T^*, \tilde{\beta}_T) - T J_T(\alpha_T^*)(\beta_T^* - \tilde{\beta}_T) = 0.$$

This yields (under the assumptions of Proposition 1 with f^0 for all functions of (α, β) evaluated at (α_0, β_0))

$$\frac{1}{T}\frac{\partial^2 \Psi_T^0}{\partial \alpha \partial \alpha'}\sqrt{T}(\alpha_T^* - \alpha_0) + \frac{1}{T}\frac{\partial^2 \Psi_T^0}{\partial \alpha \partial \beta'}\sqrt{T}(\tilde{\beta}_T - \beta_0) + \frac{1}{T}\frac{\partial^2 \Psi_T^0}{\partial \alpha \partial \beta'}\sqrt{T}(\beta_T^* - \tilde{\beta}_T)$$

$$= -\frac{1}{\sqrt{T}}\frac{\partial \Psi_T^0}{\partial \alpha} + o_p(1)$$

and

$$\frac{1}{T}\frac{\partial^2 \Psi_T^0}{\partial \beta \partial \alpha'}\sqrt{T}(\alpha_T^* - \alpha_0) + \frac{1}{T}\frac{\partial^2 \Psi_T^0}{\partial \beta \partial \beta'}\sqrt{T}(\tilde{\beta}_T - \beta_0) + \frac{1}{T}\frac{\partial^2 \Psi_T^0}{\partial \beta \partial \beta'}\sqrt{T}(\beta_T^* - \tilde{\beta}_T)$$

$$= -\frac{1}{\sqrt{T}}\frac{\partial \Psi_T^0}{\partial \beta} + o_p(1)$$

since $J_T(\alpha_T^*)$ is asymptotically equivalent to

$$-\frac{1}{T}\frac{\partial^2 \Psi_T^0}{\partial \beta \partial \beta'}.$$

We deduce that

$$\begin{bmatrix} \sqrt{T}(\alpha_T^* - \alpha_0) \\ \sqrt{T}(\beta_T^* - \beta_0) \end{bmatrix} = - \begin{bmatrix} \dfrac{\partial^2 \Psi_T^0}{\partial\alpha\partial\alpha'} & \dfrac{\partial^2 \Psi_T^0}{\partial\alpha\partial\beta'} \\ \dfrac{\partial^2 \Psi_T^0}{\partial\beta\partial\alpha'} & \dfrac{\partial^2 \Psi_T^0}{\partial\beta\partial\beta'} \end{bmatrix}^{-1} \begin{bmatrix} \dfrac{1}{\sqrt{T}} \dfrac{\partial \Psi_T^0}{\partial\alpha} \\ \dfrac{1}{\sqrt{T}} \dfrac{\partial \Psi_T^0}{\partial\beta} \end{bmatrix} + o_p(1).$$

Since

$$\sqrt{T}(\hat{\theta}_T - \theta_0) = \begin{bmatrix} \sqrt{T}(\hat{\alpha}_T - \alpha_0) \\ \sqrt{T}(\hat{\beta}_T - \beta_0) \end{bmatrix} = - \begin{bmatrix} \dfrac{\partial^2 \Psi_T^0}{\partial\theta\partial\theta'} \end{bmatrix}^{-1} \frac{1}{\sqrt{T}} \frac{\partial \Psi_T^0}{\partial\theta} + o_p(1),$$

we have

$\sqrt{T}(\alpha_T^* - \hat{\alpha}_T) = o_p(1)$ and $\sqrt{T}(\beta_T^* - \hat{\beta}_T) = o_p(1)$.

Appendix 2: I_T^* and J_T^* Are Consistent Estimators of I_0 and J_0

We will consider the consistency of I_T^* and we will deduce by analogy the consistency of J_T^*:

$$\frac{\partial\varphi}{\partial\alpha_j}(y_t, x_t, \theta_T^*, \tilde{\beta}_T) = \frac{\partial\psi}{\partial\alpha_j}(y_t, x_t, \alpha_T^*, \tilde{\beta}_T) + \frac{\partial^2\psi}{\partial\alpha_j\partial\beta'}(y_t, x_t, \alpha_T^*, \tilde{\beta}_T)(\beta_T^* - \tilde{\beta}_T)$$
$$+ \tfrac{1}{2}(\beta_T^* - \tilde{\beta}_T)' \frac{\partial^3\psi}{\partial\alpha_j\partial\beta\partial\beta'}(y_t, x_t, \alpha_T^*, \tilde{\beta}_T)(\beta_T^* - \tilde{\beta}_T),$$

where $j = 1, \ldots, p$ if $\alpha \in \mathbb{R}^p$, and

$$\frac{\partial\varphi}{\partial\beta}(y_t, x_t, \theta_T^*, \tilde{\beta}_T) = \frac{\partial\psi}{\partial\beta}(y_t, x_t, \alpha_T^*, \tilde{\beta}_T) + \frac{\partial^2\psi}{\partial\beta\partial\beta'}(y_t, x_t, \alpha_T^*, \tilde{\beta}_T)(\beta_T^* - \tilde{\beta}_T).$$

As an example, consider $I_{T\alpha_j\beta_k}^*$:

$$I_{T\alpha_j\beta_k}^* = \frac{1}{T}\sum_t \frac{\partial\hat{\psi}_t}{\partial\alpha_j}\frac{\partial\hat{\psi}_t}{\partial\beta_k} + \frac{1}{T}\sum_t \frac{\partial\hat{\psi}_t}{\partial\alpha_j}\frac{\partial^2\hat{\psi}_t}{\partial\beta\partial\beta'}(\beta_T^* - \tilde{\beta}_T) + \frac{1}{T}\sum_t \frac{\partial\hat{\psi}_t}{\partial\beta_k}\frac{\partial^2\hat{\psi}_t}{\partial\alpha_j\partial\beta'}(\beta_T^* - \tilde{\beta}_T)$$
$$+ (\beta_T^* - \tilde{\beta}_T)' \frac{1}{T}\sum_t \frac{\partial^2\hat{\psi}_t}{\partial\beta\partial\alpha_j}\frac{\partial^2\hat{\psi}_t}{\partial\beta_k\partial\beta'}(\beta_T^* - \tilde{\beta}_T)$$
$$+ \tfrac{1}{2}(\beta_T^* - \tilde{\beta}_T)' \frac{1}{T}\sum_t \frac{\partial^3\hat{\psi}_t}{\partial\alpha_j\partial\beta\partial\beta'}\frac{\partial\hat{\psi}_t}{\partial\beta_k}(\beta_T^* - \tilde{\beta}_T)$$
$$+ \tfrac{1}{2}(\beta_T^* - \tilde{\beta}_T)' \frac{1}{T}\sum_t \frac{\partial^3\hat{\psi}_t}{\partial\alpha_j\partial\beta\partial\beta'}(\beta_t^* - \tilde{\beta}_T)\frac{\partial^2\hat{\psi}_t}{\partial\beta_k\partial\beta'}(\beta_T^* - \tilde{\beta}_T),$$

where $\hat{\psi}_t = \psi(y_t, x_t, \alpha_T^*, \tilde{\beta}_T)$.

As $\text{Plim}_{T\to\infty}(\beta_T^* - \tilde{\beta}_T) = 0$, we see that $I_{T\alpha_j\beta_k}^*$ has the same limit as

$$\frac{1}{T}\sum_t \frac{\partial\hat{\psi}_t}{\partial\alpha_k}\frac{\partial\hat{\psi}_t}{\partial\beta_k},$$

which tends to I_0. The other elements of I_T^* can be treated in the same way.

Appendix 3: A_T Is Negative

Let v be the T-dimensional vector whose elements are $\mathbb{1}[y_t > 0]\, y_t$, X be the $T \times k$ matrix whose rows are $\mathbb{1}[y_t > 0]\, x_t'$, and Z be the $T \times k$ matrix whose rows are $(-\dot{h}(x_t'\tilde{\beta}_T))^{1/2}\, \mathbb{1}[y_t = 0]\, x_t'$. Note that the computation of the square root of $-\dot{h}(x_t'\tilde{\beta}_T)$ is possible since

$$\begin{aligned}\dot{h}(t) &= \frac{-t\varphi(t)}{\Phi(t)} - \frac{\varphi(t)^2}{\Phi(t)^2}\\ &= -\frac{\varphi(t)}{\Phi(t)}[t\Phi(t) + \varphi(t)]\\ &= -\frac{\varphi(t)}{\Phi(t)}\int_{-\infty}^{t}\Phi(u)\,du,\end{aligned}$$

which shows $-\dot{h}(t) > 0\ \forall t$.

With those notations we see that

$$\begin{aligned}A_T &= -v'[I_T - X(X'X + Z'Z)^{-1}X']v\\ &\leqslant 0.\end{aligned}$$

Note

1. This simple interpretation was suggested by an anonymous referee.

References

Amemiya, T. 1978. "On a Two Step Estimation of a Multivariate Logit Model." *Journal of Econometrics* 80.

Amemiya, A. 1985. *Advanced Econometrics*. Blackwell.

Bates, C., and White, H. 1985. "A Unified Theory of Consistent Estimation for Parametric Models." *Econometric Theory* 1.

Burguete, J., Gallant, A. R., and Souza, G. 1982. "On the Unification of the Asymptotic Theory of Non-linear Econometric Models." *Econometric Review* 1.

Domenich, T. and McFadden, D. 1975. *Urban Travel Demand*. North-Holland.

Fuller, W. A. 1976. *Introduction to Statistical Time Series*. Wiley.

Gouriéroux, C. 1984. *Econométrie des variables Qualitatives*. Economica.

Gouriéroux, C., and Monfort, A. 1989. *Statistique et modèles économétriques*, volume 1. Economica.

Gouriéroux, C., Monfort, A., and Trognon, A. 1984. "Pseudo-Maximum Likelihood Methods: Theory." *Econometrica* 50.

Hartley, H. O. 1961. "The Modified Gauss-Newton Method for the Fitting of Non-linear Regressions Function by Least Squares." *Technometrics* 3.

Hatanaka, M. 1974. "An Efficient Two-Step Estimator for the Dynamic Adjustment Model with Autoregressive Errors." *Journal of Econometrics* 2.

Hausman, J. A., and McFadden, D. 1984. "Specification Tests for the Multinomial Logit Model." *Econometrica* 49.

Malinvaud, E. 1978. *Méthodes statistiques de l'Économétrie*, third edition. Dunod.

Small, K. A., and Brownstone, D. 1982. Efficient Estimation of Nested Logit Models: An Application to Trip Timing. Research memorandum No. 296, E.R.P., Princeton University.

White, H. 1985. *Asymptotic Theory for Econometricians*. Wiley.

Biographical Notes

Edmond Malinvaud was born in Limoges on April 25, 1923. He attended Lycée in Limoges and then in Lyon. Later he studied at the École Polytechnique and at the Administration School of the Institut National de la Statistique et des Études Économiques (INSEE).

From 1946 to 1987 he served INSEE as Administrator and then as General Inspector. He served as Director of the École National de la Statistique et de l'Administration Économique from 1962 to 1966 and from 1971 to 1972. From 1972 to 1974 he was Director of Forecasting at the Ministry of the Economy and of Finance.

He became General Director of INSEE in 1974, and served in that capacity until 1987.

Since 1957 he has been Director of the École des Hautes Études en Sciences Sociales, and since 1987 he has been a professor at the College de France.

He has been honored as Doctor Honoris Causa by the Universities of Louvain, Bâle, Helsinki, Geneva, and Lausanne.

He has served as President of the Econometric Society (1963), of the Statistical Society of Paris (1974), of the International Economic Association (1974–1977), of the International Institute of Statistics (1980–1981), of the French Economic Association (1986–1987), and of the European Economic Association (1988).

He has been a foreign member of the American Academy of Arts and Sciences (since 1969), of the British Academy (since 1973), of the Finnish Academy of Arts and Sciences (since 1976), and of the (U.S.) National Academy of Sciences (since 1977).

Selected Scientific Publications of Edmond Malinvaud

"L'expérience travailliste et la pensée économique." *Nouvelle Revue de l'Économie Contemporaine* No. 7 (1950): 18–22; Nos. 8–9 (1950): 7–16.

"Les élasticités par rapport aux prix dans les échanges internationaux." *Journal de la Société Statistique de Paris* 91(2) (1950): 177–187.

"Possibilités d'établissement d'un indice des prix des fruits et légumes frais." *Journal de la Société Statistique de Paris* 91(3) (1950): 218–231.

"Note on von Neumann-Morgenstern's Strong Independence Axiom." *Econometrica* 20 (October 1952): 679.

"Capital Accumulation and Efficient Allocation of Resources." *Econometrica* 21 (April 1953): 233–266.

"Aggregation Problems in Input-Output Models." In T. Barna, ed., *The Structural Interdependence of the Economy*. Wiley, 1954.

"Relations entre la composition des familles et le taux de masculinité." *Journal de la Société Statistique de Paris* 96(1) (1955): 49–63.

"Quelques aspects d'un traité d'économétrie." *Cahiers du Séminaire d'Économétrie* No. 3, CNRS (1955): 74–80.

"Réflexions sur l'emploi des modèles à erreurs sur les variables." In *Les modèles dynamiques en économétrie*. Colloques internationaux du CNRS, 1956.

"L'agrégation dans les modèles économiques." *Cahiers du Séminaire d'Économétrie* No. 4, CNRS (1956): 69–146.

Initiation à la Comptabilité Nationale. Imprimerie Nationale et Presses Universitaires de France, 1957 (Second edition), 1961 (Third edition), 1964 (Fourth edition), 1973 (INSEE).

"Les variations de stocks dans les entreprises de 1950 à 1955" (with J. Vacher). *Études Statistiques*, INSEE (October-December 1958): 97–116.

"Programmes d'expansion et taux d'intérêt." *Econometrica* 27 (April 1959): 215–217.

Modèles linéaires des économies à secteurs multiples, Colectanea de Estudos-Centro de Estudos de Estatistica Economica, No. 6, Lisbon, 1959, and Collection of Groupe de Mathématique Sociale et de Statistique, École Pratique des Hautes Études, 1960.

"L'analyse statistique des salaires" (with R. Marche). *Encyclopédie française,* Vol. 9. Larousse, 1960.

"De la décision unique à la décision séquentielle." *Économie Appliquée* XIII(1) (1960): 81–109.

"L'âge mûr de la comptabilité nationale." *Journal de la Société Statistique Appliquée* 101(4) (1960): 232–242.

"The Analogy between Atemporal and Intertemporal Theories of Resource Allocation." *The Review of Economic Studies* 28 (January 1961): 143–160.

"The Estimation of Distributed Lags: A Comment." *Econometrica* 29 (July 1961): 430–433.

"Estimation et prévision dans les modèles économiques autorégressifs." *Revue de l'Institut International de Statistique* 29(2) (1961): 1–32.

"Capital Accumulation and Efficient Allocation of Resources: A Corrigendum." *Econometrica* 30 (July 1962): 570–573.

"Critères de choix des investissements." In ed. C. Bettelheim, *Choix et efficience des investissements,* Paris, 1963.

"Théorie de la régression simple." *Revue de Statistique Appliquée* XI(4) (1963): 49–73.

Méthodes statistiques de l'économétrie, Dunod, 1964 (Second edition), 1969 (Third edition), 1978 (Fourth edition), 1981 (Translations in English, Spanish, Italian, Hungarian, Russian).

"Observations sur l'étude de M. Edward Denison." *Le facteur résiduel et le progrès économique,* O.C.D.E., 1964.

"Interest Rates in the Allocation of Resources." In eds. F. H. Hahn and F. Brechling, *The Theory of Interest Rates.* Macmillan, 1965.

"La décentralisation des décisions de production." *Revue de Statistique Appliquée* XII(4) (1965): 99–105.

"Les croissances optimales." *Cahiers du Séminaire d'Econométrie* No. 8, CNRS (1965): 67–100.

"Croissances optimales dans un modèle macroéconomique." *Study Week on the Economic Approach to Development Planning.* Académie Pontificale des Sciences, 1965.

"Sur la spécification des modèles économiques." In ed. H. O. Wold, *La technique des modèles dans les sciences humaines.* Union Européenne d'Édition, 1966.

"Pour une axiomatique de la causalité." In ed. H. O. Wold, *La technique des modèles dans les sciences humaines*. Union Européenne d'Édition, 1966.

"Capital et croissance, analyse du récent ouvrage de John Hicks." *Analyse et Prévision* I(5) (May 1966): 383–390.

"Decentralized Procedures for Planning." In eds. E. Malinvaud and M. O. L. Bacharach, *Activity Analysis in the Theory of Growth and Planning*. Macmillan, 1967.

"Notes sur l'étude des procédures de planification." *Revue Canadienne d'Économique* 1 (February 1968): 16–36.

"La prise en charge des risques dans l'allocation des ressources." In eds. J. Margolis and H. Guitton, *Économie publique*, CNRS, 1968.

"Décisions en face de l'aléatoire et situation certaine approximativement équivalente." *Cahiers du Séminaire d'Économétrie* No. 11, CNRS (1969): 37–50.

"La concentration de l'industrie française s'est-elle accentuée depuis le début du siècle?" (with M. Didier). *Économie et Statistique*, INSEE, No. 2 (June 1969): 3–10.

"First-Order Certainty Equivalence." *Econometrica* 37 (October 1969): 706–718.

Leçons de théorie microéconomique. Dunod, 1969 (Second edition), 1971 (Third edition), 1975 (Fourth edition), 1982 (Translations in English, Spanish, Japanese, Russian).

"Procedures for the Determination of a Programme of Public Consumption." *European Economic Review* (Winter 1970–1971): 187–217.

"The Consistency of Non Linear Regressions." *The Annals of Mathematical Statistics* 41 (June 1970): 959–969.

"L'analyse des données."*Annales de l'INSEE* No. 4, (May-September 1970): 3–8.

"Analyse spectrale de données économiques: un essai sur l'activité dans l'industrie française." (with D. Fouquet). *Annales de l'INSEE* No. 6 (January-April 1971): 41–75.

"A Planning Approach to the Public Good Problem." *The Swedish Journal of Economics* 73 (March 1971): 96–112.

"Peut-on mesurer l'évolution du coût du capital productif?" *Économie et Statistique* INSEE, No. 22 (April 1971): 5–20.

"Letter to the Editor." *International Economic Review* 12 (June 1971): 344–345.

"L'effet d'accélération dans les investissements industriels français: une analyse simultanée des séries par branche" (with V. Thollon-Pommerol). *Annales de l'INSEE* No. 7 (May-August 1971): 73–112.

"The Allocation of Individual Risks in Large Markets." *Journal of Economic Theory* 4 (April 1972): 312–328.

"Prices for Individual Consumption, Quantity Indicators for Collective Consumption." *Review of Economic Studies* 39 (October 1972): 385–405.

"The Scientific Papers of Tjalling C. Koopmans: A Review Article." *Journal of Economic Literature* X (September 1972): 798–802.

La croissance française, un essai d'analyse économique causale de l'aprèsguerre (with J. J. Carré and P. Dubois). Éditions du Seuil, 1972 (Second edition), 1977 (English translation).

Abrégé de la croissance française (with J. J. Carré and P. Dubois), Éditions du Seuil, 1973 (Second edition), 1977 (Third edition), 1984 (Polish translation).

"Spécifications aléatoires pour l'analyse des données économiques." *Économie Appliquée* XXVI(2-3-4) (1973): 609–621.

"Induction et science économique." *Journal de la Société Statistique de Paris* 114(4) (1973): 266–278.

"Markets for an Exchange Economy with Individual Risks." *Econometrica* 41 (May 1973): 383–410.

"Une explication de l'évolution de la productivité horaire du travail." *Économie et Statistique* INSEE, No. 48 (September 1973): 46–50.

"Limits to Growth and Long Range Forecasting of Economic Aggregates." In ed. M. Marois, *Vers un plan d'action pour l'humanité, problèmes et perspectives.* North Holland, 1974.

"Propos sur les mathématiques utilisées en économie." *La Gazette des Mathématiciens* No. 3 (February 1975): 59–72.

"La science économique peut-elle ignorer la politique?" *Revue Politique et Parlementaire* 77(859) (December 1975): 10–24.

"The Theory of Economic Planning by G. M. Heal": A Book Review. *Journal of Political Economy* 83 (December 1975): 1302–1305.

"Thoughts on Planning in Western Economies." In ed. T. S. Khachaturov, *Methods of Long-Term Planning and Forecasting*, Macmillan, 1976.

"L'observation statistique des réalités économiques et sociales." l'Académie des Sciences Morales et Politiques, 8 November 1976. *Revue des Travaux de l'Académie* 2 (1976): 661–685.

"Les grands échantillons de données individuelles et leur exploitation statistique." *Journal de la Société Statistique de Paris* 118(1) (1977): 2–15.

Official Statisticians and Econometricians in the Present Day World. Tenth Geary Lecture, The Economic and Social Research Institute, 1977.

"Quel enseignement faut-il donner aux futurs cadres des services statistiques?" *Bulletin de l'Institut International de Statistique*, Indian Statistical Institute, Calcutta I (1977): 470–481.

"Une nouvelle formulation générale pour l'étude de certains fondements micro-économiques de la macroéconomie" (with Y. Younès). *Cahiers du Séminaire d'Économétrie* No. 18, CNRS (1977): 63–112.

"Some New Concepts for the Microeconomic Foundations of Macroeconomics" (with Y. Younès). In ed. G. Harcourt, *Microeconomic Foundation of Macroeconomics*, Macmillan, 1977.

The Theory of Unemployment Reconsidered. Blackwell, 1977 (Spanish translation).

Réexamen de la théorie du chômage (translated by G. Santucci, reviewed and completed by the author). Calmann-Lévy, 1980.

René Roy, 1894–1977. *Cahiers du Séminaire d'Économétrie* No. 19, CNRS (1977): 9–17. Published also in *Journal de la Société Statistique de Paris* 1 (1979).

"Economic Science and Problems of Growth." In ed. M. Marois, *Towards a Plan of Actions for Mankind*, Vol. 5, *Conclusion and Perspectives*. Pergamon, 1977.

"Macrodécisions et théorie économique." *Hommage à François Perroux*. Presses Universitaires de Grenoble, 1978.

"Nouveaux développements de la théorie macroéconomique du chômage." *Revue Économique* 29 (January 1978): 9–25.

"Some Problems of Prices and Incomes Policy in France." In eds. A. Deaton and R. Stone, *Econometric Contributions to Public Policy*. Macmillan, 1978.

"Twenty-five Rich Years for Economics." In ed. Stein Rokkan, *A Quarter Century of International Social Science*. Concept Publishing Company, 1979.

"The Costs of Economic Growth." In ed. E. Malinvaud, *Economic Growth and Resources*. Macmillan, 1979; and *Asian Journal of Economics* 1(1) (1982) 1–14.

"Macroeconomic Rationing of Employment." In eds. J. P. Fitoussi and E. Malinvaud, *Unemployment in Western Countries*. Macmillan, 1980.

Profitability and Unemployment. Cambridge University Press and Editions de la Maison des Sciences de l'Homme, 1980 (based on the Marshall lectures given at the University of Cambridge, 1978).

"Positive Economics and Development in Industrial Countries." In ed. J. Pajestka, *The Relevance of Economic Theories at the Present Day Society*. Macmillan, 1980.

"La recherche en science économique." *La Jaune et la Rouge* (June 1981): 56–59.

Théorie macroéconomique, Vol. 1, *Comportements, croissance*. Dunod, 1981; Vol. 2, *Fluctuations conjoncturelles et problèmes à court terme*, Dunod, 1982 (Spanish translation, English translation, North Holland, 1987).

"Econometrics faced with the needs of macroeconomic policy." *Econometrica* 49 (November 1981): 1363–1375. French version in *Commentaire* No. 16 (Winter 1981–1982): 542–551.

"La profitabilité comme facteur d'investissement." Communication to the Rheinisch Westfälische Akademie der Wissenschaften, Düsseldorf, 4 February 1981. Published in *Vorträge* 310 (January 1982): 7–18.

"Wages and Unemployment." *Economic Journal* 92 (March 1982): 1–12. French version in *Croissance et accumulation en déséquilibre*, eds. P. Michel and P.-Y. Hénin. Economica, 1982.

"Où en est la théorie macroéconomique?" *Revue Européenne des Sciences Sociales* XX(62) (1982): 5–23 (Conférence Luigi Solari, 12 November 1981, University of Geneva).

"The Equilibrium Concept in Economics." *Proceedings of the 6th International Congress on Logic, Methodology and Philosophy of Science*, Hannover 1979. North Holland and PWN, 1982.

"An Econometric Model for Macro-Disequilibrium Analysis." In eds. M. Hazewinkel and A. H. G. Rinnooy Kan, *Current Developments in the Interface: Economics, Econometrics. Mathematics*. Reidel, 1982.

"Data Analysis in Official Socio-Economic Statistics" (with J. C. Deville). *The Journal of the Royal Statistical Society, Series A*. 146(4) (1983): 335–361.

"Notes on Growth Theory with Imperfectly Flexible Prices." In ed. J. P. Fitoussi, *Modern Macroeconomic Theory*. Blackwell, 1983.

"The Estimation of Economic Systems and Economic Policy Simulations." *Proceedings of the 42nd Session of IIS*, Vol. XLVIII, book 1, Manila, 1983.

"From Statistics to Data Management—the French Difficulties." *Statistical Journal of the United Nations*, Vol. 1, No. 3. Economic Commission for Europe, North Holland, 1983, pp. 285–296.

Essais sur la théorie du chômage. Calmann-Lévy, 1983.

Mass Unemployment, Blackwell, 1984 (based on the Royer lectures given at Berkeley, October 1983) (Spanish and Italian translations).

"La science économique aujourd'hui." *Revue Économique et Sociale* 42 (January 1984): 35–45.

"Sociétés de statistique locales, nationales et internationales." *Journal de la Société Statistique de Paris* 125(3) (1984): 143–150.

"Il faut méditer sur Pierre Massé." *LU* No. 1 (April 1984): 18–19.

"Growth, Shortage and Efficiency by Janos Kornai": A Book Review. *Journal of Economic Literature* XXII (March 1984): 95–96.

"European Development and the World Economy." In ed. F. Bergsten, *Global Economic Imbalances*. Washington, 1984.

Eugène Morice et l'ENSAE. *Journal de la Société Statistique de Paris* 125(4) (1984): 232–237.

"The Identification of Scientific Advances in Economics." In ed. T. Hagerstrand. *The Identification of Progress in Learning*. Cambridge University Press, 1985.

"Le marché du travail en déséquilibre." *Keynes aujourd'hui: théories et politiques*. Economica, 1985.

"Unemployment Insurance." *Les Cahiers de Genève*, Vol. 10. Association Internationale pour l'Étude de l'Économie de l'Assurance, 1985.

"Sur l'analyse macroéconomique du chômage." *L'Actualité Économique* 61 (June 1985): 147–170.

"Economic and Social Statistics for Comparative Assessments." In eds. A. C. Atkinson and S. E. Fienberg, *The ISI Centenary Volume, a Celebration of Statistics*, chap. 19. 1985.

"Disequilibrium Macroeconomics in Open Economies by John T. Cuddington, Per-Olov Johanson and Karl-Gustaf Löfgren": A Book Review. *Journal of Economic Literature* XXIII (September 1985): 1196–1198.

"Pure Profits as Forced Savings." *The Scandinavian Journal of Economics* 88(1) (1986): 109–130.

"Maurice Allais, précurseur méconnu du modèle à générations renouvelées." In eds. M. Boiteux, T. de Montbrial, and B. Munier, *Marchés, Capital et Incertitude*. Economica, 1986.

"Jusqu'où la rigueur salariale devrait-elle aller? Une exploration théorique de la question." *Revue Économique* 37 (March 1986): 181–205.

"Les causes de la montée du chômage en France." *Revue Française d'Economie* 1(1) (Summer 1986): 50–83.

"Reflecting on the Theory of Capital and Growth." *The Oxford Economic Papers* 38 (1986): 367–385.

"The Discount Rate under Macroeconomic Constraint" (with D. Goudard). In ed. S. B. Jain, *Management and Role of Public Enterprises*, Vol. II. New-Delhi, 1986.

"Does Increase in Information Mean Increase in Knowledge?" In *From Tabulation to Information Society*. Central Statistical Office of Finland, Helsinki 1986.

Sur les statistiques de l'emploi et du chômage. La Documentation française, 1986.

"The Legacy of European Stagflation." *European Economic Review* 31 (February-March 1987): 53–65.

"Capital productif, incertitudes et profitabilité." *Annales d'Économie et de Statistique* No. 5 (January-March 1987): 1–36.

"La courbe de Beveridge." In Association Française de Science Économique, *Flexibilité, mobilité et stimulants économiques.* Nathan, 1987.

"The Overlapping Generations Model in 1947." *Journal of Economic Literature* XXV (March 1987): 103–105.

"The ET Interview: Professor Edmond Malinvaud." *Econometric Theory* 3 (1987): 273–295.

"The Challenge of Macroeconomic Understanding." *Banco Nazionale del Lavoro Quarterly Review* No. 162 (September 1987): 219–238.

(1) "Capital Gains and Losses," (2) "Decentralization," (3) "Intertemporal Equilibrium and Efficiency," (4) "Landry, Adolphe (1874–1956)," entries in *The New Palgrave: A Dictionary of Economics,* Macmillan, 1987.

Inaugural Lecture, 27 January 1988, Collège de France, Paris 1988.

"La compétitivité nationale." *Revue des Sciences Morales et Politiques* 143(2) (1988): 251–268.

"Econometric Methodology at the Cowles Commission: Rise and Maturity." *Econometric Theory* 4 (1988): 187–209.

Contributors

Yacine Aït-Sahalia
Ecole Polytechnique
Paris

Patrick Artus
Caisse des Dépôts et Consignations
Paris

Antoine D'Autumne
Université de Paris I (Panthéon)

Michel Balinski
Ecole Polytechnique and CNRS

Christian Baudelot
Université de Nantes

Alain Bernard
Conseil Général des Ponts et Chausées

François Bourguignon
Ecole des Hautes Etudes en Sciences Sociales (EHESS)

Dominique Bureau
Ministry of the Economy and Finance

Paul Champsaur
Ministry of the Economy and Finance

Pierre-Andre Chiappori
EHESS

Daniel Cohen
Université de Nancy

Bernard Cornet
Université de Paris I (Panthéon)

Jacques Cremer
Virginia Polytechnic Institute

Nicolas Curien
Ministry of Defense
France

Michel Deleau
European Bank for Investment
Luxembourg

Gabrielle Demange
Université de Paris XIII and Ecole Polytechnique

Jean-Pierre Florens
Université de Toulouse

Claude Fourgeaud
Université de Paris I (Panthéon)

Xavier Freixas
Université de Toulouse

Frédéric Gagey
INSEE

Michel Gensollen
France Telecom

Christian Gouriéroux
ENSAE and CEPREMAP

Jean-Michel Grandmont
CNRS and CEPREMAP

Zvi Griliches
Harvard University and NBER

Roger Guesnerie
CNRS and EHESS

Dominique Henriet
Ecole Polytechnique

Claude Henry
CNRS and Ecole Polytechnique

Serge-Christophe Kolm
CERAS and Ecole Nationale des Ponts et Chausées

Jean-Pierre Laffargue
Université de Paris I (Panthéon) and CEPREMAP

Gilbert Laffond
Conservatoire National des Arts et Metiers
Paris

Jean-Jacques Laffont
Université de Toulouse and EHESS

Jean-Paul Lambert
Saint Louis University
Brussels

Guy Laroque
INSEE

Jacques Lesourne
Conservatoire National des Arts et Metiers

Cuong Le Van
CNRS and CEPREMAP

Jacques Mairesse
ENSAE and EHESS

Pierre Malgrange
CNRS and CEPREMAP

Philippe Michel
Université de Paris I (Panthéon)

Jean-Claude Milleron
INSEE

Alain Monfort
INSEE

Pierre-Alain Muet
Observatoire Français des Conjonctures Economiques

Philippe Nasse
Ministre of the Economy and Finance

Benoît Ottenwaelter
Société Générale
Paris

Jacqueline Pradel
Université de Paris IX (Dauphine)

Pierre Picard
Université de Paris X (Nanterre) and CEPREMAP

Eric Renault
Université de Paris IX (Dauphine)

Jean-Charles Rochet
Université de Toulouse and Ecole Polytechnique

Patrick Rey
INSEE

Pierre Sicsic
Banque de France

Henri Sterdyniak
Observatoire Français des Conjonctures Economiques

Jean Tirole
Massachusetts Institute of Technology

Alain Trognon
ENSAE

Yves Younes
CNRS and CEPREMAP

The authors thank Claude Mouchot of the Université de Lyon II for his suggestions and corrections.